Woolf Studies Annual

Volume 8, 2002

PACE UNIVERSITY PRESS • NEW YORK

Copyright © 2002 by
Pace University Press
One Pace Plaza
New York, NY 10038

All rights reserved
Printed in the United States of America

ISSN 1080-9317
ISBN 0-944473-59-8 (pbk: alk.ppr.)

Member

Council of Editors of Learned Journals

∞™ paper used in this publication meets the minimum requirements of American National Standard for Information Sciences–Permanence of Paper for Printed Library Materials, ANSI Z39.48–1984

Editor

Mark Hussey   *Pace University*

Editorial Board

Tuzyline Jita Allan	*Baruch College, CUNY*
Eileen Barrett	*California State University, Hayward*
(Book Review Editor)	
Kathryn N. Benzel	*University of Nebraska-Kearney*
Pamela L. Caughie	*Loyola University Chicago*
Wayne K. Chapman	*Clemson University*
Patricia Cramer	*University of Connecticut, Stamford*
Beth Rigel Daugherty	*Otterbein College*
Anne Fernald	*DePauw University*
Val Gough	*Independent Scholar*
Sally Greene	*Independent Scholar*
Leslie Kathleen Hankins	*Cornell College*
Karen Kaivola	*Stetson University*
Jane Lilienfeld	*Lincoln University*
Toni A. H. McNaron	*University of Minnesota*
Patricia Moran	*University of California, Davis*
Vara Neverow	*Southern Connecticut State University*
Annette Oxindine	*Wright State University*
Beth Carole Rosenberg	*University of Nevada-Las Vegas*
Bonnie Kime Scott	*San Diego State University*

Consulting Editors

Nancy Topping Bazin	*Eminent Scholar and Professor of English Emerita, Old Dominion University*
Morris Beja	*Ohio State University*
Louise DeSalvo	*Hunter College, CUNY*
Carolyn G. Heilbrun	*Avalon Foundation Professor in the Humanities Emerita Columbia University*
Jane Marcus	*Distinguished Professor CCNY and CUNY Graduate Center*
Lucio Ruotolo	*Stanford University*
Brenda R. Silver	*Dartmouth College*
Susan Squier	*Pennsylvania State University*
Peter Stansky	*Stanford University*
J. J. Wilson	*Sonoma State University*
Alex Zwerdling	*University of California, Berkeley*

Many thanks to readers for volume 8: Judith Allen, Edward Bishop (U of Alberta), Diane Gillespie (Washington SU), Brenda Lyons, Jeanette McVicker (SUNY Fredonia), Krista Ratcliffe (Marquette U), Diana Royer (Miami U, OH), Molly Abel Travis (Tulane U).

Woolf Studies Annual is indexed in the *American Humanities Index*, *ABELL* and the *MLA Bibliography*.

The Society of Authors has been appointed to act for the Virginia Woolf Estate. Inquiries concerning permissions should be addressed to:

Mr. Jeremy Crow
The Society of Authors
84 Drayton Gardens
London SW10 9SB

Fax: 0171-373-5768
Tel: 0171-373-6642

Contents

Woolf Studies Annual

Volume 8, 2002

	vii	Abbreviations
Mark Hussey	1	Note from the Editor
Merry Pawlowski	3	The Virginia Woolf and Vera Douie Letters: Woolf's Connections to the Women's Service Library
	9	Index to the Women's Service Library Letters
	11	The Virginia Woolf and Vera Douie Letters
Michael Lackey	63	Virginia Woolf and T. S. Eliot: An Atheist's Commentary on the Epistemology of Belief
Maggie Humm	93	Visual Modernism: Virginia Woolf's "Portraits" and Photography
David Bradshaw	107	"Vanished, Like Leaves": The Military, Elegy and Italy in *Mrs Dalloway*
Rishona Zimring	127	Suggestions of Other Worlds: The Art of Sound in *The Years*
Stuart Christie	157	Willing Epigone: Virginia Woolf's *Between the Acts* as Nietzschean Historiography
Emily M. Hinnov	175	Shufflings of Kristeva: The Choran Moment in Virginia Woolf

GUIDE

199 Guide to Library Special Collections

REVIEWS

Susan H. Fox	215	*Outside Modernism: In Pursuit of the English Novel, 1900-30.* Lynne Hapgood and Nancy L. Paxton, Eds.; *Katherine Mansfield & Virginia Woolf: A Public of Two* by Angela Smith
Jane Lilienfeld	223	*Approaches to Teaching Woolf's* To The Lighthouse. Beth Rigel Daugherty and Mary Beth Pringle, Eds.
Evelyn Haller	227	*Virginia Woolf: Reading the Renaissance* Sally Greene, Ed.
Krystyna Colburn	232	*Virginia Woolf's London. A Guide to Bloomsbury and Beyond* by Jean Moorcroft Wilson
Jeanette McVicker	235	*The Eye's Mind: Literary Modernism and Visual Culture* by Karen Jacobs
Helen Wussow	240	*A Route to Modernism: Hardy, Lawrence, Woolf* by Rosemary Sumner
Tuzyline Jita Allan	243	*On the Winds and Waves of the Imagination: Transnational Feminism and Literature* by Constance S. Richards
Jeanne Dubino	247	*Virginia Woolf in the Age of Mechanical Reproduction*, Pamela Caughie, Ed.
Merry Pawlowski	251	*British Women Writers of World War II: Battlegrounds of Their Own* by Phyllis Lassner
Wayne Chapman	254	*Virginia Woolf and Fascism: Resisting the Dictators' Seduction* Merry Pawlowski, Ed.
Barbara Lounsberry	258	*Daily Modernism: The Literary Diaries of Virginia Woolf, Antonia White, Elizabeth Smart, and Anaïs Nin* by Elizabeth Podnieks
Notes on Contributors	263	
Policy	265	

Abbreviations

AHH	*A Haunted House*
AROO	*A Room of One's Own*
BP	*Books and Portraits*
BTA	*Between the Acts*
CDB	*The Captain's Death Bed and Other Essays*
CE	*Collected Essays (4 vols.)*
CR1	*The Common Reader*
CR2	*The Common Reader, Second Series*
CSF	*The Complete Shorter Fiction*
D	*The Diary of Virginia Woolf (5 vols.)*
DM	*The Death of the Moth and Other Essays*
E	*The Essays of Virginia Woolf (6 Vols.)*
F	*Flush*
FR	*Freshwater*
GR	*Granite & Rainbow: Essays*
JR	*Jacob's Room*
L	*The Letters of Virginia Woolf (6 Vols.)*
M	*The Moment and Other Essays*
MEL	*Melymbrosia*
MOB	*Moments of Being*
MT	*Monday or Tuesday*
MD	*Mrs. Dalloway*
ND	*Night and Day*
O	*Orlando*
PA	*A Passionate Apprentice*
RF	*Roger Fry: A Biography*
TG	*Three Guineas*
TTL	*To the Lighthouse*
TW	*The Waves*
TY	*The Years*
VO	*The Voyage Out*

The expansion of *Woolf Studies Annual* to allow for the inclusion of more material than was hitherto possible is a happy consequence of the reluctant cessation of Pace University Press's publication of an annual volume of *Selected Papers* from the Woolf conference. After seven years, the time seems right to remark on what the *Annual* sees as its function and to invite continuing interest and contributions from both established and new readers.

Woolf Studies Annual exists primarily to afford space for the publication of long articles on any aspect of the work or life of Virginia Woolf, or, indeed, of her wider milieu. Since the first issue, the *Annual*'s editors and readers have tried to provide helpful comments and suggestions to all who submit articles, whether they are ultimately published or not. In this regard, the response from those who have submitted articles assures me that we have been very successful. The *Annual* accepts about a quarter of work submitted; readers are asked to evaluate submissions according to three principal criteria: Does the work contribute significantly to scholarship on Woolf? Is the argument well-constructed and clearly expressed? Is the writer aware of existing scholarship in the field?

Looking back through eight volumes will, I hope, confirm that these criteria have not excluded particular theoretical approaches, but have ensured a high standard of scholarship whatever critical school an article might be placed in. Criticism of a writer as catholic in her interests and output as Woolf must be correspondingly diverse.

The *Annual* also seeks to provide an informed commentary on new works published about its areas of interest. Reviews of new works demonstrate the broad range of concerns in which Virginia Woolf figures significantly. Reviewers often frame their opinions within a context of previously published scholarship, reinforcing that aspect of the *Annual*'s mission which seeks to keep history visible.

Woolf Studies Annual has an archival function, too. When unpublished letters have been discovered, we have published transcriptions and commentary. Sometimes, as in volume 1's letter to St. John Hutchinson, such publications serve mainly to fill in the record. At other times, as in this volume's publication of letters between Woolf and Vera Douie, or in volume 6's annotated transcription of the *Three Guineas* letters, the *Annual* itself becomes an important adjunct to primary research. Such research is assisted also by our occasional publication of edited transcriptions of holograph material.

Finally, each year we update and add to a Guide to library collections housing materials of interest to those working on Woolf and her circle. The *Annual* thus feeds itself by assisting researchers and readers in their work.

At the end of each volume is a policy outlining how to present your work for consideration. The Editors welcome your submissions, and your suggestions for what the *Annual* might become.

Mark Hussey
for the Editorial Board

The Virginia Woolf and Vera Douie Letters: Woolf's Connections to the Women's Service Library

Merry M. Pawlowski

On a sweltering July day in 1999, I traveled the London Underground on my way to the Fawcett Library for three precious days to research Virginia Woolf's book sources for *Three Guineas*. I remember that my feet hurt, they usually do when I'm abroad and on them a lot; and I knew that I had before me a complicated journey up flights of stairs, across an above-ground walkway, and down a tiny elevator to ring the doorbell of the dungeon entrance to the crammed rooms that were the Fawcett. At the sound of my ring, a voice on the other side of the door chirped, "O, *do* come in!" It was the voice of David Doughan, librarian at the Fawcett, welcoming me back for another visit and deferentially reminding me to pay my reader's fee.

Once established at a table with plug-in facilities for my laptop computer, I happily buried myself in my work, retrieving books from rolling bookshelves, busily typing notes, and occasionally coming across a rare find—a book whose inside label proclaimed that it had been donated by "Virginia Woolf." At one point during the day, I remember proudly showing David a version of a bibliographic database guide to the footnote sources of *Three Guineas* that Vara Neverow and I had published in *Woolf Studies Annual* and sharing with him our work-in-progress, a website publication of Woolf's reading notes for *Three Guineas*.[1] Later, after lunch at a street café, I returned to lose myself once more, when David approached me and said with a hint of drama, "I have something to share with you that very few people know we have; I'll just go and get it." Moments later he returned with a file containing unpublished letters between Woolf and Vera Douie, the Fawcett's first librarian, and said, "Enjoy!" As I read, I began to realize Woolf's dedication and commitment to the Women's Service Library, as it was known until after Millicent Fawcett's death in 1929, working

---

[1]"A Preliminary Bibliographic Guide to the Footnotes of *Three Guineas*," *Woolf Studies Annual* 3 (1995): 170-210; and "Virginia Woolf's Reading Notes for *Three Guineas*: An Online Archive and Edition," now available for online subscription. This is an online edition of digital images of the three volumes of *Three Guineas* scrapbooks (Monks House Papers B16f) along with accompanying notes and contextual information. For further information, contact: mpawlowski@csub.edu or neverow@southernct.edu.

as a researcher in her queries to Miss Douie for information to bolster her arguments in *Three Guineas* and generously donating money and books to help build the library's holdings.[2] I reached the last letter, from Douie to Woolf, to be pounded emotionally by the bold, black letters written across its top which proclaimed that its intended recipient was "DEAD." I was hooked; I asked David to let me copy the letters and promised him that someday they would be published.

Before moving on to those letters, though, I think readers on this side of the Atlantic, especially those who've never had the distinct pleasure of visiting it, might need a bit of introduction to the Fawcett, now the oldest and largest library of women's history and literature in Britain.[3] In 1926, the Women's Service Library, organized by the London and National Society for Women's Service, opened with its first full-time librarian, Vera Douie (1894-1979). "Miss Douie," as she's referred to throughout Woolf's correspondence with her, served as librarian from January 1, 1926, until 1967. Douie, born in Lahore in 1894 to a wealthy Anglo-Indian family, renounced that family and insisted on living in London on her meager librarian's wages.[4] In 1943, two years after Woolf's death and three years after their last correspondence, Douie wrote a short book entitled *The Lesser Half* as a piece of campaigning literature to serve the cause of furthering women's social equality and equal compensation.[5] During the war, Douie actively campaigned for equal rights and her book was an indictment of the practice of lower compensation for women workers as well as a celebration of the abilities of women working in both World War I and World War II. Douie wrote: "in 1939, women were better equipped to serve their country than they had been in 1914, and self-reliant young women, born free from the restrictions which had hampered their mothers, were not themselves dubious of their own powers. But when the time came to use them, state and employers alike had to re-learn the lesson and were apparently just as agreeably surprised as they had been previously when the latent capacity of the women was revealed" (26).

---

[2]There is also ample evidence of Woolf's visits to the library and her use of its collection: see *L6* 145 and 232; *D4*, 145; *D5* 146.

[3]A very useful source of information on the Fawcett is the special issue of *Women's Studies International Forum* 10.3 (1987), especially the history of the Library by Rita Pankhurst.

[4]This information comes from an article entitled "'Stray Guineas': Virginia Woolf and the Fawcett Library" that Anna Snaith has kindly provided me which is forthcoming in *Literature and History*. She, too, cites her indebtedness to David Doughan, referring to a transcript of a talk entitled "Virginia Woolf, Vera Douie, and the Fawcett Library," which he shared with her.

[5]Published by the Women's Publicity Planning Association.

INTRODUCTION

During her 41 years as librarian, Douie made it her mission to accomplish two major aims in building the Fawcett's collection: to preserve the history of women's suffrage and to provide information for women seeking access to the professions. The Society's, and hence the Library's, origins were bound up with the women's suffrage movement dating back to its parent organization, The London Society for Women's Suffrage, founded in 1867 and welcoming among its members such notable names as Elizabeth Garrett Anderson and Millicent Garrett Fawcett.[6] By the 1920s, the Society had amassed a collection of pamphlets, leaflets, and government publications. The need to preserve this history of women's struggle for suffrage, along with the desire to provide a working library for women entering public life in increasing numbers as a result of the Sex Disqualification Act of 1919, provided the impetus to found the library. Vera Douie, during her tenure as Librarian transformed a small society library into a major research resource with an international reputation. In the 1930s, the Women's Service House, located at 29 Marsham Street, Westminster, housed the Library, a café and theater/lecture room; it was also a major women's center attracting prominent feminists who actively supported the Library, among them Woolf and Vera Brittain. This was the facility that Woolf knew from firsthand experience.

During the 1930s, the period of the letters between Vera Douie—or Philippa Strachey[7] acting on her behalf—and Virginia Woolf, the library had a stock of

---

[6]Millicent Garrett Fawcett (1847-1929) worked on the first suffrage committee in 1867, helped pass the Married Women's Property Act, and used her home as a base for the series of lectures which would precipitate the founding of Newnham College. In 1897, she became President of the National Union of Women Suffrage Societies She campaigned tirelessly for partial suffrage in 1916 and for full suffrage in 1928. She wrote several books, including a biography of Queen Victoria, a history of women's suffrage, and a biography of Josephine Butler, which Woolf read and used in her research for *Three Guineas*. See Virginia Woolf, *Three Guineas* (San Diego: Harcourt Brace Jovanovich, 1966), fn. 38.6, p. 169.

Elizabeth Garrett Anderson (1836-1917) was the older sister of Millicent, who, at 18, met Emily Davies and other strong activists for women's rights. In 1859, after having met America's first woman doctor, Elizabeth Blackwell, Anderson decided she wanted a career in medicine, but she faced family opposition in addition to the refusal by a number of medical schools to give her admission. Anderson eventually entered the medical profession through the "back door," passing the Society of Apothecaries examination in 1865, and, with the help of her father, established a medical practice in London. In the 1870s, along with Sophia Jex-Blake, Anderson established a London Medical School for Women. At the age of 72, Anderson joined the militant Women's Social and Political Union, narrowly missing arrest after the group stormed the House of Commons; however, she left the group in 1911 to protest their arson campaign.

[7]Philippa (Pippa) Strachey (1872-1968) was the sister of Lytton Strachey and the sister-in-law of Rachel (Ray) Strachey, author of *The Cause*, another important source of

approximately 7500 titles, a reference and enquiry service for members and non-members of the Society, and a regular program of acquisitions and donations to the collections. In 1930, Woolf was at the top of the list of speakers developed by the Junior Council of the London and National Society for Women's Service; in 1931, she gave a talk, "Music and Literature" with Ethel Smyth, for the Council; and in 1932, she became a member of the LNSWS, a fact which is recorded in the society minutes.[8] By 1933, Woolf was offering to sell her manuscript of *A Room of One's Own* to raise money for the society.

Woolf's dedication here should be placed within the context of her overall commitment to women's education and access to books and information. In 1935, for example, E. M. Forster told Woolf in the London Library that the Library Committee had been discussing whether to allow ladies to serve, when Woolf replied that they did allow ladies. "Yes yes—there was Mrs Green," said Forster, "And Sir Leslie Stephen said, never again. She was so troublesome. And I said, havent ladies improved? But they were all quite determined. No no no, ladies are quite impossible. They wouldn't hear of it." Later that night as Woolf continued to stew about the incident, she thought about her book "on Being Despised" (an early title for *Three Guineas*) and of how her name had probably come up and been rejected. "God damn Morgan for thinking I'd have taken that . . ." (*D4* 297-8). No such ridiculous prejudice against women reading, learning, and participating in public life existed at the Women's Service Library.

In fact, the opposite pertained. Writing to Ethel Smyth on June 1, 1938, Woolf told her to send Miss Douie a list of books she might be willing to donate to the library. "I think its almost the only satisfactory deposit for stray guineas, because half the readers are bookless at home, working all day, eager to know anything and everything, and a very nice room, with a fire even, and a chair or two, is provided" (*L6* 232).

---

research for Woolf's *Three Guineas*. "Pippa," as Woolf knew her, was a political activist who organized the first major march in London for women's suffrage; and in 1935, she published *Memorandum on the Position of English Women in Relation to that of English Men*, an influential source of information cited by Woolf in *Three Guineas*, fn. 25, p. 153. She was Secretary of the London and National Society for Women's Service from 1914-51, and it was at her invitation that Woolf, along with Ethel Smyth, addressed the Society in 1931, an important impetus for *Three Guineas*. Woolf records in her diary her relief at Pippa's enthusiastic response to *Three Guineas* (*D5* 149).

[8] I am again indebted to Anna Snaith for her work in researching the committee minutes and monthly library reports in the Fawcett to reveal this information. I am also grateful to her for reminding me of the incident at the London Library with Forster described in Woolf's diary, and of the remarks about the Women's Service Library in her letter to Ethel Smyth, both of which I've referred to here.

The letters contained in the archive that are transcribed here clearly indicate Woolf's commitment to enhance the library's collection. Additionally, the minutes of the Library Committee meeting for May 26, 1938, indicate the origin and scope of Woolf's involvement:

> Mrs. Virginia Woolf, jointly with her husband, had drawn up a letter addressed to women writers, which she was most kindly going to sign herself. She had also offered to give the Library books, especially biographies, in which she was much interested, and had said that she would be willing to pass on to the Library to be kept or disposed of at the discretion of the Committee. But in addition she had very generously offered to buy books for the Library, and had said that if a list of those which the Library Committee had been unable to purchase on account of lack of funds were sent to her after each meeting of the Committee, she would do what she could to supply them, and would also try to get for the Library from secondhand booksellers any old books required, especially those needed to fill any gaps in the collection of classics written by women. It was resolved that the warm thanks of the Committee should be sent to Mrs. Woolf for her great kindness, and that a list of books by famous women writers not already in the possession of the Library should be compiled for her.[9]

By the time this meeting took place, Woolf had been visiting the library and corresponding with Vera Douie to ask research questions for nearly a year. Indeed, she includes a full page description of the London and National Society for Women's Service, "What is This Society?" in her *Reading Notes*, Volume III, p. 50 (*Monks House Papers* B16f, University of Sussex Library).[10] "Through its special Library," the advertisement reads in part, "the Society acts as our Intelligence Department for all who are interested in questions affecting women's employment and opportunities." Furthermore, the knowledge of Woolf's offer to buy books helps set the context for the letter dated May 27, 1938, written by Philippa Strachey in Douie's place, which claims that the Library Committee sent Woolf "ecstatic messages which I shan't attempt to reproduce." Up to this point, the correspondence consists of reference inquiries

---

[9] The quote comes from a paper read by Christine Wise, librarian at the Fawcett Library, entitled "Virginia Woolf and the Fawcett Library" read at the Eleventh Annual Conference on Virginia Woolf held June 11-13, 2001, in Bangor, Wales, which she kindly shared with me.

[10] These three volumes of *Reading Notes* were crucial to Woolf as she developed her resources for writing *Three Guineas*. In the notebooks, Woolf included more than 300 items, among them, newspaper clippings, cuttings of articles, notes from books, letters sent to her from various individuals and organizations, manifestoes, and a pamphlet. The letters to Vera Douie published here clearly demonstrate the importance of the Library to Woolf's research, and I've established as many cross references among names and titles in the letters, notes or clippings in the notebooks, and footnotes in *Three Guineas* as I could find to illustrate that fact.

by Woolf answered by Vera Douie, but the tenor of the letters changes once Woolf makes her offer to buy books to fill the Library Committee's requests. Beginning June 3, 1938, either Vera Douie or Philippa Strachey acknowledges and thanks Woolf for the gifts of the following books: Dorothy McDougall's *Madeleine de Scudery,* Zaimi's *Daughter of the Eagle,* Cole's *Marriage Past and Present, Ouïda,* Batten's *My Life,* Barnard's *Madame de Maintenon and Saint-Cyr,* Earhart's *Last Flight,* Haldane's *From One Century to Another, Miss Weeton: Journal of a Governess* (Vols. 1 and 2), Lindbergh's *Listen! The Wind,* McLeod's *Heloise,* Armitage's *The Taylors of Ongar,* Percival's *The English Miss,* Anderson's *Elizabeth Garrett Anderson,* Ferber's *A Peculiar Treasure,* a set of 12 Hannah More pamphlets, More's *Thoughts on the Importance of the Manners of the Great to General Society,* Sender's *Autobiography of a German Rebel,* and Carpenter's *Our Convicts* and *Juvenile Delinquents.*

In 1940, five months before Woolf's death and Douie's last letter to her, the Women's Service House sustained severe damage from bombs. Woolf wouldn't survive to read Douie's description of the fortuitous survival of the Library's collection and its removal from Westminster to the Society of Oxford Home-Students. Even after Woolf's death, though, Leonard continued her commitment to the Library, donating books and advising the Librarian about which works of criticism on Woolf to procure. The Society had changed its name to the Fawcett Society in memory of Millicent Fawcett and her daughter Philippa Fawcett, both of whom gave financial assistance to the Library. The Library followed suit, calling itself the Fawcett Library until just recently. In March, 1977, the Library moved to its most recent location at the (then) City of London Polytechnic University, now known as the London Guildhall University. Currently, the Library, now called the Women's Library, is moving to its new location in Old Castle Street, adjacent to its present location, with exhibition and gallery space, a conference room, a reading room with open access Library material and electronic access to information, and much more. In an updated way, the new Library location promises to serve as an inviting and pleasant space for reading and research about women's issues, much like the space at 29 Marsham Street that Woolf cherished.

I am honored that David Doughan shared with me the letters which follow; and I am happy to share them with readers who, though convinced of Woolf's fierce dedication to women's access to books and to education and her feminist involvement in the affairs of her time, can always applaud more evidence of such activity.

Index to the Women's Service Library Letters between Virginia Woolf and Vera Douie and Virginia Woolf and Philippa Strachey July 1937-March, 1941

1. Librarian (Vera Douie) to Mrs. Woolf, with attachment – July 3, 1937
2. Virginia Woolf to Miss Douie – July 9, 1937
3. Virginia Woolf to Miss Douie – October 21, no year written
4. Librarian to Mrs. Woolf – October 21, 1937
5. Virginia Woolf to Miss Douie – December 17, 1937
6. Librarian to Mrs. Woolf – December 20, 1937
7. Virginia Woolf to Miss Douie – December 21, 1937
8. Virginia Woolf to (Miss Douie), with addressed envelope – Sunday, no date written
9. Librarian to Mrs. Woolf – March 3, 1938
10. Virginia Woolf to (Miss Douie), with addressed envelope– Friday, no date written
11. P.[hilippa] S.[trachey] to Virginia – May 27, 1937
12. Librarian to Mrs. Woolf – June 3, 1938
13. Virginia Woolf to Miss Douie – June 8, 1938
14. Librarian to Mrs. Woolf, with attachment – June 30, 1938
15. Librarian to Mrs. Woolf – July 14, 1938
16. Virginia Woolf to Miss Douie – August 13, 1938
17. P.[hillipa] S.(trachey] to Virginia – August 16, 1938
18. P.[hillipa] S.[trachey] to Virginia – August 16, 1938
19. Librarian to Mrs. Woolf – September 2, 1938
20. Librarian to Mrs. Woolf – October 31, 1938
21. Virginia Woolf to Miss Douie – November 13, 1938
22. Librarian to Mrs. Woolf – November 15, 1938
23. Librarian to Mrs. Woolf – November 16, 1938
24. Librarian to Mrs. Woolf – December 2, 1938
25. Librarian to Mrs. Woolf – December 10, 1938
26. Librarian to Mrs. Woolf – February 9, 1939
27. Librarian to Mrs. Woolf – February 11, 1939
28. Librarian to Mrs. Woolf – March 3, 1939
29. Librarian to Mrs. Woolf – March 9, 1939

30. Librarian to Mrs. Woolf – March 30, 1939
31. Librarian to Mrs. Woolf – April 4, 1939
32. Librarian to Mrs. Woolf – May 4, 1939
33. Librarian to Mrs. Woolf – May 13, 1939
34. Librarian to Mrs. Woolf – July 4, 1939
35. Librarian to Mrs. Woolf – July 6, 1939
36. Librarian to Mrs. Woolf – July 28, 1939
37. Virginia Woolf to Miss Douie – July 30, no year written
38. Librarian to Mrs. Woolf – July 31, 1939
39. Librarian to Mrs. Woolf – March 11, 1940
40. Virginia Woolf to Miss Douie – March 14, no year written
41. Librarian to Mrs. Woolf – April 22, 1940
42. Librarian to Mrs. Woolf – May 31, no year written
43. Librarian to Mrs. Woolf – June 14, no year written
44. Librarian to Mrs. Woolf – July 25, 1940
45. Librarian to Mrs. Woolf – September 13, no year written
46. Librarian to Mrs. Woolf – March 26, no year written

The following letters are reproduced with the kind permission of The Women's Library, London Guildhall University.

London & National Society for Women's Service

(Formerly London Society for Women's Suffrage. Dating from 1866)

Non Party. Affiliated to the National Council of Women

President—The Rt. Hon. The Viscount Cecil of Chelwood, K.C.
Hon. Treasurer—The Hon. Mrs. Spencer Graves.
Chairman of Executive—Miss Ethel Watts.
Secretary—Miss Philippa Strachey.

29 Marsham Street
Westminster, S.W.1

Telephone: Victoria 9542

1
Typed
July 3, 1937

<u>LIBRARY</u>

3rd July, 1937

Dear Mrs. Woolf,

Miss Strachey is not here to-day, and I am sure she would like to answer your question regarding the Debate in the Lords herself when she comes on Monday, but in the meantime I am sending you a copy of the report on Mr. Baldwin's speech about women in the Civil Service which appeared in the "Daily Telegraph" on April 1st, 1936.[1]

I am always delighted to look up any facts I can for members, and it is surprising really how wide the scope of the Library now is. Our charges for

---

[1] Woolf references this speech in *Three Guineas*, fn 25.2, p. 153, but doesn't quote it or elaborate on its message. The newspaper article in which the speech appears is not found in her *Reading Notes* (Monks House Papers B16f, Vols. 1, 2, and 3), so it appears that the only source for the footnote was the information sent to her here by Douie. However, there are clippings which report two other speeches by Baldwin in her notebooks, Vol. II, p. 6, and Vol. III, p. 7. In this and the letters which follow, I have endeavored to establish the links among Woolf's correspondence with Douie, her use of the Library, her resources

"information" are 6d. for small easily-obtainable items, and 1/- per hour for larger pieces of research.

Yours sincerely,

Librarian

Mrs. Woolf,
    52, Tavistock Square,
        W. C. 1.

Attachment to Letter 1
Typed
Undated

PREMIER PAYS TRIBUTE TO WOMEN

Better than Men in Keeping Secrets

PROVED IN CIVIL SERVICE

A striking tribute to woman's capability, loyalty and power was paid yesterday by Mr. Baldwin. He was presiding at a meeting at 10, Downing-street to launch the Newnham College Building Fund Scheme.

The Premier was referring particularly to women in the Civil Service.

---

in the volumes of her *Reading Notes*, and her sources as cited in *Three Guineas*. Citations from the *Three Guineas* footnotes will include the primary footnote number, the number of the citation within the footnote if applicable, and the page number from the 1966 Harcourt Brace Jovanovich edition. Citations from the *Reading Notes* will include the volume number and the page number. Further information may be obtained by subscribing to the online edition and archive: "Virginia Woolf's Reading Notes for *Three Guineas*: An Online Archival Edition" (contact me at mpawlowski@csub.edu); from Brenda Silver's invaluable guide to all of Woolf's reading note manuscripts, *Virginia Woolf's Reading Notebooks* (Princeton UP, 1983); and from Primary Source Media's *Major Authors on CD-ROM: Virginia Woolf.*

"Many of them", he said, "are in positions in the course of their daily work to amass secret information. Secret information has a way of leaking very often, as we politicians know to our cost.

"I have never known a case of such a leakage being due to a woman, and I have known cases of leakage coming from men who should have known a great deal better."

He was not prepared to say that any conclusion had been formed or was even necessary—whether women were as good as, or better than men, but he believed that women had worked in the Civil Service to their own content, and certainly to the complete satisfaction of everybody who had had anything to do with them.

SCOPE FOR WOMEN

"I should like to pay my personal tribute to the industry, capacity, ability and loyalty of the women I have come across in Civil Service positions," he went on.

"I was surprised to find from inquiries that in many fields of commerce and industry, and local and municipal administration, there is much work already done by University-trained men, but hardly any advantage seems to have been taken of University-trained women.

"Yet I am quite confident that in all these spheres there must be room just as room has been found in the Civil Service. I hope very much that the men who are in control of great businesses, and the administration of great municipalities, will take into serious consideration, not the swamping of their offices, of course, but of finding opportunity and occasion for the use of what I believe to be the very fine and admirable material that is not being used to the greatest advantage in those quarters at present."

2
Handwritten on letterhead
July 9, 1937

From **Leonard Woolf, 52 Tavistock Square, W.C.1.** *Museum* 2621
("Mrs" underlined handwritten in ink above "Leonard")

9th July 1937

Dear Miss Douie

Many thanks for sending me the information I wanted. I will certainly apply to you again if I may. I enclose stamps, with thanks.

Yrs sincerely

Virginia Woolf

3
Handwritten on letterhead
October 21 (1937)

From **Leonard Woolf, 52 Tavistock Square, W.C.1.** *Museum* 2621
("V" handwritten in ink over the first two letters of "Leonard")

21st Oct

Dear Miss Douie,

I don't know who (or whom) this should be paid to. So I have left a blank.

Many thanks for your help

Yrs sincerely

Virginia Woolf

4
Typed
October 21, 1937

<u>LIBRARY</u>

21st October, 1937

Dear Mrs. Woolf,

It is most kind and generous of you to send us a subscription of 10/ - for Library enquiries, and I do hope you will manage to find a large number of questions to ask us, so that I shan't feel we are taking the money under false pretences!

I enclose an official receipt, with many thanks.

Yours sincerely,

Librarian

Mrs. Woolf
    52, Tavistock Square,
        W. C. 1.

5
Handwritten on letterhead
December 17, 1937[2]

From **Leonard Woolf, 52 Tavistock Square, W.C.1.** *Museum* 2621
("V" handwritten in ink over the first two letters of "Leonard")

17th Dec. 37.

Dear Miss Douie,

    I will bring the books back, or most of them next week. I'm sorry to be so late.
Can you tell me if there is any way in which I can find out what are the endowments of the Cambridge colleges, both for men & women at the present time?[3] Also am I right in thinking that Miss J. A. Clough received no salary when Principal of Newnham?[4] I have said so, but cannot find my authority.

                          Yrs sincerely

                            Virginia Woolf.

---

    [2]This letter was published by Joanne Trautmann Banks in "Some New Woolf Letters." *Modern Fiction Studies* 30, 2 (Summer 1984): 175-202.
    [3]The *Reading Notes* contain a great many references to endowments and income for the universities, especially Oxford. One clipping which serves as an example is entitled "More Money for Universities," unidentified newspaper, dated February 29, 1936 (Vol. II, p. 19). The article reports on over one million pounds in state grants to be given to universities in Great Britain.
    [4]Woolf's typed notes from her reading of Blanche Clough's *A Memoir of Anne Jemima Clough* (Edward Arnold, 1897) appear in Vol. 1, p. 48 of her *Reading Notes*. In her footnotes to *Three Guineas*, Woolf refers to the *Life of Anne J. Clough*, fn 1.2, p. 145. This reference is likely an error, as bibliographical checks turn up only the title *A Memoir of Anne Jemima Clough*. In two subsequent footnotes, though, Woolf refers to the correct title, the *Memoir*, in fn 33, p. 164; and fn 12, p. 176.

6
Typed
December 20, 1937

<u>LIBRARY</u>

20th December, 1937

Dear Mrs. Woolf,

Many thanks for your post card. I have asked Miss B. A. Clough, who confirms that her aunt, Miss A. J. Clough, received no salary when Principal of Newnham.

With regard to endowments, Miss Clough thinks she would perhaps be able to get you some material. I will let you know if she is successful. All we have in the Library is a RECORD OF BENEFACTORS OF NEWNHAM COLLEGE MADE IN 1921[5] (of which I believe there is a later edition) and Lady Stephen's GIRTON COLLEGE, which has a Biographical Index giving a list of founders and benefactors. The date of this is 1932.

I have myself an old book on the Cambridge Colleges (men's) which includes tables of benefactors, but not, as far as I remember, the amount contributed! In any case, I will try to remember to bring it to the Library, so that you may see it when you return the books, as you kindly say you will this week.

---

[5]In this regard, I think it useful to mention a letter from Joan Pernel Strachey, who, from 1923-1941, was Principal of Newnham College. The form letter, dated February 19, 1936, appears in Woolf's *Reading Notes*, Vol. 2, p. 7, and asks for Woolf to consider becoming a Patron of the College for the purposes of fundraising.

The Library will be shut from the evening of December 23rd to the morning of January 3rd.

Yours sincerely,

Librarian

Mrs. Woolf
    52, Tavistock Square,
        W. C. 1.

7
Handwritten on letterhead
December 21, 1937

**52,
Tavistock Square,**
W. C. 1.
Telephone: Museum 2621

Dec. 21st 37

Dear Miss Douie,

    Many thanks for your information. Please don't bother yourself, or let Miss Clough bother any more about the endowments. The only question I was trying to answer was, what were the large legacies to the Cambridge Men's Colleges during the past 3 or 4 years (I have got the facts about the old endowments) I rather think that Johns or Christs was ~~given~~ made a very large bequest by a private man : & wanted to use this to illustrate an argument accurately if I could. But its not worth bothering about. I expect some University calendar would give it me.

I will send the books, or some back by post tomorrow, as I cant come in.

Yours sincerely

Virginia Woolf

8
Handwritten on letterhead
Sunday

From **Leonard Woolf, 52 Tavistock Square, W.C.1.** *Museum* 2621

Sunday

Could you give me the name of a book on the present position of women in France, & the author?[6]

Virginia Woolf

Attachment to Letter 8
Addressed Envelope, Handwritten
Postmarked 12 AM, 28 Feb, 1938

Miss Douie
The L. S.^{ty} for W. ^{omens} Service
Marsham Street
Westminster
SW

[6]Woolf may have received the answer to her question in person since a letter with the title of the book in question does not appear in this correspondence. The book she references in *Three Guineas*, fn 3, p. 173, is *The Position of Women in Contemporary France* by Frances Clark (London: P. S. King & Son, 1937).

9
Typed
March 3, 1938

LIBRARY

Dear Mrs. Woolf,

I am so sorry I was out when you came this afternoon, but I had to go and look at some books we are hoping to buy secondhand at a very cheap rate.

Here is the last edition that was published of Mrs. Fawcett's most useful pamphlet, WHAT THE VOTE HAS DONE.[7] To bring it up to date I enclose a little typed list of the legislation passed since. We shall be glad to have it back when you have done with it, as there is only one other copy.

I am sending also THE STORY OF THE DISARMAMENT DECLARATION which has lists of peace societies at the end, and which gives an interesting account of one particular effort for peace organised by women. They also did a great part of the work in connection with the Peace Ballot in 1935. I am afraid I cannot say how many women are actually engaged in working for peace.

Other peace societies not mentioned in the disarmament pamphlet are: -

England.
British Commonwealth Peace Federation.
International Arbitration League.
International Peace Campaign.[8]
International Peace Society.

---

[7] Woolf references this publication in *Three Guineas*, fn. 14, p. 149, quoting from Millicent Fawcett's *Josephine Butler*, "'This publication . . . was originally a single-page leaflet; it has now (1927) grown to a six-page pamphlet, and has to be constantly enlarged.'"

[8] Woolf included a circular from this organization in her *Reading Notes*, Vol. 3, p. 24, which describes the activities of the organization and asks for a donation. The brief pamphlet, signed by the Viscount Cecil, is a single sheet folded in half and printed on all four sides.

Peace Pledge Union.
University of London War and Peace Society.
Women's International Boycott to Prevent War.
Women's World Committee against War and Fascism, - British Branch.

<u>Abroad.</u>

International Christian Peace Fellowship.
International Committee for the Co-ordination of Forces making for Peace.
Inernational Consultative Group for Peace and Disarmament.
International League for Peace and Freedom.
War Resisters' International.
World Committee against War and Fascism.
World Union of Women for International Concord.
World Youth Community for Peace, Freedom and Progress.

Yours sincerely,

Librarian

Mrs. Woolf,
    52, Tavistock Square,
        W. C. 1.

10
Handwritten on letterhead
Undated

From **Leonard Woolf, 52 Tavistock Square, W.C.1.** *Museum* 2621
("V" handwritten in ink over the first four letters of "Leonard")

Many thanks for sending me the information, which is what I needed. I will return the pamphlet.

                                                Virginia Woolf

Friday

Attachment to Letter 10
Addressed Envelope, Handwritten
Postmarked 8:15 pm, March 4, 1938

                       Miss Douie

                       Women's Service

                              29 ~~56~~   Marsham Street

                                        SW. 1

11
Typed
May 27, 1938

27th May, 1938

Dear Virginia,

The Library Committee met yesterday and their demeanour when they heard of this new method of getting books quite came up to my expectations. They sent you ecstatic messages which I shan't attempt to reproduce.

We have a fair number of applications for books from the Central Library and receive a report every month of those they have asked for which we have not been able to supply. There is always a proportion of rubbish in this but there were two this time which we thought you might like to put on your list of oddities to look out for in the second hand shops : -

    Babington.   MEMOIR OF CHARLOTTE ELIOT. 1875.
    Lewis (Ed).   EXTRACTS FROM THE JOURNALS AND CORRESPONDENCES OF MISS BENNY, 1783 — 1825.

Re New Books.

The only one we hankered for and rejected on the score of economy was : -

    Zaimi, Nexhmie. DAUGHTER OF THE EAGLE – THE AUTOBIOGRAPHY OF AN ALBANIAN GIRL. Blackie. 7/6d.

We deferred buying

    Cole, Margaret. MARRIAGE PAST AND PRESENT. Dent. 7/6d.

because we imagined that Mrs. Cole might very likely give you a copy which you could pass on to us. If she doesn't, we think we ought to get this ourselves because it is in the general run of things and not in the luxury department.

We also considered

McDougall, Dorothy	MADELEINE DE SCUDERY Methuen.	12/6d.

but no one knew whether it was worth having, and we thought you might perhaps be able to have a look at it and form a judgment. We have nothing about her in the library beyond an account in Julia Kavanagh's FRENCH WOMEN OF LETTERS, 1868, so that if this is a good book it would be welcome. On the other hand if it turns out to be a cumberer of shelves itself, it might reveal the existence of some French or other authority which would be worth looking out for instead.

Miss Douie is going to examine the collection of classics with a view to gaps. I am shocked to find that we don't possess that heavenly work DEERBROOK. We have a good number of Miss Martineau's in old editions and Miss Douie seems to turn up her nose at the idea of a modern DEERBROOK, so if you chance on a second hand copy of that do get it for us.

P[hilippa]. S[trachey]. [handwritten]

12
Typed
June 3, 1938

LIBRARY

3rd June, 1938

Dear Mrs. Woolf,

Your perfectly delightful gift of MADELEINE DE SCUDERY, MARRIAGE PAST AND PRESENT and DAUGHTER OF THE EAGLE has just arrived, and I hasten to thank you in the name of the Library Committee for your generosity to us.

It is quite wonderful of you to say you will give us new books, and that we may send you each month a list of those we are unable to buy owing to lack of funds. We shall look forward to receiving many a treasure, and are most highly appreciative of your kindness to us.

Yours sincerely,

Librarian

Mrs. Woolf,
    52, Tavistock Square,
        W. C. 1.

13
Typed on letterhead
June 8, 1938

Monk's House,
Rodmell,
near Lewes,
Sussex

8th June 38

Dear Miss Douie,

    Many thanks for your letter. I sent the book on Mlle de Scudery although Miss Strachey was doubtful if it was worth having. But I had not had time to look at it myself; and some review said it was a serious book. I am very glad to send you books; though sometimes I may have to refrain. But please do not think it necessary to write and thank me. I'm sure you have enough letters to write; and a card to say they have come safe is all that is needed. I am keeping an eye on catalogues in case the old books you need should turn up; but as you know this is a question of luck. If you send me the names I will make a note of them.

> Here is a cheque from Lady Gerald Wellesley – sent direct to me in spite of the address given. Would you take charge of it, and answer her officially? Her address is:
>
> > Lady Gerald Wellesley,
> > Penns in the Rocks
> > Withyham Sussex.
>
> She says she has great sympathy with the library; it would be worth sending her circulars.
>
> > Yours sincerely,
> >
> > Virginia Woolf [handwritten]

14
Typed
June 30, 1938

<u>LIBRARY</u>

30th June, 1938.

Dear Mrs. Woolf,

At its last meeting, the Library Committee asked me to convey to you their warmest thanks for the three books you so kindly gave us last month. There is no doubt that the members much prefer them to the dull, though doubtless instructive, books provided for them by the Committee, for they have all been continually out, and have been greatly appreciated by their readers.

It seems dreadful to forward you another list of "wants" so soon, but you said we might tell you after each Committee what we should have like to have, but had been unable to buy through lack of funds. This month there are two, Jean Batten's MY LIFE (Harrap) 8/6d., and Yvonne ffrench's [sic] OUIDA

(Cobden-Sanderson) 8/6d. The latter, especially, sounds fascinating, and was very well reviewed by "The Times".

I am also sending you at last a list of the Works by Famous Women Writers not possessed by the Library. I am afraid you will think the selection a little arbitrary—indeed I frankly admit that it is. The tremendous list of books by Harriet Martineau has been included through sheer favouritism, because we have already a very large collection by her, and it is always my ambition to complete it. Similarly, Mrs. Opie appears while many another writer perhaps equal in merit has been left out. But there again, we have a good collection already to which it would be pleasant to add. Other books, such as Mary Wollstonecraft's MARY, A FICTION, are, we know, quite beyond the dreams of avarice, but as their absence undoubtedly constitutes a "gap" they have been included all the same.

With many thanks for all your kindness,

Yours sincerely,

Librarian.

Mrs. Woolf

Attachment to Letter 14
Typed
Undated

LIST OF THE WORKS OF FAMOUS WOMEN WRITERS NOT

POSSESSED BY THE MILLICENT FAWCETT LIBRARY

Jane Austen

PRIDE AND PREJUDICE
FRIENDSHIP AND LOVE

Sarah Fielding

THE LIVES OF CLEOPATRA
AND OCTAVIA
THE HISTORY OF OPHELIA

Anne Bronte

TENANT OF WILDFELL HALL
AGNES GREY

Charlotte Bronte

JANE EYRE

Emily Bronte

WUTHERING HEIGHTS

Fanny Burney

CAMILLA
THE WANDERER

Maria Edgeworth

POPULAR TALES
BELINDA
EMILIE DE COULANGES
THE MODERN GRISELDA
PATRONAGE
HARRINGTON
THOUGHTS ON BORES
ORMOND

Elizabeth Gaskell

(any except DARK NIGHT'S
WORK, LIFE OF CHARLOTTE
BRONTE, MARY BARTON,
NORTH & SOUTH, RUTH and
WIVES & DAUGHTERS

Eliza Heywood

BETSY THOUGHTLESS
COURT OF CARIMANIA
JEMMY & JENNY JESSAMY
LIFE'S PROGRESS THROUGH
    THE PASSIONS
SECRET HISTORIES:
    NOVELS & POEMS

Mary de la Riviere Manley

THE NEW ATLANTIS
HISTORY OF QUEEN ZARAH
POWER OF LOVE IN SEVEN NOVELS

HELEN

George Eliot

AMOS BARTON
SCENES FROM CLERICAL LIFE
ROMOLA
FELIX HOLT
IMPRESSIONS OF THEOPHRASTUS SUCH
AGATHA

Harriet Martineau

Early Religious Works, 1823-1832
FIVE YEARS OF YOUTH
GUIDES TO SERVICE. THE MAID-OF-ALL-WORK : THE HOUSEMAID :
    THE LADY'S MAID : THE DRESSMAKER (Published
    anonymously)
DEERBROOK
THE MARTYR AGE OF THE UNITED STATES OF AMERICA
THE SETTLERS AT HOME
THE PEASANT AND THE PRINCE
THE CROFTON BOYS
LETTERS ON MESMERISM
DAWN ISLAND
EASTERN LIFE, PAST AND PRESENT
HOUSEHOLD EDUCATION
INTRODUCTION TO THE HISTORY OF THE PEACE, FROM 1800 TO 1815
HALF A CENTURY OF THE BRITISH EMPIRE
LETTERS ON THE LAWS OF MAN'S NATURE AND DEVELOPMENT
MERDHIN
GUIDE TO WINDERMERE
A COMPLETE GUIDE TO THE ENGLISH LAKES
THE FACTORY CONTROVERSY
CORPORATE TRADITIONS AND NATIONAL RIGHTS
THE ENDOWED SCHOOLS OF IRELAND
SUGGESTIONS TOWARDS THE FUTURE GOVERNMENT OF INDIA
ENGLAND AND HER SOLDIERS
HEALTH, HUSBANDRY AND HANDICRAFT

Mary Russell Mitford

RIENZI
BELFORD REGIS
RECOLLECTIONS OF A LITERARY LIFE
ATHERTON

Hannah More

THOUGHTS ON THE IMPORTANCE OF THE MANNERS OF THE GREAT
    TO GENERAL SOCIETY
VILLAGE POLITICS
SPIRIT OF PRAYER

Amelia Opie

DANGERS OF COQUETRY
SIMPLE TALES
MADELINE
DETRACTION DISPLAYED
TALES OF THE HEART

Ann Radcliffe

CASTLES OF ATHLIN AND DUNBAYNE
GASTON DE BLONDEVILLE

Mary Shelley

VALPERGA
THE FORTUNES OF PERKIN WARBECK
LODORE
FALKNER
JOURNAL OF A SIX WEEKS' TOUR

Mary Wollstonecraft

MARY, A FICTION
A VINDICATION OF THE RIGHTS OF MEN

15
Typed
July 14, 1938

<u>LIBRARY</u>

14th July, 1938.

Dear Mrs. Woolf,

    We were surprised at receiving OUIDA and Jean Batten's MY LIFE yesterday evening, and I am sure they will be the occasion of great delight to large numbers of members. Ouida, in fact, has been eagerly snapped up already, and I am sure Jean Batten will begin her flight from hand to hand as soon as her presence in the Library is known.

    With many thanks for this and your other kindnesses,

                      Yours sincerely,

                        Librarian

Mrs. Woolf,
    52, Tavistock Square,
        W. C. 1.

16
Handwritten on letterhead
August 13, 1938

From **Leonard Woolf, Monk's House, Rodmell, Lewes, Sussex.**
("Mrs" underlined handwritten in ink above "Leonard")

13th Aug. 38.

Dear Miss Douie,

    I wonder if you could very kindly help with a quotation with which I could answer the enclosed letter from Time and Tide?
    I found so many statements, from schoolmasters, objecting to women teaching boys ~~tha~~ after 14 that I compressed them into one, & thus did not give a reference. The note books in which my cuttings are kept are in London, & I cannot get at them.[9] If you could supply me with something bearing out my statement, I should be very grateful. Would you kindly return the cutting.
I am awaiting another library list!

                                  Yours sincerely
                                         Virginia Woolf.

---

[9]Woolf is referring to Monks House Papers B16f, Vols. 1, 2, and 3, demonstrating here the importance of her gathering material to enter in these scrapbooks as her research and sources for *Three Guineas*. Even though *Three Guineas* came out in June, 1938, Woolf received and responded to many letters in the aftermath, as ably demonstrated in Anna Snaith's "Three Guineas Letters," *Woolf Studies Annual* 6 (2000) : 17-168.

17
Typed
August 16, 1938

[handwritten] Acknowledged with thanks by V.W.

August 16th, 1938.

Dear Virginia,

Miss Douie is away on her holiday, and so I am making shift to answer your letter.

I fear the root of it all is that you have made an error in saying "a conference of <u>headmasters</u>" instead of "a conference of <u>schoolmasters</u>".

The various teachers' associations are very confusing. The Headmasters' Association and the Headmistresses' Association are "Olympic bodies"; the Assistant Masters' Association and the Assistant Mistresses' Association are in a minor degree "Olympic". All four of these are concerned with secondary education.

Then there comes the National Union of Teachers which includes both men and women teachers in elementary schools. This though not "Olympic" is the official association for this class of teacher. It has a large majority of women members and a large majority of men on its Executive Committee, though this year its President is a woman. Somewhere about 1922 it resolved that it was in favour of Equal Pay, and this resulted in a break away of about 2000 men teachers who formed themselves into the National Association of Schoolmasters with the object of maintaining higher pay for men than women and preventing women from having any dominion over anything male above the age of seven. This was followed by another break away from the N.U.T. of a large body of the more militant of the women teachers who considered that the Resolution was and would remain nothing but a pious one and who formed themselves into the National Union of Women Teachers with the object of actively working for Equal Pay and complete equality of the sexes in their profession.

-2-

Both these dissident societies (though much smaller than the N.U.T.) have branches all over the place and are full of life and hold annual conferences which are very fully reported in the press.

The cuttings you have collected must be, I feel certain, reports of meetings of the National Association of Schoolmasters – for all their branches and their annual conferences continually pass the noxious resolutions which you rolled into one.

The reference which I think most clearly bears you out is a Times report of April 14th, 1936, of a resolution unanimously carried by their conference on the preceding day.

> " 1) That in all boys schools men teachers only should be appointed. 2) That all mixed schools other than infants'should be under a headmaster, with as many male assistants as would ensure that the boys came under the predominating influence of men."

This year the report is not so clear and the resolution itself doesn't fit in quite so well with what you say. The Conference took place on April 18th, 1938, and the Times of the following day says: —

> "A resolution was accepted expressing concern about the present attitude of the authorities to the staffing of mixed schools, which reduced the attractiveness of the profession to men . . .
> . . . . . . (The speaker) asked what man of mettle was going to proffer his life's services as an assistant, and even that service to be spent possibly under the orders of a woman."

The Association publishes a paper called "The Schoolmaster" in which their tenets are incessantly advocated, and I should think Mr. Willson could be referred to that, but I fear you will be bound to say that by a slip you have written the word "head" instead of "school" masters, for I feel sure he is right in thinking that the Headmasters Conference would never announce such a doctrine.

This is a very long preachment, but I have told you the whole history so that you should know what lies behind the point at issue.

P[hilippa].S[trachey]. [handwritten]

18
Typed
August 16, 1938

[Handwritten] 17th Aug. Mrs. Woolf replies that she will send all three books.

August 16th, 1938.

Dear Virginia,

I am answering the last remark on your card in a separate letter for the sake of convenience.

The Library Committee met on the day before Miss Douie left for her holiday or she would no doubt have greedily written to tell you that there were three luxury books rejected this month: -

Mona Wilson	Jane Austen and Some Contemporaries Cresset Press - 10/6.
H. C. Barnard	Madame de Maintenant and St. Cyr. Second hand at the Times Library 6/ - . (Published at 10/6)

Both these we should like very much especially the first, though the second is also believed to be good.

The third on the list was Lady Oxford's "Myself when Young". I expect you will have seen this and will be able to judge whether it is worth having. In any case it is rather expensive—12/6—and it might be got second-hand from the Times later on if you thought it desirable. If purely twaddling don't lets have it.

Mrs. L. Woolf,
    Monk's House
        Rodmell,
            Lewes.

19
Typed
September 2, 1938

<u>Library</u>   September 2nd., 1938.

Dear Mrs. Woolf,

    Thank you very much indeed for the very welcome gift of Barnard's <u>Madame de Maintenon and Saint-Cyr</u> received this morning. It was so kind of you to give us a brand new copy in place of the second-hand one for which we modestly asked, and it is certain to be greatly appreciated by members, as I need hardly say all your delightful presents have been. I myself have, alas, seen very little of them, as they are all continually out, many of them with long waiting lists of eager applicants.

                Yours sincerely,

                Librarian

Mrs. Woolf.
52 Tavistock Square,
W.C.1.

20
Typed
October 31, 1938

Library.

31st October, 1938.

Dear Mrs. Woolf,

      Very many thanks for your kind message regarding a balance in the bank which I received from Mrs. Strachey. The reason why we have not recently troubled you with petitions for books is that we do not have a Library Committee in August or September. Our appetite for new books has however been whetted rather than the reverse by long abstinence.

      The Committee ask me to say that they would very much appreciate it if you were able to give us MISS WEETON: THE JOURNAL OF A GOVERNESS, 1807-1811[10] (Oxford University Press) 12/6, Amelia Earhart's LAST FLIGHT[11] (Harrap) 9/ -, and Miss Haldane's FROM ONE CENTURY TO ANOTHER[12] (Machehose) 12/6. The last two have reached the second-hand stage, and can be got from the Times Book Club for about half price.

      They also ask me to say, in regard to your other kind offer to fill gaps in our antique section that they are particularly anxious at the present time to acquire a copy of Mary Wollstonecraft's VINDICATION OF THE RIGHTS OF MAN, 1798, as the National Central Library recently asked us for the loan of it in vain. They would therefore be most grateful if, when you are

---

    [10]Miss Weeton's Journal is referenced in *Three Guineas*, fn 32, p. 164, and in the *Reading Notes*, Vol 2, p. 37.

    [11]*Earhart's Last Flight* is referenced in *Three Guineas*, fn 46, p. 186; and while Woolf does not include notes in her *Reading Notes* from this work, she does include clippings about women aviators in Vol. 2, p. 6 and Vol. 3, p. 28.

    [12]Haldane's work is referenced in *Three Guineas*, fn 1.3, p. 145; fn 11.4, p. 148; fn 4.3, p. 174, and in the *Reading Notes*, Vol. 3, p. 52, where her note indicates Haldane's exclusion from a party at Cambridge where her brother, among others, received their degrees. Haldane listened to speeches and watched through a peephole from another room. "The whole surroundings seemed mediaeval," wrote Haldane.

scanning the pages of second-hand catalogues, you could keep a special look-out for it. Not, I fear, that it is likely to reward even the most earnest search, for I believe it is only rarely that a copy comes on the market—and then it is probably beyond the dreams of avarice.

With many thanks for your generosity to us,

Yours sincerely,

Librarian.

Mrs. Woolf,
    52 Tavistock Square, W.C.1.

21
Handwritten on letterhead
November 13, 1938

From Leonard Woolf   52, Tavistock Square, W.C.1.
                                                Telephone: Museum 2621

[Mrs written across the "L" of Leonard]

13th Nov 38

Dear Miss Douie,

I am sending the books, after some delay, but I was away. I have had no luck with the second hand booksellers lately, or I would have tried to fill up some of your gaps. I will keep a look out for the Mary Wollstonecraft in particular.

Yrs sincerely

V. Woolf.

22
Typed
November 15, 1938

Library.

15th November, 1938.

Dear Mrs. Woolf,

     LAST FLIGHT and FROM ONE CENTURY TO ANOTHER arrived yesterday, and we were, of course, delighted to welcome them to their new home. Not that, they will be quietly remaining there long, for I am glad to say that all the books you give us have the modern habit of gadding about and spend very little time on their shelves! In fact, Amelia Earhart never reached hers, but was eagerly carried off by a borrower the moment she was catalogued.

     It is very good of you to say you will look out specially for the VINDICATION OF THE RIGHTS OF MAN. I am afraid very few copies come into the market.

With very many thanks,

Yours sincerely,

Librarian.

Mrs. Woolf
     52 Tavistock Square,
        W.C.1.

23
Typed
November 16, 1938

<u>Library.</u>

16th November, 1938.

Dear Mrs. Woolf,

Thank you very much indeed for MISS WEETON: JOURNAL OF A GOVERNESS, which arrived this morning, and which will, I am sure, give delight to many readers.

It is a great joy receiving all these beautiful new books.

Yours sincerely,

Librarian.

Mrs. Woolf
      52 Tavistock Square,
          W.C.1.

24
Typed
December 2, 1938

<u>Library.</u>

2nd December, 1938.

Dear Mrs. Woolf,

When the Library Committee met last week they had one book on their list which they wondered if you would be so very kind as to give them. It was Mrs. Lindbergh's LISTEN! THE WIND, (Chatto and Windus), 7/6.

The book was particularly well reviewed, and those who have read it appear to admire it greatly. I am sure if you are able to give it us many readers will bless your name, as indeed they do already for the gift of so many fascinating books.

Yours sincerely,

Librarian.

Mrs. Woolf
    52 Tavistock Square,
        W.C.1.

25
Typed
December 10, 1938

<u>Library.</u>

10th December, 1938.

Dear Mrs. Woolf,

LISTEN! THE WIND has just made its very welcome appearance. Thank you so much.

I am sure it will give a great deal of pleasure to large numbers of readers here in the Library, and that they will all bless you for your bounty.

Yours sincerely,

Librarian.

Mrs. Woolf
    52 Tavistock Square,
        W.C.1.

26
Typed
February 9, 1939

<u>Library.</u>

9th February, 1939.

Dear Mrs. Woolf,

The Library Committee at its last meeting wondered if you would add to your kindness in giving us MISS WEETON: THE JOURNAL OF A GOVERNESS, Vol I, by generously presenting us with the second volume, which has just been published (Oxford University Press, 15/-).

They will be deeply grateful if you feel able to do so, and so, I am sure, will the number of enthusiastic borrowers who read the first volume, and are longing to read the second. Miss Weeton has, in fact, been nearly, but not quite, as popular as "Ouida".

Yours sincerely,

Librarian.

Mrs. Woolf
    52 Tavistock Square,
        W.C.1.

27
Typed
February 11, 1939

<u>Library.</u>

11th February, 1939.

Dear Mrs. Woolf,

MISS WEETON has just arrived and we are delighted to welcome her. Thank you so much.

I am afraid she had a sad life, but her history is now being eagerly read by members of the Society, who are all most grateful to you for giving them the opportunity.

Yours sincerely,

Librarian.

Mrs. Woolf
    52 Tavistock Square,
        W.C.1.

28
Typed
March 3, 1939

Library.

3rd March, 1939.

Dear Mrs. Woolf,

The Library Committee at its meeting last week wondered if you would be able to add to all your former kindness by giving us Enid McLeod's HELOISE (Chatto and Windus) 12/6?

The book has been well reviewed and would be a most delightful addition to the Library, and a very pleasant change from the heavy statistical and depressing industrial literature on which we are compelled to spend our hard-won pennies.

Yours sincerely,

Librarian.

Mrs. Woolf
    52 Tavistock Square,
        W.C.1.

29
Typed
March 9, 1939

<u>Library.</u>

9th March, 1939.

Dear Mrs. Woolf,

    Thank you very much indeed for so kindly giving us HELOISE for the Library.

    She will be a great ornament to the Biographical Section, and we are delighted to have her to add to our galaxy of famous women of all ages. The temptation to be the first borrower is too great for me to resist it, although I usually think it only fair to give the general public a chance first!

Yours sincerely,

Librarian.

Mrs. Woolf
    52 Tavistock Square,
        W.C.1.

30
Typed
March 30, 1939

<u>Library.</u>

30th March, 1939.

Dear Mrs. Woolf,

I am afraid this is the usual monthly begging letter. At its meeting last week, the Library Committee wondered whether you would add to all your former kindness by giving us THE TAYLORS OF ONGAR, by D.M. Armitage, (Heffer), 10/6d.

It deals with all the Taylor family, but Jane and Ann figure largely in its pages, and it appears to be a most delightful book about very remarkable and unusual people. Though one knows them better for their ORIGINAL POEMS FOR INFANT MINDS, the girls no less than the boys seem to have been apprenticed to the family trade of copperplate engraving, which must have been very unusual at that period.

HELOISE has not been in at all since you so kindly gave her to us last month.

Yours sincerely,

Librarian.

Mrs. Woolf
52, Tavistock Square,
LONDON, W.C.1.

31
Typed
April 4, 1939

<u>Library.</u>

4th April, 1939.

Dear Mrs. Woolf,

     Thank you very much for THE TAYLORS OF ONGAR, which has just arrived.

     It looks a most delightful book, and will, I am sure, give pleasure to many readers. The Library Committee feels quite unable to express adequately their gratitude to you for giving them books which people really enjoy reading, and I have no doubt that the members of Women's Service are entirely of the same mind.

                            Yours sincerely,

                                    Librarian.

Mrs. Woolf
52, Tavistock Square,
LONDON, W.C.1.

32
Typed
May 4, 1939

<u>Library.</u>

4th May, 1939.

Dear Mrs. Woolf,

The Library Committee at its last meeting wondered if you would be able to add to all your former kindness by giving us Alicia Percival's THE ENGLISH MISS (Harrap) 10/6d.

It appears from the reviews to be not only a fascinating but a thoroughly sound piece of work, and the illustrations, if the one I enclose is typical, are certainly charming.

Yours sincerely,

Librarian.

Mrs. Woolf
    52, Tavistock Square,
        LONDON, W.C. 1.

33
Typed
May 13, 1939

13th May, 1939.

Dear Mrs. Woolf,

Thank you very much indeed for so kindly giving us Alicia Percival's THE ENGLISH MISS.

I see it is recommended by the Book Society, and it looks an altogether charming book – a very welcome oasis in our rather arid collection of useful but not always very lively literature.

                    Yours sincerely,

                       Librarian.

Mrs. Woolf
52, Tavistock Square,
LONDON, W.C. 1.

34
Typed
July 4, 1939

                      4th July, 1939.

Dear Mrs. Woolf,

  The Library Committee at its last meeting wondered whether, in accordance with your very generous offer to present us with books we were unable to purchase ourselves, it would be possible for you to give us ELIZABETH GARRETT ANDERSON by Louise Garrett Anderson (Faber & Faber), 10/6d., and A PECULIAR TREASURE, by Edna Ferber (Heinemann), 12/6d. It would be a great pleasure to us to have them.

  Knowing our grasping nature, you must have been quite surprised at receiving no requests from us last month. This was not due to a change for the better in our dispositions, but was due to the fact that all the books published about then seemed so dull that we hadn't the heart to ask for them.

Yours sincerely,

Librarian.

Mrs. Woolf
52, Tavistock Square,
LONDON, W.C. 1.

35
Typed
July 6, 1939

6th July, 1939.

Dear Mrs. Woolf,

    Thank you so much for your kind present of ELIZABETH GARRETT ANDERSON and A PECULIAR TREASURE.

    It is most delightful to have them, and I am sure in their different way they will give pleasure to many readers.

I feel the fact that one member remarked the other day that she always found the very books she wanted to read here in our Library is almost entirely due to your generosity.

Yours sincerely,

Librarian.

Mrs. Woolf
52, Tavistock Square,
LONDON, W.C. 1.

36
Typed
July 28, 1939

<u>Library.</u>

28th July, 1939.

Dear Mrs. Woolf,

This time, the Library Committee is not crying to you for help in replenishing its stocks of new books, but for an ancient treasure.

We have at the moment the opportunity to acquire a set of 12 separately bound pamphlets relating to the bitter controversy which raged over Hannah More's endeavour to start schools for the poor in rural Somerset. To find so large a number all on the market at once is, of course, extremely unusual. Indeed, most of the individual pamphlets probably found their way into early 19th Century waste-paper baskets, and few can have survived till this day. Alas, the price is £3, and this is a special reduction made by Mr. David Low, the Secondhand Bookseller, who is rather a friend of the Library.

We are extremely diffident about asking you to give us these, but it does seem a pity to miss what would be so valuable and interesting an addition to our antique section. There will be no further Library Committee till the end of October, and even after that, if you did feel able to give us the Hannah More pamphlets, we would give an undertaking not to ask you for anything for a month or two. Indeed, we should not have the face to act otherwise!

The pamphlets are at present in the Library on approval. I know the time is rather short, as we close for a month on August 4th, but if you are in London, and would care to come and see them, they will be here for inspection.

Yours sincerely,

Librarian.

Mrs Woolf
52, Tavistock Square,
LONDON, W.C. 1.

37
Handwritten on letterhead
July 30 [1939]

From *Leonard Woolf, Monk's House, Rodmell, near Lewes, Sussex.*

~~2~~   30 July

Dear Miss Douie,

Yes, certainly I will give the money for the pamphlets. I don't know that I want to read them myself, but I'm sure the Library ought to have them. I shall not be in London for some weeks, but hope to look in some time to see them.

I enclose cheque for £3

Yr sincerely V. Woolf

38
Typed
July 31, 1939

31st July, 1939.

Dear Mrs. Woolf,

    Thank you so very much indeed for your noble gift to enable us to buy the Hannah More pamphlets.

    They will be a very interesting and important addition to the Library. If not unique, the collection must be extremely rare, and we are indeed fortunate that your bounty has enabled us to acquire it.

    I cannot say that the controversialists err on the side of charity!

    With again many thanks,

                                    Yours sincerely,

                                    Librarian.

Mrs. Woolf
Monk's House,
Rodmell,
Near Lewes,
Sussex.

39
Typed
March 11, 1940

1541

<u>Library.</u>

March 11th, 1940

Dear Mrs Woolf,

    Now that the war has made so much difference to everyone's finances, I do not know whether you will still be able to continue your very kind practice of presenting the Library with books. But if it is possible for you to do so, the Library Committee wondered whether you would be so kind as to give us a book which is advertised for sale for 8/6d in David Low's Catalogue No. 29.

    This is Hannah More's THOUGHTS ON THE MANNERS OF THE GREAT TO GENERAL SOCIETY, New edition, 1809, with presentation inscription by the author.

    I am afraid, since your gift last July of the 12 pamphlets on the controversy over her schools in Somerset, you may think we are becoming almost too attached to Hannah More! But that is the way things happen; once you start acquiring a good collection of one writer, you can't help going on trying to complete it. Apart from the very interesting pamphlets, we have quite a fair collection of her works. Indeed, it is now a race between Hannah More and Harriet Martineau to see which gets completed first!

                      Yours sincerely,

                            Librarian.

Mrs. Woolf
    52, Tavistock Square
        W. C. 1

40
Handwritten on letterhead
March 14 [1940]

From *Leonard Woolf, Monk's House, Rodmell, near Lewes, Sussex.*

14th March

Dear Miss Douie,

> I am sorry for the delay but I am in bed with influenza. I shall be glad to give the book you mention, if you will order it & send me the bill. Of course I cannot be certain about the future, but if you will let me know from time to time I will do my best.

> Yrs sincerely
> V. Woolf

41
Typed
April 22, 1940

1541

April 22nd, 1940

Dear Mrs Woolf,

I am delighted to say Mr David Low has now found Hannah More's THOUGHTS ON THE IMPORTANCE OF THE MANNERS OF THE GREAT TO GENERAL SOCIETY. He brought it along in person this morning, with many apologies for the delay.

It is a great acquisition to the Library, not only in increasing our collection of her Works, but in giving us for the first time an example of her handwriting and signature, for we have nothing from her in our Autograph Collection.

It is most good of you to give us the book, and we are extremely grateful. I enclose the bill as you said I might do, with many thanks.

Yours sincerely,

Librarian.

Mrs. Woolf
    52, Tavistock Square,
        W. C. 1

42
Typed
May 31 [1940]

May 31st

Dear Mrs Woolf,

It scarcely seems to be the time for thinking about books for the Library, but at its last meeting the Library Committee instructed me to write and ask you whether you would be so very kind as to give us Toni Sender's AUTOBIOGRAPHY OF A GERMAN REBEL (Routledge), 7/6d. We are very diffident about asking for it, but you did say when you last wrote that you would continue your generous practice of presenting books to the Library as long as possible, and this emboldens us to make the request. I enclose a review for your inspection.

The Library Committee were quite entranced with the inscribed copy of Hannah More's THOUGHTS ON THE IMPORTANCE OF THE MANNERS OF THE GREAT TO GENERAL SOCIETY.

                Yours sincerely,

                Librarian

Mrs Woolf
    Monk's House,
        Rodmell,
           Nr Lewes,
              Sussex

43
Typed
June 14 [1940]

                June 14th

Dear Mrs Woolf,

We are very delighted to have Toni Sender's AUTOBIOGRAPHY OF A GERMAN REBEL, which arrived this morning. Thank you so much.

It is most good of you to give it us for the Library, and I know it is one of those books – like so many of the others you have given us – which will be constantly out on loan. In fact, we have already been asked more than once if we had it.

                Yours sincerely,

                Librarian

Mrs Woolf,
    Monk's House,
        Rodmell,
           Lewes

44
Typed
July 25, 1940

                                          1541

                                July 25th, 1940

Dear Mrs Woolf,

    At their meeting yesterday the Library Committee had their attention drawn to two items by Mary Carpenter included in a catalogue sent us by E.M. Lawson of Sutton Coldfield. They are :-

        OUR CONVICTS, 2 Vols. 1864   15/-, and
        JUVENILE DELINQUENTS, 1st Ed. 1853   7/6d

Both are, I believe, hard to come by, and we are most anxious not to let slip the chance of acquiring them.

    Though the very day after the new budget provisions were announced seems hardly the most appropriate time to importune one's friends for gifts, the Committee desired me to write and ask you, if you felt able to do so, to be so very kind as to give us one of them. Even we have not the face to ask for both, and indeed, we feel very diffident about asking at all, but such an opportunity may not occur again, and we are emboldened by the fact that you very kindly said we were to go on making our requests.

The Library will be shut from August 1st to September 1st inclusive.

Yours sincerely,

Librarian

Mrs Woolf,
    Monk's House,
        Rodmell,
            Lewes,
                Sussex

[Handwritten note in bottom right hand corner] Mrs. Woolf telephoned would give us both books, & instructed us to tell Lawson to send bill to her. Sent letter of thanks.

45
Typed on letterhead
September 13 [1940]

September 13th

Dear Mrs Woolf,

I believe Miss Strachey has already thanked you for the two books by Mary Carpenter you so kindly gave us, but I feel I must write too and say how delightful it was to see them here on my return from my holiday,

I gather she failed to show as much enthusiasm as she might have over these new treasures! But they are indeed a great acquisition, not only because they are important in the history of penal reform, and moreover hard to get, but also because we already have her REFORMATORY SCHOOLS, and there is something particularly attractive about completing a set.

With very many thanks,

Yours sincerely,

Librarian

Mrs Woolf
   Monk's House,
      Rodmell,
         Lewes,
            Sussex

46
Typed
March 26 (1941)

[Handwritten note at top center] 1937-40
DEAD

Women's Service Library
12, Charlbury Road
Oxford
March 26th

Dear Mrs. Woolf,

Since we last appealed to your bounty in July 1940, much has happened to the Library. Following the bad air-raid damage to Women's Service House in

October, when though much was destroyed the Library itself was mercifully spared, it was decided that the only wise course was to remove our books from the dangerous purlieus of Westminster if another home could possibly be found for them. Through the generosity of the Society of Oxford Home-Students, we have been given hospitality in their new Library in the Woodstock Road, and have transferred Women's Service Library there, lock, stock and barrel, or, in other words, complete even to its own shelving, equipment and librarian.

In these circumstances, it has not been possible to hold any meetings of the Library Committee, and Miss Strachey and I are wondering if you will let us write to you direct without their authority, to ask if you are still able to continue your kind gifts of books. The two on which we are at the moment casting covetous eyes are Dame Katherine Furse's HEARTS AND POMEGRANATES (Peter Davies), 15/-, and Blanche Dugdale's FAMILY HOMESPUN (Murray), 9/-. If you are able to give us one or other, or even both, we shall, of course be eternally grateful, but we know how difficult times are at present from the financial point of view, and we do our begging with the utmost diffidence.

Many [sic] I also take this opportunity of saying how greatly I enjoyed reading ROGER FRY, and of thanking you for the pleasure it gave me.

Yours sincerely,

Librarian

Mrs Woolf,
    Monks House
        Rodmell, Lewes.

[Handwritten note at bottom] Mrs Woolf died before receiving this

Virginia Woolf and T. S. Eliot: An Atheist's Commentary on the Epistemology of Belief [1]

Michael Lackey

I.

Not all atheists are atheistic.[2] Such is one of the major discoveries of many late-nineteenth and early-twentieth century intellectuals.[3] Perhaps most direct on this point is Jean-Paul Sartre, who claims that many atheists remain believers because they unwittingly adopt a mentality that is distinctive to the believer.[4] For Sartre, "there is no human nature, since there is no God to conceive it" (36). Given this logic, those who believe in human nature are believers, even if they call themselves atheists, which is why Sartre specifically faults Enlightenment thinkers: "the atheism of the *philosophers* discarded the idea of God, but not so much for the notion that essence precedes existence" (36). What troubles Sartre so much is the Enlightenment philosopher's failure to realize that believing in human nature (an essence) presupposes a theological orientation towards the world. Marcel Proust makes a similar point in *Swann's Way* when his narrator observes: even after the death of the Gods, "when a belief vanishes, there survives it . . . an idolatrous attachment to the old things which our faith in them

---

[1] I would like to thank Suzette Henke, Val Gough, and Pierre-Eric Villeneuve for patiently listening to my arguments about Woolf's atheism and for helping me to formulate my own position. I would also like to thank Pamela Caughie and the readers from *Woolf Studies Annual* who read earlier versions of this essay and advised me in better focusing and organizing my ideas.

[2] In my essay, "Atheism and Sadism: Nietzsche and Woolf on Post-God Discourse," I detail the various types of atheism (nihilism, absurdism, atheism) emerging in the late-nineteenth and early-twentieth centuries. According to my taxonomy, nihilists and absurdists remain believers despite themselves. Only those who have identified and exorcised the theological prejudices inherent in language are true atheists according to my model. This point will become clear later in this essay.

[3] For a discussion of the gradual intellectual development leading towards "absolute atheism" (4), see James Thrower's book *Western Atheism: A Short History*. Thrower focuses on epistemology and science, whereas my work focuses on language.

[4] Richard Rorty makes a similar observation when he claims that the "very idea that the world or the self has an intrinsic nature ... is a remnant of the idea that the world is a divine creation, the work of someone who had something in mind, who Himself spoke some language in which He described His own project" (*Contingency* 21). Given Rorty's logic, a person who believes in human nature is implicitly a believer.

did once animate" (324). Though the sea of faith may have receded, the operative assumptions from the age of belief remain intact.

Not surprisingly, many atheist writers overstate their atheism in order to highlight their "absolute atheist" perspective.[5] For instance, Nietzsche praises Arthur Schopenhauer for being "the *first* admitted and inexorable atheist among us Germans" (*Gay* 307). "Unconditional honest atheism," according to the Übermensch philologist, "is the only air we breathe, we more spiritual men of this age!" (*Genealogy* III.27) Sigmund Freud also makes this point rather emphatically when he refers to himself as "a completely godless Jew" (*Psychoanalysis* 64) and "an out-and-out unbeliever" (*Letters* 453), and in the 1953 novel *The Outsider*, Richard Wright's Cross Damon claims that "Modern consciousness is Godlessness .... Godlessness in a strict sense" (274). In a "Sketch of the Past," Virginia Woolf follows suit by claiming that "certainly and emphatically there is no God" (72).

For writers like Nietzsche, Freud, Woolf, Sartre, and Wright, understanding the world in absolute atheistic terms is not just a hair-splitting semantic game; it is crucial to their projects as intellectuals. In the following pages, I look closely at Woolf's emphatic atheism in relation to T. S. Eliot's rhetoric of belief. The relationship between these two is fraught with much ambivalence, and while it has generated excellent studies of a powerful literary rivalry, an imbalance in gender relations, and divergent aesthetic philosophies, no one has yet done a focused analysis of the religious tensions between the two.[6] The virtue of such a study will be to explain Woolf's need to refer to herself as certainly and emphatically atheistic. Moreover, it will bring into sharper focus two separate responses to the modernist plight with regard to knowledge.[7]

---

[5]David Berman also takes note of the atheist's tendency to make an emphatic declaration of unbelief. Such a person he refers to as a "thorough atheist" (218-221).

[6]For useful studies of the relationship between Woolf and Eliot, see Lyndall Gordon's "Our Silent Life: Virginia Woolf and T. S. Eliot"; Hermione Lee's *Virginia Woolf* (432-447); Bonnie Kime Scott's *Refiguring Modernism. Volume One: The Women of 1928* (128-38); and Erwin R. Steinberg's "*Mrs. Dalloway* and T. S. Eliot's Personal Wasteland."

[7]In *Rich and Strange*, Marianne DeKoven makes note of two divergent responses to modernism: "Antimodernists generally consider the fragmentation and disjunctiveness so broadly characteristic of modernist form a capitulation to nihilist political despair concerning the possibility of representing a unified interpretive synthesis of the life of modern society. Promodernists consider the same phenomenon montage or polysemy: form that is nonlinear, decentered, or open and therefore antihierarchical and antiphallogocentric" (9). My approach to the period is similar to DeKoven's, although I focus on the theolog-

II.

In Woolf's corpus, there is much paranoia the moment a believer comes upon the scene, a fear and dread that unhinges characters and sends them spiraling out of emotional and rhetorical control.[8] For instance, George Carslake of "A Simple Melody" resents the power religious people have over language.[9] Whatever phrase he uses, however mundane, tinkles "in his ear with a sham religious flavour," for the religious, according to Carslake, colonize discourse, appropriating and then fashioning it to serve their ends. "'Getting home'," for example, "the religious had appropriated that. It meant going to Heaven." Given the believer's control of language, Carslake feels "trapped into the words. 'To believe in God'" (203), a discovery that clearly anticipates Mrs. Ramsay's feeling in *To The Lighthouse*. In a weak moment, Mrs. Ramsay says to herself: "We are in the hands of the Lord." But immediately questioning the validity of such a claim, she says: "Who had said it? Not she; she had been trapped into saying something she did not mean" (63). More significantly, after reflecting on the degree to which she has been *trapped* into belief Mrs. Ramsay searches "into her mind and heart, purifying out of existence that lie, any lie" (64). This reflective act of self-purification stands in stark contrast to Mr. Ramsay, for just after she affirms her atheism, Mr. Ramsay laughs to himself as he thinks of the older David Hume, who had "grown enormously fat" and was "stuck in a bog." Consistent with the theme of being trapped into belief, an old woman rescues the skeptical philosopher from the bog "on condition he said the Lord's prayer" (73).

Perhaps the most poignant and clever example of a person being trapped into belief is found in the painfully precarious predicament of a minor character from *Jacob's Room*. Mrs. Jarvis, a friend of Betty Flanders, is the unhappy wife of a

---

ical/atheist divide—antimodernists, like Eliot, tend to be believers, while promodernists, like Woolf, tend to be atheists.

[8]There have been a handful of studies on Woolf's atheism, but to date only Susan E. Lorsch has the background in atheist literature to make sense of Woolf's distinctively atheistic project. Though Lorsch's work is first-rate scholarship, her model is only an initial phase in the process of understanding Woolf's atheism. For Lorsch, God's death leads to the designifcation of nature, but according to more recent studies, especially in the post-structuralist tradition, atheism leads to the designification of the "human" (the death of the subject). As should be obvious, my work does not refute Lorsch's; it merely builds on what she has intelligently begun. Other scholars who have discussed Woolf's atheism include Makiko Minow-Pinkney, Mark Hussey, Val Gough, and Martin Corner.

[9]In my essay, "The Gender of Atheism in Virginia Woolf's 'A Simple Melody,'" I examine Woolf's development as an atheist from 1915 through 1927, focusing specifically on atheistic language. I claim that Woolf became acutely aware in 1925 of the rhetorical strategies believers use to trap atheists into belief, a discovery that significantly impacts her representation of atheism in "A Simple Melody" and *To The Lighthouse*.

clergyman. That Mrs. Jarvis is unhappily married is certain, for she occasionally threatens to leave her husband and ruin his career as a clergyman (27). To deal with her unhappiness, she frequently walks the moors alone and reads poetry. Interestingly, the narrator comments on the dangers of such walks for a clergyman's wife: "Short, dark, with kindling eyes, a pheasant's feather in her hat, Mrs. Jarvis was just the sort of woman to lose her faith upon the moors" (27). But Mrs. Jarvis "did not lose her faith, did not leave her husband, never read her poem through, and went on walking the moors" (27). The narratorial intrusion suggests that losing her faith would be a logical response to her current situation, but even more striking is the way the narrator describes the sequence of events, if Mrs. Jarvis were to lose her faith: loss of faith would lead to her leaving her husband which would then lead to her finishing her poem. But since she did not lose her faith, she continues to walk the moors, something she does "when she was unhappy" (27).

Towards the end of the novel, Woolf gives her reader more substantial reasons for taking Mrs. Jarvis' inchoate atheism more seriously. Once again, we find the depressed woman walking the lonely moors at night, and "[n]either did Mrs. Jarvis think of God" (132). This interjection is striking, for Mrs. Jarvis may not have been thinking about a Jane Austen novel or the First World War, but Woolf's narrator chooses to tell us specifically that the unhappy woman was not thinking about some divine being. Yet, despite not thinking about God, the human and historical landscape is strewn with religious traps that ensnare her within the discourse of belief:

> Mrs. Jarvis found it difficult to think of herself to-night. It was so calm. There was no wind; nothing racing, flying, escaping. Black shadows stood still over the silver moors. The furze bushes stood perfectly still. Neither did Mrs. Jarvis think of God. There was a church behind them, of course. The church clock struck ten. Did the strokes reach the furze bush, or did the thorn tree hear them? (132)

Wherever she turns, whatever she does, "[t]here was a church . . . , of course." If Woolf were a typical religious thinker, like later Evelyn Waugh or Flannery O'Connor, this scene could be read as an invitation to experience the healing powers of God's grace, a twitch on the spiritual thread bringing Mrs. Jarvis into the loving bosom of the Heavenly Father. However, Woolf's reading of the discourse of belief is anything but complimentary. Indeed, religious rhetoric is more a conceptual imposition than a spiritual invitation, so the church can be seen as a ubiquitous tyrant rather than an earthly sanctuary. The narrator makes this clear when she says that the "measured voice" of those who "believed in God" continues "to impose itself upon time and the open air" (133). And such an imposition is exactly what makes Mrs. Jarvis a melancholy mourner. In other words, like Carslake and Mrs. Ramsay, Mrs. Jarvis feels trapped into belief.[10]

Given the subtle but sophisticated traps that Woolf's believers use to ensnare atheists, we can understand Clarissa Dalloway's response to Miss Kilman in *Mrs. Dalloway*. For Clarissa, who "thought there were no Gods" and who "evolved this atheist's religion of doing good for the sake of goodness" (78), the presence of the evangelical Kilman hurls her into a state of confusion (126) and hatred (13), as the self-righteous believer consistently asserts her superiority (12). Such paranoia in the presence of believers is not merely the stuff of fiction, for Woolf responds with the same kind of confusion to T. S. Eliot's 1927 conversion. On hearing that *The Waste Land* poet "has become Anglo-Catholic, believes in God and immortality, and goes to church," Woolf tells her sister: "I was really shocked. A corpse would seem to me more credible than he is. I mean, there's something obscene in a living person sitting by the fire and believing in God" (*L3* 457-58). Because of the believer's tendency to impose upon time and the open air, being in a believer's presence can be dangerous, which explains why Woolf claims that Eliot "may be called dead to us all from this day forward." Consistent with the response of her fictional characters, Woolf fears the presence of believers, so when Eliot has his conversion, she considers him a threat, an *imposing* force that must be avoided.

III.

But to what degree is Woolf's paranoia justified? Is she not making much ado about nothing of substance? Significantly, after T. S. Eliot's conversion, he led a campaign to re-Christianize the world, and a close look at his poetry and lectures will perhaps explain Woolf's uncharitable response to believers. After his conversion, Eliot found himself in a rather awkward position. The religious Eliot was beginning by 1928 to launch an ambitious campaign to re-Christianize the Western world. But having seemingly been a part of a secularist tradition, Eliot felt himself to be a faithful David against the Goliath of secular modernism.[11] Indeed, in his 1934 essay "Religion and Literature," Eliot condemns the corrupting influence of his time precisely because of its secular orientation: "What I do wish to affirm is that the whole of modern literature is corrupted by what I call Secularism, that it is simply unaware of, simply cannot understand the meaning of, the primacy of the supernatural over the natural life: of something which I assume to be our primary concern" (108). To counteract the godless ten-

---

[10]In *A History of Atheism in Britain*, Berman develops an excellent theoretical model for analyzing the strategies believers use to manipulate nonbelievers into belief (1-43).

[11]For a useful discussion of Eliot's conversion and subsequent attempt to Christianize culture, see Peter Ackroyd's *T. S. Eliot: A Life* (149-77).

dencies of his age, Eliot evolved a philosophy of converting people to belief, not on a conscious, but on an "*un*conscious" level.[12] It is for this reason that he faults G. K. Chesterton's overtly Christian approach to literature: "What I want is a literature which should be *un*consciously, rather than deliberately and definitely, Christian" ("Religion" 99). But what exactly is this unconscious Christian literature Eliot speaks of? From 1933 through 1948 Eliot worked towards a definition as he developed a philosophy of conversion that would enable him to lead the culture's infidels down the epistemological straight and narrow, even if they professed fidelity to a pagan creed, or no creed at all. The task would be to make believers of unbelievers without letting the unbelievers know what happened to them.

When converting others, Eliot is not so much concerned, as he argues in *The Idea of a Christian Society*, with "the conscious formulation of the ideal aims of a people, but the substratum of collective temperament, ways of behaviour and unconscious values which provides the material for the formulation" (14). Although Eliot acknowledges that his project resembles totalitarian systems of his time period, he is not sympathetic to the fascist tendency to "partly impose by force upon its peoples" (14).[13] According to Eliot, if there is going to be a stable political structure, the people must adopt his Christian system naturally and "*un*consciously."

The goal, therefore, is "to train people to be able to think in Christian categories" (*Idea* 22). This does not mean that everyone in the culture will be Christian. In fact, Eliot claims that a community with many Christians will not necessarily result in a "Christian organisation of society" (27). Moreover, a community with many nonbelievers could be profoundly Christian, for what constitutes a Christian organization of society are "ways of behaviour and unconscious values." So if non-Christians conduct themselves in a Christian manner, then the society could be called Christian. Most important is that "the Christian faith be ingrained" (23), the "conviction in the heart of the individual" (41). And since most people blindly accept the culture's ideals, were Eliot able to Christianize his culture, the people would be Christian, even if they professed fidelity to another creed.

---

[12]In *T. S. Eliot and Ideology*, Kenneth Asher discusses how Eliot's association with the Jacques Maritain-inspired group known as the Moot contributed significantly to Eliot's philosophy of converting people on an unconscious level. The group debated whether it is better to "advocate active revolution" or to "engage in a more subtle and conspiratorial indoctrination" (85). Eliot opted for the latter.

[13]Asher has done the most extensive work analyzing the degree to which Charles Maurras's fascist political philosophy influenced Eliot (11-59).

Here we come to the crux of Eliot's argument: "a skeptical or indifferent statesman, working within a Christian frame, might be more effective than a devout Christian statesman obliged to conform to a secular frame" (22). For Eliot, most important is the construction of this "Christian frame," "a unified religious-social code of behaviour" (27), and as far as he is concerned, few people need to be conscious of the governing principles of this political system. In fact, Eliot specifies who should be in the know: "it is only from the much smaller number of conscious human beings, the Community of Christians, that one would expect a conscious Christian life on its social level" (23). While the "Community of Christians" is given a privileged epistemological status in discerning the governing principles of the Christian frame, later these same figures are given the perceptual power to know "the supernatural end" of those in the community. And to punctuate their privileged epistemological status, Eliot concludes the paragraph by referring to them as "those who have the eyes to see it" (27). As an emotional and psychological reward for such a penetrating comprehension of the supernatural ends of the community, these spiritual leaders will experience "beatitude" (27), the heavenly bliss of having an omniscient perspective of the culture's governing principles.

No doubt, Eliot sees himself as an expositor of a Chosen-People creed, and while he tolerates nonbelievers, he will do so only so long as they do not pose a threat to the "unified religious-social code." That the Christian is now singularly Chosen, Eliot makes clear in his poem "Journey of the Magi." The narrator records his experience of having witnessed Christ's birth, but as a non-Christian, he does not know whether to call it a birth or a death: "this Birth was/ Hard and bitter agony for us, like/ Death, our death." Christ's birth invalidates "the old dispensation," resulting in the genesis of a newly Chosen religion. And for those who have not accepted the God-Man Christ, like the narrator, despair and alienation are the only alternatives:

> But no longer at ease here, in the old dispensation,
> With an alien people clutching their gods,
> I should be glad of another death. (68-69)

The logic of the poem suggests that the narrator intuits that his religion is now false, and Eliot confirms this by referring to the narrator's people as 'alien.' Furthermore, while Eliot's "Community of Christians" is honored with an uppercase reference, the false gods are degraded by referring to them in the lower case ("their gods"). And for the narrator, who now recognizes that his gods have been displaced, he can only wish for death.

This Chosen-People status is the cornerstone of Eliot's political philosophy, for in establishing his "Christian frame," he can tolerate anyone, except those who call into question the metaphysical foundations of his socio-religious system. He is very direct on this point in his 1933 lecture, *After Strange Gods*:

> The population should be homogeneous; where two or more cultures exist in the same place they are likely either to be fiercely self-conscious or both to become adulterate. What is still more important is unity of religious background; and reasons of race and religion combine to make any large number of free-thinking Jews undesirable. (22)

Eliot's scurrilous remark is totally consistent with his religious orientation. Deeply committed to the metaphysical Christian frame, Eliot must repress the instinct for freedom, that impulse to construct an alternative discourse about the human and the world. Because Jews subscribe to an alternative system, they are for Eliot automatically free-thinking. But it is specifically because they are free-thinking that they pose the most serious threat to his Christian frame.[14] Were Eliot able to indoctrinate Jews with Christian values, they could remain within the community, secretly living a Christian lifestyle while believing they live as Jews. But as a people belonging to a powerful, long-standing tradition, and specifically being free-thinking, the Jews cannot be so easily indoctrinated.[15] For this reason, they must be expelled from the community. Eliot makes this point directly when explaining why the coexistence of "two standards" will have a devastating psychological impact on the religiously grounded society: "The effect on the mind of the people of the visible and dramatic withdrawal of the Church from the affairs of the nation, of the deliberate recognition of two standards and ways of life, of the Church's abandonment of all those who are not by their wholehearted profession within the fold—this is incalculable; the risks are so great that such an act can be nothing but a desperate measure" (*Idea* 39). Because allowing two competing standards to coexist would undermine the single-minded pursuit of the divinely legitimated Truth, dividing the people's mind with regard to the legitimacy of the "Universal Church" (43), Eliot calls for the expulsion of only those traditions that pose a serious threat to the existence of the "one Church" (43). In other words, the Jews are death, death to the living Truths of the Christian Community, because they pose a serious threat to the Christian

---

[14] For an excellent study of Eliot's anti-Semitism, see Anthony Julius's *T. S. Eliot, Anti-Semitism, and Literary Form*.

[15] James Carroll systematically identifies the various overt and covert strategies Christians have used throughout the ages to indoctrinate Jews, ranging from mandating ghettos, placing the Talmud on the Catholic Church's official "Index of Forbidden Books," to forcing Jews to choose between death and conversion. His book sheds considerable light, not just on Christian strategies to force consent, but also the increasingly dangerous consequences for those who resist conversion.

frame. Were it possible to assimilate them effectively into a Christian frame, they could remain. But to preserve Truth and Justice, Eliot has no choice but to expel from the community that which would undermine the faith of the God-appointed Chosen People.

To understand the psychological necessity of banishing dissident voices, we need to take into account Eliot's distinction between tradition and orthodoxy. In *After Strange Gods*, Eliot, through his understanding of tradition, specifically discusses the necessity of an intense emotional bond for the development of his Christian community. To his mind, tradition is "a way of feeling and acting which characterizes a group throughout generations" (31), so it "is of the blood, . . . rather than of the brain" (32); moreover, it includes "all those habitual actions, habits and customs, from the most significant religious rite to our conventional way of greeting a stranger, which represents the blood kinship of 'the same people living in the same place'" (18). In contrast to tradition is orthodoxy. While tradition may be connected with feelings, values, and the unconscious, "*orthodoxy* is a matter which calls for the exercise of all our conscious intelligence" (31). Because orthodoxy presupposes "conscious intelligence," we can assume that orthodox truths can only be apprehended by the rational intellect. Though humans can apprehend orthodox Truths, such Truths are not dependent on the human community for their existence. In other words, where a tradition, which presupposes an emotionally bound social group, can exist only in the context of a human community, orthodoxy can exist even if there were no humans. Eliot is unambiguous on this point: "while tradition, being a matter of good habits, is necessarily real only in a social group, orthodoxy exists whether realized in anyone's thought or not" (32). And as a Christian, Eliot specifically calls for a tradition of "Christian orthodoxy" (22).

But to establish a Christian orthodox tradition is rather difficult if there is an "influx of foreign populations" (15) or if the society has been "invaded by foreign races" (17). Here we return to the "alien" people of "The Journey of the Magi." Should such foreign races invade Eliot's Christian society, they would be welcome if they agreed to efface their identity, if they accepted their own psychological death. This explains Eliot's claim when delivering his *After Strange Gods* lecture that his 1933 Virginia audience has "been less industrialized and less invaded by foreign races" (17). That Virginia had a large African American population does not mean that it has been invaded by a foreign race, according to Eliot. African Americans are invisible or dead; they have no identity, or if they do, it is one that has been effectively subsumed into the Christian frame (Julius makes a similar observation about Eliot's treatment of Virginia African Americans [25]). So when Eliot discusses "foreign races," he does not mean people who are foreigners; he means those who refuse inscription within the Christian frame.

We are now ready to draw some conclusions about Eliot's psychology as a believer. In *After Strange Gods*, he makes a plea for orthodoxy, but in *The Idea of a Christian Society*, orthodoxy is replaced by the Christian frame. Eliot acknowledges that alternative traditions can exist, but given his view of one "Universal Church," there can be only one orthodoxy or one Christian frame. Consequently, "a whole generation might conceivably pass without any orthodox thought" (*After* 32). The best of all possible worlds for Eliot would be a tradition that strives to be orthodox, and as an orthodox Christian, Eliot believes that he must secure the political foundations for a Christian frame to come into being. But to be an orthodox Christian, one need not proclaim oneself a Christian. What Eliot's orthodoxy assumes is a specific relationship to language. Independent of the human community, there is a Truth, so language is merely an attempt to give that Truth a specific form. According to this system, different traditions can construct various discourses in order to access the Truth, but since there is only one Truth, most languages will be mere perversions. As a believer, Eliot must accomplish two things if he wants to make unconscious believers of nonbelievers. First, he must get the nonbeliever to accept the existence of an orthodox Truth. Second, he must get the nonbeliever to conform his/her life to that Truth. Once Eliot accomplishes these two tasks, he will have made believers out of his culture's infidels.

IV.

Taking into consideration Eliot's doctrine of "spiritual perception" (*Notes* 103) and the Christian frame, we can now give a fuller account of Woolf's need to make an overstated claim on behalf of atheism. Belief in God is a trap. But Woolf, like Eliot, is not concerned with a person's overt religious orientation. For Eliot, a person could be a Muslim, Buddhist, or Jew and still be Christian, should this person naturally and unconsciously experience the world within the context of the Christian frame. And the function of the spiritually enlightened Community of Christians is to organize society such that people adopt the Christian frame without actually being aware of this. Given this philosophy of the unconscious believer, Woolf insists that to be an atheist, a person needs to do more than just deny God's existence; this person must reject the believer's frame, the governing assumptions of the system of belief. That Woolf was hyperconscious of the distinction between an overt declaration and an unconscious orientation is clear in her first five novels, where she examines in considerable detail how many self-proclaimed atheists are believers despite themselves. The difference between Peter Walsh and Clarissa Dalloway perhaps best captures the essence of this distinction. Not "for a moment did" Clarissa "believe in God" (29), whereas Peter Walsh is by "conviction an atheist perhaps" (57).[16] An atheist categorically denies God's existence, so saying that Peter is an "atheist perhaps" makes him more of an agnostic, and since Woolf's father wrote voluminously about agnosticism, she was familiar with this discourse.[17] Peter is no anomaly in Woolf's corpus, for a casual glance at the male atheists in the first four novels will indicate a consistent pattern—that the males, while seemingly atheists, are really believers. For instance, in *The Voyage Out* Terence Hewet, a male who touts a progressive feminist ideology, flaunts his apostasy (144), though he betrays a covert faith by attending church (229). In *Night and Day*, Ralph Denham and Katharine Hilbery are both nonbelievers who reject a church wedding, but Ralph's "doubts" about having a church wedding, "which were always raised by Katharine's presence, had vanished completely" now that Katharine's mother suggests a church wedding in a private conversation with Ralph (489). In *Jacob's Room*, though Jacob and Timmy Durrant make jokes about God, we find the two in church. But more important is their decision on the issue of allowing women to take part in a "service in the King's College Chapel" (32). Jacob responds negatively, not just because bringing a woman into the Chapel is like "bringing a dog into church," but also because the women who would come would be "as ugly as sin" (33). The pattern is consistent: Woolf's early male atheists reject God, and yet there are subtle hints (church attendance) that suggest a fidelity to God, a gesture that makes many of her males "atheists perhaps," but not really atheists.

In stark contrast to the atheist perhaps is the emphatic atheist. For example, once Rachel Vinrace passionately declares in *The Voyage Out*, "I don't believe in God" (250), she makes it clear that she will attend church no more (261). In like manner, on the shelf which held "the last relics of religious belief" (*ND* 343), Katharine Hilbery keeps only school books, and to punctuate her atheism, she refuses to be married in a church (489). Like Woolf, who claims that "certainly and emphatically there is no God," "not for a moment did" Clarissa "believe in

---

[16]No critic has yet distinguished the emphatic atheist from the "atheist perhaps" in Woolf's works, and as a consequence, there has been some confusion when dealing with the atheism in Woolf's novels. For instance, Mark Hussey discusses Woolf's atheism in *Mrs. Dalloway*, and while he acknowledges that Woolf's work is that of "an avowed atheist," he does not distinguish between Peter Walsh's "atheism perhaps" and Woolf's emphatic atheism (97). If I have been sufficiently attentive to Woolf's careful distinction, then Clarissa's and Woolf's atheism is significantly different from Peter's.

[17]Woolf specifically calls attention to her father's agnosticism ("Leslie" 75). In her novels, however, there is not a single reference to agnosticism, though there are many references to atheism.

God." And as for Mrs. Ramsay, she has the self-reflective capacity to purify out of existence the lie that we are in the hands of the Lord. In sum, certainly not believing in God is different from being an "atheist perhaps."

In the next part of this essay, I want to examine Woolf's emphatic atheism by looking closely at her writings from 1928 through 1931, a period, I argue, that represents Woolf's most sophisticated thinking on the topic. Within the context of the modern period, Woolf understood the epistemological implications of twentieth-century language philosophy in a way that Eliot simply could not. Like Foucault, Woolf understood that "the death of God profoundly influenced our language" ("Father's" 86). The early Woolf (1915-1927), like Henri Bergson and Martin Heidegger, valorizes time over space, thereby conceiving "reality" in terms of temporal relations instead of a spatialized substance.[18] While this development had radical implications, especially on narrative technique (stream-of-consciousness), it did nothing to challenge the idea that the world possesses a prediscursive conceptual nature.[19] In other words, the correspondence theory of truth remained intact, though the reality that language now signified was a set of relations instead of an essential substance. Woolf's most radical development during her middle period (1928-1931), however, was to reject the correspondence theory of truth in whole, an intellectual development that Nietzsche made in the last two years of his writing (1886-1888)[20] and Wittgenstein made start-

---

[18]Before 1928 Woolf ontologized the temporal flux, a philosophical move that does nothing to challenge the theological assumptions implicit in the correspondence theory of truth. For instance, in her 1924 essay "Montaigne," she claims: "Movement and change are the essence of our being" (63). From essays like "Modern Fiction" to "Mr. Bennett and Mrs. Brown," Woolf reifies life as motion, but by 1928, she began to understand that such a reification presupposes a conceptual reality to which our language is held bound. It was during this period that Woolf started to abandon the correspondence theory of truth in whole.

[19]In "Physics, Sound, and Substance: Later Woolf," Gillian Beer has done some of the most important work on Woolf's understanding of life as a set of relations, and while I find Beer's work compelling, especially her focus on the new physics, I think she ultimately reads Woolf's later novels within the context of a relational correspondence theory of truth. To my mind, Pamela Caughie sheds more light on Woolf's project by focusing on the language problematic, though she does not take into consideration the vital role Woolf's atheism plays in this project. In perhaps one of the most insightful passages on Woolf's philosophy of language, Caughie says: "To speak of rhetoric as either revealing or concealing, to speak of appearance as either natural or contrived, is to set up a false opposition; it is to assume that we can get beyond or beneath the linguistic paradigm, in which rhetorical and sexual differences function, to some natural state, some natural discourse" (80-81).

ing in the 1930s.[21] The Woolf of 1928 discovers that, because God is dead, neither the world nor the self possesses a conceptual nature.[22] Put differently, atheism has a profound effect on the relationship language has to that which it signifies.

V.

As a believer, Eliot assumes the existence of a truth independent of humans—"orthodoxy exists whether realized in anyone's thought or not."[23] The task, therefore, is to cultivate and perfect an epistemological capacity for apprehending such truths, and in his 1948 essay, he outlines this project by showing how "[e]sthetic sensibility must be extended into spiritual perception, and spiritual perception must be extended into esthetic sensibility" (*Notes* 103). By directing the community's gaze towards orthodoxy, Eliot's community of Christians could lead the culture's apostates to orthodox Truth. But not all people want to accept Eliot's system, so he resorts to a strategy of training people, on an unconscious level, to think in Christian orthodox terms. So while there can be a surface diversity, Eliot believes that his Community of Christians must target the "substratum of collective temperament, ways of behaviour and unconscious values" (*Idea* 14) as a way of bringing into existence the anonymous orthodox Christian. In *Notes Towards the Definition of Culture*, Eliot makes this point when he endorses diversity on a conscious level, while working towards orthodox unity on an unconscious level: "The unity with which I am concerned must be largely unconscious" (125). Woolf, by contrast, suggests that "it would be better to give up seeking for the truth" (*Room* 41). As should be

---

[20]For an excellent discussion of the development of Nietzsche's philosophy of language, see Maudemarie Clark's *Nietzsche on Truth and Philosophy* and Sarah Kofman's *Nietzsche and Metaphor*.

[21]For an excellent discussion of Wittgenstein's language philosophy, specifically in the context of Woolf's works, see Caughie's book. Also, for a useful discussion of Wittgenstinian language and reification, see Richard Rorty's "Wittgenstein, Heidegger, and the Reification of Language."

[22]For extremely insightful discussions of the effect of atheism on the deconstruction of "reality," see Jacques Derrida's "Force and Signification," *Of Grammatology* and "The Theater of Cruelty and the Closure of Representation"; and Michel Foucault's "The Discourse on Language," *The Order of Things: An Archaeology of the Human Sciences*, "A Preface to Transgression," and "What is an Author?"

[23]In contrast to Eliot, Rorty says: "Truth cannot be out there—cannot exist independently of the human mind—because sentences cannot so exist, or be out there. The world is out there, but descriptions of the world are not. Only descriptions of the world can be true or false. The world on its own—unaided by the describing activities of human beings—cannot" (*Contingency* 5). Later Woolf is clearly in the same tradition as Rorty.

obvious, Woolf's suggestion cuts at the heart of Eliot's philosophy, for her position opens the door to an epistemic pluralism that Eliot's orthodoxy precludes. Indeed, Eliot insists that "the deliberate recognition of two standards and ways of life" would be devastating, so he would find Woolf's rejection of truth precisely the kind of threat to orthodoxy that must be eliminated.[24]

In what follows I want to show why Woolf was such a threat to Eliot by examining the link between her atheism and the destruction of the correspondence theory of truth. In her 1928 novel *Orlando*, Woolf hit upon a brilliant idea for identifying precisely the radical implications of shifting from a culture of belief that honors unity to an atheistic culture in a strict sense—she traces the life of a single character through five centuries. Born in Elizabethan England, Orlando is raised a traditional Christian who entertains fantasies of lopping off Pagan heads. It is important to note that two sets of binary oppositions are established in the opening pages: Christian/Pagan, male/female. The novel begins with the young Christian—for there could be no doubt about his religion—"in the act of slicing at the head of a Moor" (13). Contra the standard readings of this passage, I want to suggest that the narrator literally means, "there could be no doubt of his sex" or religion.[25] With God in his heaven, all is right with essentialized subjects, so Orlando could playact the male, Christian role expected of a boy "whose father, or perhaps his grandfather, had struck it [the Moor's head] from the shoulders of a vast Pagan" (13).

Before a radical questioning of binary oppositions could occur, the God-hypothesis would first have to be refuted, or at least challenged, and such a questioning did occur during the reign of King James (1603-25), the age in which Galileo's discovery of the telescope (1610) confirmed that the earth is not the center of the universe. The new world view forced God out of the Ptolemaic heavens and undermined the church's traditional belief in the hierarchical chain of being, leaving the early-modern human with no justifiable ground for his/her established standing in the cosmos. So the church, which relinquished neither its power nor its teaching, had to assert itself more forcefully, lest humans fall prey to the "madness" (46) of an undifferentiated universe.

---

[24]As Bonnie Kime Scott notes in *Refiguring Modernism*, when discussing the moral turpitude of literary modernism, Eliot specifically uses Woolf as an example (126), and it is certainly Woolf's rejection of God and truth that would have led him to draw such a conclusion.

[25]Pamela Caughie argues that "our doubt is aroused" about Orlando's sex, because, in calling attention to his sex, the "stress on what is obvious makes it seem unnatural. The stress on an innocent pronoun makes it suspect" (78). Minow-Pinkney argues along similar lines, but she focuses on the text's obsession with disguise (*Virginia* 132).

Not coincidentally, Orlando meets Sasha, a young Russian girl, when King James is in power (31), and during a conversation with her, Orlando notes that only "a knife's blade separates" seeming contraries (45). Because there is no legitimate ground for making clear categorial distinctions, the passage continues, the philosopher "bids us take refuge in the true Church . . . which is our only harbour, port, anchorage, etc., he said, for those tossed on this sea" of a non-differentiatable world (46). Indeed, the narrator goes out of his way to explain how Orlando's mind operates during the age of belief: "For that was the way his mind worked now, in violent seesaws from life to death stopping at nothing in between" (46). Initially, Orlando questions the religious epistemology of binary oppositions, but by turning to the church, he reduces his non-differentiatable experience of the world to an either/or. But let us look at a passage that occurs much later in the text. This time, for the female Orlando, "everything was partly something else, and each gained an odd moving power from this union of itself and something not itself so that with this mixture of truth and falsehood her [Orlando's] mind became like a forest in which things moved; lights and shadows changed, and one thing became another" (323). Early in the novel, Orlando's mind worked "in violent see-saws from life to death stopping at nothing in between," but now her mind is "like a forest in which things moved ... and one thing became another." Woolf is obviously inviting us to consider what causes this radical shift in the way Orlando's mind works, and since Woolf's narrator unambiguously connects Orlando's world of binary oppositions to the church, we can assume that removing the church's dogmatic authority would liberate Orlando's mind.

To indicate that the church has lost credibility, Woolf's narrator documents Orlando's experience in front of St. Paul's church on two different occasions. The first time, just after Orlando has turned to the church, Orlando sees that "the Abbey windows were lit up and burnt like a heavenly, many-coloured shield (in Orlando's fancy): now all the west seemed a golden window with troops of angels (in Orlando's fancy again) passing up and down the heavenly stairs perpetually" (53). Notice how the narrator distances himself from Orlando's interpretation by suggesting that the experience only occurs in Orlando's "fancy." The narrator obviously does not trust Orlando's judgment at this moment. Now let us consider St. Paul's at the end of the eighteenth century: "Orlando then for the first time noticed a small cloud gathered behind the dome of St. Paul's. As the stroke sounded, the cloud increased, and she saw it darken and spread with extraordinary speed" (225). There are no narratorial qualifications this time. But more importantly, as the great cloud shrouds St. Paul's, England is hurled into the age of doubt: "All was dark; all was doubt; all was confusion. The Eighteenth Century was over; the Nineteenth Century had begun" (226).[26] The church's simple binary oppositions no longer obtain in a post-God world, for now that the church has been covered in darkness, it is impossible to ground clear categorial distinctions as the philosopher does during the reign of King James. Hence the confusion and darkness.

If, in the age of belief, truth and meaning precede language, then humans must evolve an epistemology that will enable them to access those truths. For atheists like Woolf, however, God's death leads to the de-divinization of language, which means that defining the human, much less anything else, is simply nonsense. In the context of *Orlando*, this means that "Nothing is any longer one thing" (305). For Eliot, an orthodox Truth, like God, preexists language. Therefore, prediscursive truth (orthodoxy) is what it is whether the human community accesses it or not. But if there is no God, truth and meaning are produced in and through language, which explains how "one thing became another" in Orlando's post-God world. We see this most clearly when Orlando reflects on the complexities of her "being" as a subject. Late in the novel, Orlando calls out: "Orlando." But for the narrator, since "two thousand and fifty-two people" (308) sometimes inhabit a person at any given moment, locating a single self simply makes no sense. But let us say, just for the sake of argument, that we could find a language that would accurately signify each of the 2052 people within an individual body, Woolf's narrator would still consider this project naïve and misguided, because in a post-God world, a stable meaning or an orthodox truth does not exist. Put differently, in contrast to theological discourse, which presupposes the existence of a stable God-created Truth (Eliot's orthodoxy) independent of language and the human, post-God discourse evolves meaning in and through the materiality of the signifier. Derrida is quite compelling on this score: "To write is to know that what has not yet been produced within literality has no other dwelling place, does not await us as prescription in some *topos ouranios*, or some divine understanding. Meaning must await being said or written in order to inhabit itself, and in order to become, by differing from itself, what it is: meaning" ("Force" 11). Language is a tool for producing meaning; it is not an instrument for accessing a prediscursive truth.[27] In the context of *Orlando*, once God is dead and the church no longer dominates, "humans" can then liber-

---

[26]That Woolf considers Western civilization beyond the age of belief she makes clear not only in *Orlando* but also in *A Room of One's Own*: "And when the age of faith was over and the age of reason had come, still the same flow of gold and silver went on" (9). But like Sartre and Proust, Woolf considers many thinkers from the age of reason unconscious believers.

[27]Once we acknowledge that language produces meaning rather than signifying a prediscursive truth, Judith Butler's project follows quite logically—"discourse produces the effects that it names" (*Bodies* 2).

ate language within the body, creating multiple conceptual systems, some of which allow for the possibility of one thing becoming another. It is such an experience of "subjectivity" that Woolf's narrator endorses in *Orlando*.

VI.

Woolf's 1931 novel, *The Waves*, differs significantly from *Orlando*. In 1928, Woolf documents the way the mind works first in the age of belief and then in the age after God's death. In a sense, Woolf uses Orlando to examine the process whereby a person (and a culture) undergoes a transformation from being a believer to an emphatic atheist. The focus, therefore, is on a person's and a culture's development towards a full-fledged atheistic philosophy. *The Waves*, however, differs from *Orlando* because Woolf focuses more on a believer's (Neville's) particular attempt to coerce a nonbeliever (Bernard) into belief. Put differently, the sweeping historical analysis of *Orlando* gives way to a microscopic examination of a subtle psychological skirmish between a believer and an atheist. That Woolf decided to write such a novel as *The Waves* during this time makes perfect sense if we consider that Eliot had already begun his project of converting and re-Christianizing Western civilization—he published "Journey of the Magi" in 1927 and "Ash Wednesday" in 1930. Though there is a sense of triumph for the atheist in *Orlando*, Eliot's campaign surely gave Woolf reason to reconsider to what degree her culture had been effectively secularized. *The Waves* is Woolf's response, so I claim, to the apparent shift back to an age of belief.

Gillian Beer claims that the character of Louis from *The Waves* is modeled on T. S. Eliot ("*Waves*" 87), and while I find Beer convincing on this point, it appears that Neville better embodies Eliot's sneaky religious philosophy. Neville and Eliot have a tendency to coerce a person into belief by manipulating individuals at an unconscious level. More specifically, Eliot and Neville, as poets, wish to *contract* people into a single and unified subject. By contrast, a character like Bernard, who has no time for God or the church, rejects a correspondence theory of truth as he embraces an atheistic philosophy of pluralism and diversity. Such a view deeply offends Neville, mainly because he is an expositor of the unconscious philosophy of a single and unified truth.

But let us consider more carefully the relationship between Bernard and Neville. Bernard considers most people simple-minded, because they are governed by a single idea, "all save Neville, whose mind is far too complex to be reduced by any single activity" (77). And yet, Neville, as master of deception, admits that his complex exterior belies a profoundly concentrated and focused commitment to a single idea: "Nobody guessed the need I had to offer my being to one god" (52). He is right, for Bernard has not a clue about Neville's secret desire, and yet, when Neville later gives Bernard a poem as a token of their friendship, Bernard makes some discoveries that reveal Neville's secret intent. After reading the poem, Bernard feels a strange "line that is spun from us lengthening its fine filament across the misty spaces of the intervening world. He is gone; I stand here, holding his poem. Between us is this line" (89). Later in the novel, Neville clarifies the meaning of "this line": "I am merely 'Neville' to you, who see the narrow limits of my life and the line it cannot pass. But to myself I am immeasurable; a net whose fibres pass imperceptibly beneath the world. My net is almost indistinguishable from that which it surrounds" (214). On the surface, Neville is merely Neville to us, but on an unconscious level ("a net whose fibres pass imperceptibly beneath the world"), he is a potent force that seeks to eliminate pluralism by reducing it to unity (recall Eliot, who admits plurality and diversity on the conscious level, but who claims: "The unity with which I am concerned must be largely unconscious"). As a believer, Neville seeks to convert Bernard, and this means *contracting* Bernard into a single and unified subject. In other words, Neville believes that people possess a nature, and the task is to discover one's true self. Not surprisingly, Neville says of himself: "I am one person—myself" (87). And as a manipulative believer, Neville insists that others must subscribe to this philosophy: "To be contracted by another person into a single being," Bernard says to himself after reading Neville's friendship poem, "how strange ... For I am more selves than Neville thinks" (89). Woolf's decision to use the word *contract* highlights the power of the poetic word. As a legal word, contract indicates Bernard's condition as a political subject—the social or political contract recognizes him as a single self. As a poetic word, contract underlines the power poetry has to materialize a reality within the body of another. Taken together, the word suggests the political power of the poetic word to control a person's genesis within the context of the body politic.

For Woolf the atheist, because there is no God, Neville's attempt to contract Bernard into a single and unified being presupposes a violent epistemology that leads to an extreme form of rhetorical *subjection*. We see this subjection most clearly through Woolf's critique of the "violent language" of the West. Throughout the novel, Neville fawns on Percival, who is described as a God:

> By applying the standards of the West, by using the violent language that is natural to him, the bullock-cart is righted in less than five minutes. The Oriental problem is solved. He rides on; the multitude cluster round him, regarding him as if he were—what indeed he is—a God. (136)

Commenting on this passage, Lorsch claims that Percival represents Christ (147-48), while Kathy J. Phillips argues that he is a symbol for "Osiris, Attis, and

Adonis" (30). But these interpretations miss the point. Woolf is not interested in portraying one God over another; she is interested in the way that the God-concept functions to colonize. Put differently, Woolf exposes the way the God-concept is used as a convenient device behind which colonizers can veil their individual wills to power. According to this interpretation, Percival is no God, because there is no God. On the contrary, God is nothing more than a person in power pretending to be divine in order to justify using his "violent language" of conquest.

So Neville's usage of language to contract Bernard into a single and unified being is essentially linked to his belief in God. Stated differently, to deny the existence of an individual identity that is waiting to be correctly named ("I am one person—myself") is to strike at the heart of belief in God ("there is no human nature, since there is no God to conceive it," Sartre claims), so Neville must contract others into a single self in order to justify offering his "being to one god." By contrast, Bernard, who does not presuppose that truth preexists language, uses discourse, not to signify or represent a human subject as God has created it, but to produce a plethora of "selves" within a human body. This means that subjects are brought into conceptual being through language, and were humans not to be named, they would not come to be as subjects. Bernard is to the point on this score: "When I cannot see words curling like rings of smoke round me I am in darkness—I am nothing" (132). At this point, Bernard has effectively reversed the directionality of signification. Knowledge of the world and self would be possible if there were knowledge to be had, but as Bernard observes: "To speak of knowledge is futile. All is experiment and adventure" (118). Language no longer functions to represent a prediscursive truth, because there is no longer such a truth to be known; rather, language, as experiment, brings into conceptual being that which it names. Therefore, to be is to be named, a point that Neville makes when he claims that "[n]othing should be named lest by doing so we change it" (81). Given this uncanny power of language, when humans verbally interact with one another, there is always the danger of taking conceptual possession of the other, of subjecting the other into grammatical being through one's own verbal will to power, a point Bernard makes when he notes the role language and perception play in his genesis as a subject: "To be myself (I note) I need the illumination of other people's eyes, and therefore cannot be entirely sure what is my self" (116). Without the look of the other, Bernard cannot come to know himself, and yet, in the moment he confers on others the power to illuminate his own subjectivity, he becomes subject to their formative power. Bernard makes this claim even more forcefully when he suggests, like Judith Butler, that he can only come into being as a subject through his interactions with others: "But I only come into existence when the plumber, or the horse-dealers, or whoever it may be, says something which sets me alight.... Thus my character is in part made of the stimulus which other people provide, and is not mine, as yours are" (133). To put this in Butler's words, individuals "enjoy intelligibility only to the extent that they are, as it were, first established in language. The subject is the linguistic occasion for the individual to achieve and reproduce intelligibility, the linguistic condition of its existence and agency. No individual becomes a subject without first becoming subjected or undergoing 'subjectivation'" (*Psychic* 11). Given this logic, were people not to *say* anything, Bernard would not come to be as a subject ("When I cannot see words curling like rings of smoke round me I am in darkness—I am nothing"), for it is only through language that he achieves intelligibility as a subject.

Bernard's refusal to be contracted into a single and unified being poses the greatest threat to a person like Neville, who secretly offers his being to one God. For many, God may be dead and gone on a conscious level, but by manipulating Bernard at an unconscious level, Neville can at least make his friend, as Eliot claims, "*un*consciously, rather than deliberately and definitely," a believer. By rejecting Neville's philosophy of a single and unified subject, however, Bernard rejects God at the deepest level imaginable, because he implicitly rejects the believer's primary assumption—"orthodoxy exists whether realized in anyone's thought or not." Significantly, though Bernard nearly succumbs to Neville's philosophy, he eventually realizes how manipulative his friend can be. And by the end of the novel, Bernard finally comes to terms with his post-God experience of the world: "For this is not one life; nor do I always know if I am man or woman, Bernard or Neville, Louis, Susan, Jinny or Rhoda—so strange is the contact of one with another" (281). Here Bernard does not offer his reader a relational model of "subjectivity"; he merely comments on his own puzzlement with regard to contact with other people. Were Bernard to offer us a systematic model for conceptualizing the "self" in relational terms, he would be guilty of the believer's crime of accepting on faith the existence of a conceptual "reality" (an orthodox truth) independent of language. But Woolf's emphatic atheists do not make this mistake, for they reject not only God, but also the theological assumptions born in the age of belief.[28] What Woolf is doing here, and we have already seen this in *Orlando*, is examining how post-God language and cultural contact produce new subjects. As a believer, Neville demands that Bernard (and everyone else) discover his true self, a self that has an essential nature, but for a nonbeliever like Bernard, the task is to use language to create multiple selves.

---

[28]Like Woolf, Nietzsche considered the rejection of faith in God essentially linked to the rejection of faith in grammar. In a sense, my work on Nietzsche and Woolf has been an extended meditation on the following claim from Nietzsche: "I fear we are not getting rid of God because we still believe in grammar" (*Twilight* 48).

The post-God "subject," therefore, seeks, not a language to best signify the self's multiple selves, but a creative method for generating an endless variety of "selves" within an individual body. And as Woolf consistently suggests during this period, it is only in a post-God age that such a creative experience of multiple subjectivities could occur.

If my reading of Woolf is convincing, then I think we can safely take issue with Minow-Pinkney's claim that *"The Waves* is a depressive text, plagued with disbelief in the validity of signification" ("How" 94). While the 1931 novel is certainly "plagued with disbelief in the validity of signification," and while Minow-Pinkney is right to connect this disbelief with Woolf's atheism, I do not think we can call this experience depressive or despairing. Listen to what Woolf says about the consequences of faith in her essay "Reading": "What, one asks, as considerations accumulate, is ever to stop the course of such a mind, unroofed and open to the sky? Unfortunately, there was the Deity. His faith [Sir Thomas Browne's] shut in his horizon. Sir Thomas himself resolutely drew that blind. His desire for knowledge, his eager ingenuity, his anticipations of truth, must submit, shut their eyes, and go to sleep" (173). Here we have a stunning reversal of Eliot's philosophy. For the religious poet, orthodox truths exist whether a person realizes them or not. The goal of the orthodox Christian, therefore, is to discover, through "conscious intelligence," such truths. For Woolf, like Nietzsche, God's existence leads to fatalism because the highest human achievement would be to discover the Creator's prefabricated verities. For this reason, atheism means liberation; it means freeing the "human" from the tyranny of God and orthodoxy; it means the freedom to create interesting variations of that being once known as the Human. In a world where there is a God, there is no room for creative freedom. Therefore, for Woolf, atheism was not an occasion for despair because language could no longer signify. On the contrary, it was an occasion for rejoicing, because language now has the power to create many selves within one body. If anything, what makes *The Waves* a depressive text are characters like Neville and Percival, who refuse to abandon the violent language of the West in favor of post-God discourse, that ever-shifting language of experiment and adventure.

VII.

In his brilliant essay, "A Preface to Transgression," Foucault observes: "The death of God is not merely an 'event' that gave shape to contemporary experience as we now know it: it continues tracing indefinitely its great skeletal outline" (32). Atheism is not a one-time event beginning with the rejection of God's existence; it is a process in which the culture exorcises from itself the ontotheological spirits that continue to inform its intellectual systems despite the apparent absence of the God-concept.[29] Both early Eliot (1909-1927) and early Woolf (1915-1927) had to confront their culture's and time's atheism, and by 1927, the two made decisive choices that would radically impact their writings for the rest of their careers.[30]

Eliot's early poetry was heavily influenced by a nihilistic version of atheism, which is atheism in an infant stage of development. For the nihilist, after God's death everything is *"nada y pues nada"* (383), to quote Hemingway. In the first half of the twentieth century, modernist writers and post-Husserlian phenomenologists commonly ontologized nothingness. For instance, Wallace Stevens suggests that once heaven is considered a tomb, we can look forward to a "spiritous passage into nothingness" ("Of Heaven Considered as a Tomb"), and by nothingness, he means that "[n]othing that is not there and the nothing that is" ("The Snow Man"). For phenomenologists, nothingness is a mystical but real presence as intense as the Platonic Good or the numinous God of the cloud of unknowing. Though Heidegger resists calling nothingness a "being" (104) or an "object" (110), he does claim that nothingness has a prediscursive conceptual essence the nature of which humans must discover: "If the nothing itself is to be questioned as we have been questioning it, then it must be given beforehand. We must be able to encounter it" (100). Ironically, to presuppose that Nothingness preexists language is to treat it as God, a point that Kafka, with characteristic wit, makes in a discussion with Max Brod: "'We are nihilistic thoughts that came into God's head'" (75). To be absolutely nothing in a Heideggerian sense, God must have spoken humans ("nihilistic thoughts") into existence; therefore, nihilism presupposes God.

Throughout Eliot's career atheism means not the absence of a prediscursive truth, but emotional and psychological annihilation by that preexistent entity known as Nothingness. As early as 1910, Eliot devoted himself to the pursuit of the prediscursive "pure Idea" and the "Absolute,"[31] and by 1922, with the publi-

---

[29]Nietzsche makes this point emphatically: "God is dead; but given the way of men, there may still be caves for thousands of years in which his shadow will be shown.—And we—we still have to vanquish his shadow, too" (*Gay* 167).

[30]Significantly, Berman considers 1927 "the high-water mark of British atheism" (233).

[31]In *T. S. Eliot: An Imperfect Life*, Lyndall Gordon intelligently demonstrates that 1910 marks "the beginning of Eliot's religious journey" (49). This is ironic for two reasons. First, critics like I.A. Richards, who claim that *The Waste Land* embodies the lost generation's atheistic disillusionment, fail to see that the poem ultimately embraces rather than rejects belief, though it is a belief that has gone through various stages of doubt. Second, because Eliot only understood an atheism (nihilism) that was in an infant stage of development, the Modernists who looked to *The Waste Land* for a definitive atheist statement only got an atheistic vision that was quickly becoming obsolete.

cation of *The Waste Land*, he suggests that in a world in which "the empty chapel" is "only the wind's home," all that humans can know, see, and experience is nothing:

> "What is that noise now? What is the wind doing?"
>   Nothing again nothing.
>   "Do
> You know nothing? Do you see nothing? Do you remember
> Nothing?" (118-23)

This nothing functions as an ultimate category, a meta-concept that effectively explains the "nature" of "Being," and for Eliot, if it turns out that there is no God, then nothing is the ultimate concept by which all things are measured.

Once Eliot made his famous declaration of faith in 1927, he aligned himself with an institution that denounced atheism as nihilism and provided him with an epistemology that justified his view. It is at this point that Eliot went on the attack, denouncing atheists as people who cannot be moral[32] and who cannot love.[33] Moreover, it is after 1927 that Eliot developed an epistemology of "spiritual perception" that enables him to see the "pure Idea" and the "Absolute" that he sought as a young man.

Ironically, while Eliot was formulating an epistemology in which humans can only know either the Absolute or Nothing as a pre-existent meta-category of "Being," many intellectuals were moving beyond an epistemology that takes a meta-conceptual reality as a legitimate object of inquiry. This development was important, especially for believers and nihilists, because both had the same relationship to language: they assumed that there is an ultimate truth out there (God or Nothing) and that the community must find a language that best embodies that truth. Nietzsche was obviously one of the most radical and forceful critics of such a view of language, claiming in 1888 that he had abolished both the real and the apparent worlds, but it would be in the writings of Woolf, Ferdinand de Saussure, and Wittgenstein that a post-God vision of language would be most intelligently developed.[34] In 1916, with the posthumous publication of *Course in General Linguistics*, Saussure developed a scientific model for analyzing lan-

---

[32]As Gordon observes, Eliot condemns the atheistic and heretical writings of Irving Babbitt and D.H. Lawrence (275), while Bonnie Kime Scott shows how Eliot denounced Woolf's immorality.

[33]As Gordon (238) and Alfred Kazin note, for Eliot, "the love of man and woman is only made possible by a higher love, that of God; or else it is simply 'the coupling of animals'" (207).

[34]In my article, "Killing God, Liberating the 'Subject': Nietzsche and Post-God Freedom," I examine Nietzsche's philosophy of language, showing specifically how he

guage, which led him to conclude: "There are no pre-existing ideas, and nothing is distinct before the appearance of language" (112). For early Wittgenstein (1921), the world has a logical form, which can be expressed through a showing theory of language, but after 1930, he discarded the idea of the world's logical form, a view that led him to focus all his attention on the way various language games produce ever-changing conceptual fields.

Wittgenstein and Saussure did not associate the developments in their philosophies of language with God's death, but the French poststructuralists, who drew heavily from Nietzsche's work, indicate precisely how essential atheism is to their projects. For instance, in "Force and Signification," Derrida claims that the distinguishing feature of modernism is the "absence of divine writing" (10). According to the traditional view, the world was like "the infinite manuscript read by a God, who, in a more or less deferred way, is said to have given us use of his pen" (10), but now that God is dead, the world is no longer a text to be read. For the Derrida in *Of Grammatology*, the culture must understand that language, as formerly understood, "is essentially theological" (14).[35] Once we identify this theological prejudice inherent in language, we can begin the process of "de-divinizing" language, as Rorty refers to it, by showing how "there is no linguistic sign before writing" (*Grammatology* 14), a project that bears a striking resemblance to Wittgenstein's and Saussure's.[36]

As an atheist, the Woolf of 1928 through 1931 began to trace more clearly the distinctive skeletal outline of a post-nihilist vision of atheism. Through "spiritual perception," Eliot claims epistemological access to a God-created truth (orthodoxy), but Woolf exposes that truth, not as a conceptual reality dangling in a Christian heaven of ideas, but as a production of the violent language of the West. If there is no prediscursive truth, then language is experiment and adventure instead of accurate representation, but to enable language to assume this new function, deconstructing God and Nothingness is a political necessity.[37] And for

---

eventually (1886-1888) was able to make consistent sense of a post-God vision of language.

[35]Derrida says: "The sign and divinity have the same place and time of birth. The age of the sign is essentially theological" (*Grammatology* 14).

[36]The writers who are in the same tradition as Derrida include: Sarah Kofman, Michel Foucault, Gilles Deleuze, Felix Guattari, and Richard Rorty.

[37]In light of the deconstruction of representation and the subject, there has been a recent attempt to formulate a postmodern model of ethics that takes into account the valuable insights of poststructuralism regarding the hegemonic function of morality to marginalize certain groups of people. While Woolf would have been sympathetic to this project, I have argued elsewhere that she would have been inclined, like many atheists in her tradition, to dispense with morality altogether. Instead of morality, she evolves, I argue, a philosophy of "flowering into intimacy," a way of human relatedness that makes morality

Woolf, until her culture kills God and Truth, there will be no possibility for "humans" to produce multiple "selves" within individual bodies.

---

insignificant and irrelevant. For a discussion of Woolf's understanding of intimacy, see my dissertation, *Killing God, A Labor of Love: Post-God Intimacy in Nietzsche and Woolf*. My work in progress concerns Woolf, D. H. Lawrence, Sigmund Freud, Nella Larsen, and William Faulkner in which I detail a post-God and post-morality vision of human intimacy.

Works Cited

Ackroyd, Peter. *T. S. Eliot: A Life*. New York: Simon and Schuster, 1984.
Asher, Kenneth. *T. S. Eliot and Ideology*. Cambridge: Cambridge U P, 1998.
Beer, Gillian. "Physics, Sound, and Substance: Later Woolf," *Virginia Woolf: The Common Ground*. Ann Arbor: U of Michigan P, 1996. 112-124.
———. "*The Waves*: 'The Life of Anybody,'" *Virginia Woolf: The Common Ground*. Ann Arbor: U of Michigan P, 1996.
Berman, David. *A History of Atheism: From Hobbes to Russell*. London and New York: Routledge, 1988.
Brod, Max. *Kafka: A Biography*. New York: Schocken Books, 1963.
Butler, Judith. *Bodies That Matter: On the Discursive Limits of 'Sex'*. New York and London: Routledge, 1993.
———. *The Psychic Life of Power: Theories in Subjection*. Stanford: Stanford U P, 1997.
Carroll, James. *Constantine's Sword: The Church and the Jews*. Boston and New York: Houghton Mifflin Company, 2001.
Caughie, Pamela. *Virginia Woolf & Postmodernism: Literature in Quest & Question of Itself*. Urbana and Chicago: U of Illinois P, 1991.
Clark, Maudemarie. *Nietzsche on Truth and Philosophy*. Cambridge: Cambridge U P, 1990.
Corner, Martin. "Mysticism and Atheism in *To The Lighthouse*." *Studies in the Novel*. 13:4 (1981): 408-23.
DeKoven, Marianne. *Rich and Strange: Gender, History, Modernism*. Princeton: Princeton U P, 1991.
Deleuze, Gilles. *Foucault*. Trans. Sean Hand. Minneapolis: U of Minnesota P, 1986.
Deleuze, Gilles and Felix Guattari. *A Thousand Plateaus: Capitalism and Schizophrenia*. Trans. Brian Massumi. Minneapolis: U of Minnesota P, 1987.
Derrida, Jacques. "Force and Signification," in *Writing and Difference*. Trans. Alan Bass. Chicago: U of Chicago P, 1976.
———. *Of Grammatology*. Trans. Gayatri Chakravorty Spivak. Baltimore and London: Johns Hopkins U P, 1976.
———. "The Theater of Cruelty and the Closure of Representation," in *Writing and Difference*. Trans. Alan Bass. Chicago: U of Chicago P, 1976.
Eliot, T. S. *After Strange Gods: A Primer of Modern Heresy*. New York: Harcourt, Brace and Company, 1934.
———. "The Journey of the Magi," *The Complete Poems and Plays 1909-1950*. New York: Harcourt Brace, 1958.
———. *The Idea of a Christian Society*, in *Christianity and Culture*. New York: Harcourt Brace & Company, 1977.
———. *Notes Towards the Definition of Culture*, in *Christianity and Culture*. New York: Harcourt Brace & Company, 1977.

——. "Religion and Literature," *Essays Ancient and Modern*. London: Faber and Faber, 1945.
——. *The Waste Land. The Complete Poems and Plays 1909-1950*. New York: Harcourt Brace, 1958.
Foucault, Michel. "The Father's 'No'," in *Language, Counter-Memory, Practice: Selected Essays and Interviews*. Trans. Donald F. Bouchard and Sherry Simon. Ithaca: Cornell U P, 1977.
——. *The Order of Things: An Archaeology of the Human Sciences*. New York: Random House, 1970.
——. "A Preface to Transgression," in *Language, Counter-Memory, Practice: Selected Essays and Interviews*. Trans. Donald F. Bouchard and Sherry Simon. Ithaca: Cornell U P, 1977.
——. "What is an Author?" *The Foucault Reader*. Ed. Paul Rabinow. New York: Pantheon Books, 1984.
Freud, Sigmund. *Letters of Sigmund Freud*. Trans. Tania & James Stern. New York: Basic Books, 1960.
——. *Psychoanalysis and Faith: The Letters of Sigmund Freud and Oskar Pfister*. Trans. Eric Mosbacher. New York: Basic Books, 1963.
Gordon, Lyndall. "Our Silent Life: Virginia Woolf and T.S. Eliot," *Virginia Woolf: New Critical Essays* Ed. Patricia Clements and Isobel Grundy. London: Vision Limited Press, 1983. 77-95.
——. *T. S. Eliot: An Imperfect Life*. New York and London: W.W. Norton & Company, 1998.
Heidegger, Martin. "What is Metaphysics?" *Martin Heidegger: Basic Writings*. Ed. David Farrell Krell. San Francisco: Harper & Row, 1977.
Hemingway, Ernest. "A Clean, Well-Lighted Place," *The Short Stories of Ernest Hemingway*. New York: Charles Scribner's Sons, 1966. 379-83.
Hussey, Mark. *The Singing of the Real World: The Philosophy of Virginia Woolf's Fiction*. Columbus: Ohio State UP, 1986.
Julius, Anthony. *T. S. Eliot, Anti-Semitism, and Literary Form*. Cambridge: Cambridge U P, 1995.
Kazin, Alfred. *God and the American Writer*. New York: Alfred A. Knopf, 1997.
Kofman, Sarah. *Nietzsche and Metaphor*. Trans. Duncan Large. Stanford: Stanford U P, 1993.
Kojecky, Roger. "A Christian Elite," *T. S. Eliot and Social Criticism*. London: Faber and Faber, 1971. 159-170.
Lackey, Michael. "Atheism and Sadism: Nietzsche and Woolf on Post-God Discourse," *Philosophy and Literature* 24, 2 (2000): 346-363.
——. "The Gender of Atheism in Virginia Woolf's 'A Simple Melody,'" *Studies in Short Fiction* 35(1) (Winter 1998): 49-63.
——. *Killing God, A Labor of Love: Post-God Intimacy in Nietzsche and Woolf*. Ann Arbor: Bell and Howell, 2001.

———. "Killing God, Liberating the 'Subject': Nietzsche and Post-God Freedom," *Journal of the History of Ideas* 60, 4 (October 1999): 737-754.
Lee, Hermione. *Virginia Woolf.* New York: Alfred A. Knopf, 1997.
Lorsch, Susan E. *Where Nature Ends: Literary Responses to the Designification of the Landscape.* London and Toronto: Associated University Presses, 1983.
Miller, J. Hillis. *The Disappearance of God: Five Nineteenth-Century Writers.* Cambridge: Harvard U P, 1963.
Minow-Pinkney, Makiko. *Virginia Woolf & the Problem of the Subject.* New Brunswick: Rutgers U P, 1987.
———. "'How then does light return to the world after the eclipse of the sun? Miraculously, frailly': A Psychoanalytic Interpretation of Woolf's Mysticism." *Virginia Woolf and the Arts.* Ed. Diane F. Gillespie and Leslie K. Hankins. New York: Pace U P, 1997.
Nietzsche, Friedrich. *The Gay Science.* Trans. Walter Kaufmann. New York: Penguin, 1990.
———. *On the Genealogy of Morals.* Trans. Walter Kaufmann and R. J. Hollingdale. New York: Random House, 1989.
———. *Twilight of the Idols.* Trans. R. J. Hollingdale. New York: Random House, 1990.
Phillips, Kathy J. *Virginia Woolf Against Empire* Knoxville: U of Tennessee P, 1994.
Proust, Marcel. *Swann's Way* Tr. C.K. Scott Moncrieff. New York: Random House, 1970.
Rorty, Richard. *Contingency, Irony, and Solidarity.* Cambridge: Cambridge U P, 1989.
———. "Wittgenstein, Heidegger, and the Reification of Language," *The Cambridge Companion to Heidegger.* Ed. Charles B. Guignon. Cambridge: Cambridge U P, 1993. 337-357.
Sartre, Jean-Paul. "The Humanism of Existentialism," *Essays in Existentialism.* Secaucus, N. J.: Carol Publishing Group, 1999.
Scott, Bonnie Kime. *Refiguring Modernism. Volume One: The Women of 1928.* Bloomington and Indianapolis: Indiana U P, 1995.
Steinberg, Erwin R. *"Mrs. Dalloway* and T. S. Eliot's Personal Wasteland,*" Journal of Modern Literature* 10, 1(1983): 3-25.
Stevens, Wallace. *The Collected Poems of Wallace Stevens.* New York: Random House, 1982.
Thrower, James. *Western Atheism: A Short History.* Amherst: Prometheus Books, 2000.
Wilson, A. N. *God's Funeral.* New York and London: W. W. Norton & Company, 1999.
Woolf, Virginia. *The Complete Shorter Fiction of Virginia Woolf.* Ed. Susan Dick. New York: Harcourt Brace, 1989.

——. *The Diary of Virginia Woolf.* 5 vols. Ed. Anne Olivier Bell. New York: Harcourt Brace Jovanovich, 1977-1984.
——. *Jacob's Room.* 1922. New York: Harcourt Brace, 1950.
——. *The Letters of Virginia Woolf.* Eds. Nigel Nicolson and Joanne Trautmann. 6 vols. New York: Harcourt Brace Jovanovich, 1975-1980. Volume 3.
——. *Mrs. Dalloway.* 1925. New York: Harcourt Brace, 1981.
——. "Mr. Bennett and Mrs. Brown," *The Captain's Death Bed and Other Essays* New York: Harcourt Brace Jovanovich, 1978.
——. *Moments of Being* 2nd ed. Ed. Jeanne Schulkind. New York: Harcourt Brace, 1966.
——. "Montaigne." *The Common Reader: First Series*. Ed. Andrew McNeillie. New York: Harcourt Brace & Company, 1984.
——. *Night and Day.* 1919. New York: Harcourt Brace Jovanovich, 1948.
——. *Orlando: A Biography.* New York: Harcourt Brace, 1956.
——. "Reading," *The Captain's Death Bed and Other Essays* New York: Harcourt Brace Jovanovich, 1978.
——. *A Room of One's Own.* 1929. New York: Harcourt Brace, 1989.
——. *Three Guineas.* 1938. New York: Harcourt Brace, 1966.
——. *To The Lighthouse.* 1927. New York: Harcourt Brace, 1981.
——. *The Waves.* 1931. New York: Harcourt Brace, 1959.
——. *The Voyage Out.* 1915. New York: Harcourt Brace Jovanovich, 1954.
Wright, Richard. *The Outsider.* San Francisco: Harper Collins, 1993.

Visual Modernism: Virginia Woolf's "Portraits" and Photography

Maggie Humm

Virginia Woolf's neglected short fictions "Portraits" provide an appropriate point at which to examine broader issues of visuality and gender in modernism (*CSF* 242-6*)*. "Portraits" did not appear in print until Susan Dick's first edition of the short fiction was published in 1985. Although limited in length to five published pages, these experimental pieces, as much as Woolf's better known visual fictions "Blue and Green" and "The Mark on the Wall," display many of the same virtues as Woolf's novels being impressionistic collages of significant experiences. "Portraits" figure the problem of representation in modernity as a tension between characters' memories and what they observe in fluid, feminine "snapshots."

It is now a critical commonplace that gender shapes the visible spaces of modernity in the sense that the public space of the street or the theater is an arena for the staging of gendered gazes.[1] For example, it is generally agreed that one of the key figures of modernity is the flâneur, or observing male stroller, free to move about the public space and able to direct his gaze equally at women and at goods for sale (Pollock, *Vision* 71). Although more recent work by Deborah Parsons and Elizabeth Wilson has problematized the flâneur figure, certainly canonical modernist art, for example Manet's *Olympia*, articulates this masculine gaze at the body of woman (Parsons; Wilson). Charles Harrison argues, in "Degas' *Bathers* and Other People," that this issue was central to the "first period of the development of modernism in painting—say in the fifty years between 1860-1910" (61). Harrison suggests that by the 1870s, "the modernity of a painting's composition would be recognized" by its representations of looking. Griselda Pollock argues in *Vision and Difference* that the sexual politics of looking in modernist paintings utilize binary positions of looking/being seen, activity/passivity in which women figures are passive, the objects of an implied or evident male voyeuristic gaze (87). But if modernism's most distinctive visual feature is an implied male spectator, then what role has a female spectator? Can texts by women about female (and male) spectators produce different ways of looking?

---

[1] In *Differencing the Canon*, Griselda Pollock deftly sketches a semiotics of modernist spaces as arenas of sexuality.

Virginia Woolf's short fictions "Portraits" adopt a different position of viewing than this customary gender binary because Woolf uses a specifically photographic, rather than painterly, vocabulary like a camera negotiating vertical and horizontal frames of portrait and landscape.[2] This enables the urban spaces of modernity in these stories to become places of relationships rather than sites of a dominating male gaze. That Woolf was highly familiar with photography is becoming better known (Gillespie, "'Her Kodak'"). Even from childhood Woolf was an inveterate photographer. In 1897, aged fifteen, Woolf was staying in Bognor when "[T]he Frend [camera] arrived from Becks, in a new box, all rubbed up and beautiful, smelling strongly of Jargonel. We tried shutting Nessa up in the cupboard to put in the films, but there were too many chinks. Then she suggested being covered by her quilt, and everything else that I could lay hands on—She was accordingly, buried in dresses and dressing gowns, till no light could penetrate. Soon she emerged almost stifled having forgotten how to put the film in. I hustled her back again into her burrow" (*PA* 34). Woolf's precocious understanding of photographic processes quickly registers an interest in album-like visual narratives. By February 14, 1897, Woolf stages photographic seriality. "We photographed Simon 6 times - on the chair with a coat and pipe, and lying on the ground . . . After tea, Nessa and I developed in the night nursery" (*PA* 35).[3] Although seriality was a usable, heuristically productive force in much of modernist art, for example in the paintings of Cézanne, the major artist in Fry's 1910 Post Impressionist exhibition, I feel that Woolf's early interest in multiple photography equally presages the later "Portraits" in which Woolf adopts an almost photographic seriality.

Virginia Woolf belonged to the first generation of women to be active photographers and cinema-goers from childhood. The years from Woolf's birth in 1882 to the writing of "Portraits" were the years in which photography became a career option for women (Gover). Like Woolf, many modernist women writers, including H. D. and Dorothy Richardson, owned "vest-pocket Kodaks." All these writers used domestic photography to express a degree of self-definition that allowed their private worlds to be a resource in their more public writing.[4] As I have detailed elsewhere, throughout her career as an innovative modernist

---

[2]Of course, as my perceptive reader pointed out, Woolf does not divest "Portraits" of sounds (trains, markets) and smells (urine, petrol). Woolf's "Portraits" do offer much information about sounds and smells, but, importantly, Woolf uses the visual surface in particular as a framework for unrevealed information.

[3]Mitchell A. Leaska, the editor of *A Passionate Apprentice*, identifies Simon as the dog of Arthur Studd, a family friend and painter.

[4]I discuss this theme in more detail in my forthcoming book, *Modernist Women and Visual Cultures* (Edinburgh U P).

writer Woolf, together with Leonard, took, developed and mounted in albums over one thousand domestic photographs (Humm).

Virginia Woolf was also familiar with photographic challenges to representation, for example, the photography of her great-aunt Julia Margaret Cameron. Using a wet collodian process, Julia Cameron took hundreds of photographs of friends and family, including portraits of Woolf's mother, between 1864 and Cameron's death in 1879 (Smith). Cameron's long exposures of three to seven minutes often resulted in a relativism of focus which Cameron preferred. Woolf shared Cameron's disregard for sharp images, and *Freshwater*, Woolf's play about Cameron, describes Cameron's use of visual metaphors. Together with Roger Fry, Woolf edited and introduced a book collection of Cameron's photographs and bound her photography albums with the same purple ribbon used by Cameron for her albums. Both photographers shared an interest in the domestic and in chiaroscuro, the play of light and shadow. Woolf's continuous attention to photography's visual effects must inevitably impact on all her work including "Portraits." In particular photography influences the sphere of memory, a key feature of "Portraits" and of modernist sensibility in general.

In "Portraits" Woolf stages a number of gendered gazes shaped by a photographic syntax. While experimental writing, per se, is neither uniquely "feminine" nor uniquely modernist, Woolf's "Portraits" are characteristically modernist because they utilize phenomenality to subvert classic realism. At a formal level, "Portraits" achieve an impact not simply by means of narrative elements alone but through Woolf's striking patterns. The two distinguishing features of "Portraits" are their spatial arrangements of visual associations and a repression of chronological narrative. But the visual associations interact inside each narrator's memory pictures, so that there is a major emphasis on affect, and on pictorial mediations. This dualistic stratagem, which pitches formal arrangements against the affect of memory pictures, allows Woolf to explore the aesthetics of modernism while dramatizing gender differences.

Virginia Woolf's "Portraits" are eight miniature stories, each between one and three paragraphs in length. Although in most the sex of the narrator is not clear, in portraits 4 and 5 we follow the thoughts of female characters, portraits 2 and 3 suggest a female narrator, and three portraits view female subjects, suggesting that "Portraits" as a whole focuses on women looking at the modern world. Each story has a different focus, takes a different photograph, of what Walter Benjamin calls the unconscious optics of modernity or the ways in which photographs can register moments outside immediate perception.[5] As Susan Dick's immaculate editorial gloss on the fictions suggests, "Portraits" are proba-

---

[5] I discuss Benjamin's ideas more fully in relation to Woolf's own photography in "Virginia Woolf's Photography and the Monk's House Albums."

bly part of a collaborative work called "Faces and Voices" which Woolf and Vanessa Bell were discussing in February 1937 (*CSF* 307). Although the Monk's House Papers, University of Sussex Library Archives, number the "Portraits" as five, Dick supplied the titles of "Portraits" 4 to 8 from evidence in Woolf's manuscripts and points out that the eighth portrait derives from "The Broad Brow," one of the "Three Characters," another version of which is published as "Middlebrow" in *The Death of the Moth* (307).

Woolf's own account of "Portraits"' generative moment of composition, Friday, February 19, 1937, reveals how such image/texts, for her, are an irresistible testimonial to epistemological novelty. In her diary Woolf records, "I've written this morning 3 descriptions for Nessa's pictures: they can be printed by us no doubt, & somehow put into circulation. But then theres in my drawer several I think rather good sketches; & a chapter on biography. Clearly I have here in the egg a new method of writing criticism. I rather think so" (*D5* 57). And Woolf described in her diary the following day, "I discussed a book of illustrated incidents with Nessa yesterday; we are going to produce 12 lithographs for Xmas, printed by ourselves" (*D5* 58). There are strong connections between lithography and photography. As Beatrice Farwell suggests in *The Cult of Images*, the early English calotype process replicated lithographic imagery, and photography and lithography existed interchangeably with each other for several decades. Lithographs can share the demotic snapshot quality of photographs whose conventions lithographs often mimic.

Diane Gillespie, in *The Sisters' Arts*, comprehensively explores the impact of painting on Woolf's fiction and Woolf's uses of visual iconography. Gillespie touches briefly on "Portraits." In the two paragraphs, Gillespie points out that "Portraits" is a "compendium of techniques" perhaps "recalling Sickert's paintings of everyday life," and that the characters "talk about paintings and people, objects and sights we cannot see" (172). Certainly Woolf argued, in *Walter Sickert: A Conversation*, "let us hold painting by the hand a moment longer, for though they must part in the end, painting and writing have much to tell each other. They have much in common" (22). But an aesthetic investment in photography is equally a significant pressure on Woolf's writing, as Gillespie expertly acknowledges elsewhere (Gillespie, "'Her Kodak'"). Recurring references to photographic activities occur in many of Woolf's novels, for example, *Jacob's Room*, as well as in her diaries and letters. There are other ways in which photography might be represented in writing. Photography arrests moments in time, capturing non-linear gestures and attitudes hitherto invisible to spectators. Photography graphically highlights personally significant details such as favorite objects, as Woolf does so often in her writing. In addition, photography's composition by field mirrors Woolf's juxtaposition of the quotidian with deep philosophical ideas.

There have been a number of critiques in the last few years on the relationship between photography and twentieth-century literature.[6] Nancy Armstrong's recent and important study, *Fiction in the Age of Photography*, describes how nineteenth-century literature (in works such as *Wuthering Heights*, *Alice's Adventures in Wonderland*, and *The Picture of Dorian Grey*) often referred to "what either was or would become a photographic commonplace," for example, representations of the picturesque or city streets (5). Armstrong's is a sophisticated argument that photography and nineteenth-century fiction shared the same tasks of miniaturizing rural Britain and producing spatial classification systems because "realism and photography were partners in the same cultural project" of classifying the world (26).

In Armstrong's chapter on modernism, she argues that "modernism's assault on mass culture and femininity" came from a distrust of the body as an aesthetic strategy. Armstrong devotes her attention to how modernist writers and photographers, such as D. H. Lawrence and Edward Weston, eroticize their aesthetic experiments (247). Armstrong attacks Woolf's "Mr. Bennett and Mrs. Brown" specifically here for reducing realism to "a mere caricature of itself" and argues that "the modernist concept of authenticity was a post-photographic way of imagining one's relation to the real" (245-6). While Armstrong's is a very nuanced account of nineteenth-century writing, I feel that her description of modernism and photography is overly focused on the pornographic at the expense of representations of visual memories, and her attack on Woolf misplaced. Psychoanalysis teaches us that we frequently displace onto other races, classes and genders features of ourselves which we would like to disavow.[7] Psychoanalysis would see the excess in Woolf's classic attack on Arnold Bennett's realism as exemplary of such a kind of displacement. In other words, I feel that Woolf does not caricature realism per se, but that Woolf's critique betrays her fascination with but troubled view of realism and popular culture, which would include domestic photography. Woolf might wish to disavow realism ideologically while not rejecting tropes of realism such as those of domestic photography for example, in her writing.

[6]Recent critical work includes Marianne Hirsch's now classic text *Family Frames: Photography, Narrative and Postmemory* (1997), Judith F. Davidov *Women's Camera Work: Self/Body/Other in American Visual Culture* (1998), Jessica Evans (ed.) *The Camerawork Essays: Context and Meaning in Photography* (1997), Linda Rugg *Picturing Ourselves: Photography and Autobiography* (1997), Bridget Elliott and Jo-Ann Wallace *Women Artists and Writers* (1994).

[7]See Phil Cohen's extensive work, among others.

What Woolf was calling her "new method of writing criticism" in her concomitant diary can be glimpsed in "Portraits'" fresh spatial arrangements of people and objects. "Portraits" resembles an album of eight synchronic moments in the lives of bourgeois women and men in modernity. The fictions are creative modernist image/texts which utilize scopic devices of looks or gazes. "Portraits" have very different types of narrator: some stories totally lack an obvious authorial inscription, others have carefully delineated middle class and gendered figures and are set in differing contexts, including France, London and Florence. The title of the first portrait, "Waiting for Déjeuner," recalls Manet's *Dejeuner sur l'herbe*(1863) (*CSF* 242). Although, in general, Roger Fry's hostility to Impressionism was consistent, he chose Manet as the forerunner of Post Impressionism, as the title of Fry's 1910 exhibition, "Manet and the Post-Impressionists," makes clear. December, 1910, was, of course, a significant moment for Woolf, Fry's friend. Manet's painting acknowledges a Renaissance engraving by Marcantonio Raimondi (1520) after Raphael's *Judgement of Paris*, drawing on a detail of a late Roman sarcophagus in the Villa Medici, Rome. Woolf immediately subverts any evident indebtedness to canonic art history with a snapshot synchronicity of historical relativities. Elephants "squelch," as the cinema announces "the new Jungle film" (*CSF* 242). The notion that the past is simultaneously part of the present was encouraged by a scientific zeitgeist freighted with the idea that the external visible world cannot easily be measured and was relative to a viewer, and Woolf frequently concerns herself with issues of visible and invisible visuality, for example, her use of two kinds of photography in *Three Guineas*.[8] Persian women groom children while "Monsieur and Madame Louvois" wait by the Seine for their lunch of tripe (*CSF* 242).

Unlike Woolf's short fiction "Mark on the Wall," the focus here is less on the narrator and more on a blurring of subjective and objective evident in Woolf's choice of appellation for her portrait of the two principals who are called "Louvois" (*CSF* 242). "Monsieur and Madame Louvois stared at the mustard pot and the cruet ... and the eyes of Monsieur and Madame Louvois lit with lustre" (*CSF* 242). The description resembles the way in which a camera takes a literal image of a subject. But the portrait hovers between two kinds of photography. On the one hand Monsieur and Madame Louvois are described realistically, and on the other the portrait is also like a study revealing subjective personalities which Woolf knowingly announces in her emblematic choice of name. "Louve" is the French noun for she-wolf and louvoyer means to tack about or dodge. The portrait is, then, no brief entremet but a performative self portrait of mocking self deflection as the Louvois wait for a luncheon of tripe.

[8]This was the major theme of Bloomsbury's philosopher G. E. Moore in his "The Refutation of Idealism."

The second portrait, "The Frenchwomen in the Train," resembles Van Gogh's paintings of peasant women. Both equally exaggerate women's laboring bodies. "Here the bull neck bears baskets of grapes" (*CSF* 243). But unlike Van Gogh's eroticized topographic bodies, in Woolf's photographic *mis-en-scène* the woman is alternatively impressionistic, with "undulating shoulder," and precise (*CSF* 243). The portrait is a quite extraordinarily visual and sensual description of a parodic, peasant landscape in which a "butting ram, men astride it," surround a monumental woman with "wild pig eyes" (elsewhere in Woolf's work a synonym for the Duckworth brothers) (*CSF* 243). But, just as Griselda Pollock argues in terms of Van Gogh that this production of fantastic peasant women "brought him close to the scenes and bodies of his childhood memories," so Woolf's portrait also might register parental memories (Pollock, *Differences* 60). For example, Woolf suggests that the woman "would be running through Clapham on her way to Highgate to renew the circle of china flowers on the grave of her husband," and Woolf's parents and half-sister are buried in Highgate cemetery (*CSF* 243).

Yet although the exaggeration of the portrait resembles Van Gogh's topographies, the vocabulary of Portrait 2 resembles the connotative and denotative quality of photographic language. Roland Barthes used these terms to characterize the meanings of different elements in a photograph (195). Denotative describes the literal meaning of elements such as an object or a gesture so that we recognize what we are seeing. In Woolf's Portrait a woman is sitting in a train carrying a bag. But beyond the level of denotative meanings lie connotative meanings which refer to the ways in which movements or expressions are also "codes" reflecting underlying meanings. The woman "at the Junction . . . sits in her corner[,] on her knee a black bag," and simultaneously the woman "bears on her immense and undulating shoulder the tradition; even when her mouth dribbles" (*CSF* 243). Woolf breaks up the ordered denotative world of a realist photograph by saturating the woman with connotative photographic signs like intimations of an archaic fantasy of the maternal.

My argument about Woolf's photographic techniques, gender and modernism requires me to unpack a little more this issue of how women and men look in modernity. Griselda Pollock, in *Differencing the Canon*, calls for modernist criticism to read "for *the inscriptions of the other otherness of femininity*, that is, for those traces of the unexpected articulation of what may be specific to female persons in the process of becoming subjects—subjected, subjectified and subjectivised—in the feminine through the interplay of social identities and psychic formations within histories" (102).[9] The contemporary psychoanalyst and

---

[9]Pollock's sophisticated take on "difference" argues against a patriarchal binary male/female in favor of more complex registers of representation.

artist Bracha Lichtenberg Ettinger, on whom Pollock has written a great deal, has created the term matrix to describe more specifically Pollock's "unexpected articulation" and what might be specific to women in the process of becoming subjects (22). Lichtenberg Ettinger argues that art visualizes strata of subjectivity and chronologies through objects in a field which can reveal inscriptions of the feminine. Lichtenberg Ettinger herself utilizes photographic fields in which repeated photographic images of family members become examples of a sub-symbolic filter, the internal/external traces of the matrixial encounter in the womb. In some ways Woolf's attention to a circulation of looks in "Portraits'" memory pictures, across the boundaries of chronological time, suggests similar matrixial recognitions. That is to say, in Woolf's "Portraits," narrative images often play denotative and connotative roles as in photography in order for the subject/narrators of "Portraits" to appear as subjects flowing between a consciousness of everyday life and the unconscious world beyond the normally visible. I have stressed this idea of representing unconscious associations in order to specify theoretically Woolf's investment in denotative and connotative photographic vocabulary. In the case study of "Portraits" certain recurring features of Woolf's writing can be read as a photographic means of representing strata of feminine subjectivity.

Portrait 3, a mere eleven lines, has a clearly identified narrator "sitting in the courtyard of the French Inn" who scopically views a woman "sitting in the sun" (*CSF* 243). As Richard Morphet points out, Bloomsbury paintings also focused with "unusual insistence" on the arresting gaze and on eyes (29). For example, in Vanessa Bell's portrait of Mary Hutchinson "the look the eyes give is accentuated" as well as the eyes' shape (29). But in "Portraits" the scene is photographic more than painterly, employing shapes and light within the frame. Woolf suggests a female gaze with a narrator physically close to the woman but able to stare with non-voyeuristic attention to details of breast and skin. "Her face was yellow and red; round too; a fruit on a body; another apple, only not on a plate. Breasts had formed apple-hard under the blouse on her body" (*CSF* 243). The portrait lingers on the physiognomy of the woman like a camera and the narrator's reflections touch on those aspects of mentality which can only be visible in close up photography.

The unnamed female of Portrait 4 more closely resembles self-reflexive female narrators elsewhere in Woolf's fiction—for example, *Mrs. Dalloway*—as the narrator floats between past and present while enjoying a snatched day with her son before he returns to Rugby school. Like an album of snapshot pictures, the piece functions associatively. For example, the character observes that the hors d'oeuvres already lack sardines and that George, her son, has "the eyes of a carp" (*CSF* 244). Woolf highlights the terms of representation in the same way in which many modernist photographers exaggerated features of faces: El Lissitzky, the Russian constructivist photographer's *Constructor* (1904), for example. Russian constructivist photography did not simply aim to "reflect" the world but to make a cognitive transformation of the world through an "explicit thematisation of the art of the everyday" (Roberts 20). The head in Lissitzky's *Constructor* is represented by a surplus of physiognomic details; for example, Lissitzky places an eye in the constructor's adjacent hand in order to suggest a relationship between the physical and the mental (Clarke 191). Similarly George and the narrator's past "sandy haired boy" are identified visually by Woolf like photographic portraits by means of physiognomy (*CSF* 244). Like constructivist photography, Woolf de-familiarizes objects through the use of an unexpected angle as a means of expanding the experience of the everyday (Roberts). In narratives, memory pictures most often work by means of visual associations. Like screen memories, the character's recollections have the quality of dreams in their associative displacements and repressions. Although she easily remembers a past male admirer, the character is yet unable to discuss sexuality with her son, to be "more like a father" (*CSF* 244). Freud's term *Nachträglichkeit* similarly refers to deferred actions where the past works on the present yet memory-traces can be re-transcribed.

The constructedness of biography itself is exposed in subsequent portraits. Portrait 5 is a brief monologic pastiche of middle class materialism and its institutionalized values. A bourgeois woman eating "white sugared pastry" enjoys her social superiority: "at the Hospital the men used to call me Little Mother" (*CSF* 244). Woolf leaps into a surreal visual image of the woman's "scent bottle which she carried in a gland in her cheek with which to sweeten the sometimes malodorous emanations of her own not sufficiently appreciated character" (*CSF* 244). Woolf carefully portrays a psychological state of mind by means of an exact image. In this way Portrait 5 resembles the manipulation of images by modernist photographers such as the American Alvin Langdon Coburn, whose Cubist portraits break with surface reality. To photograph *Vortograph* (1917), for example, Coburn used mirrors to create a sense of multiple perspectives, manipulating photography to create metaphoric images as Woolf does here with the scent bottle (Clarke 188). Coburn's portrait has been likened to earlier combination printing in which a print is built up from several negatives (Clarke 188). Woolf similarly turns the psycho-social detail of the woman's life into object images such as the scent bottle.

Like prints in a photo album each portrait flickers towards another. The male of Portrait 6 is dislocated by contemporary life where a "felt hat with a dent in it" has displaced "a topper" (*CSF* 244). An immediate precedent and influence on Woolf's portrait is the conclusion of Marcel Proust's *Swann's Way*, published in 1913 and immediately highly praised by Roger Fry. "I no longer found the grey 'toppers' of old . . . they passed before me in a desultory, haphazard, meaningless fashion" (Proust 510). There are many references to Woolf's love of Proust in her diaries and letters, particularly in Woolf's letters to Roger Fry. "Oh. If I could write like that! I cry. And at that moment such is the astonishing vibration and saturation and intensification that he procures—there's something sexual in it—that I feel I *can* write like that" (*L2* 525). Like Marcel, the male of Portrait 6, "I who should have been born in the eighties," lives in a world which is now almost entirely memorial, made up of his family's memories, of "Oscar [Wilde] being witty" and "prostitutes in Piccadilly," and a time with "society, graded like one of those ices wrapped in frilly paper" (*CSF* 245). Although the portrait is not realistic it is photographic. The male narrator thinks of his relationship to his family in photographic terms with visual clues determining status, such as, "should have carried a cane, like my father" (*CSF* 244).

The compositional structure of a photo album also shapes the last two portraits. Portrait 7 is dedicated to Vernon Lee, "the pen-name of author Violet Page," a pacifist lesbian, remembered in three momentary snapshots: at Talland House, in Florence, and in the 1917 Club, places which all figure in photographs in Woolf's own family albums.[10] The narrator, again another parodic bourgeois ("No, I don't paint myself; but then one appreciates art all the better perhaps"), coheres an identity only by means of association with minor cultural figures (*CSF* 245). A more extensive version of Portrait 8, written as a letter to *The New Statesman*, appears as "Middlebrow" in *The Death of the Moth*. Unlike Portrait 8, the more detailed "Middlebrow" is a somewhat mannered essay, a linear narrative in which Woolf's persona defines herself as highbrow uniting with lowbrows against middlebrows and their love for "Queen Anne furniture (faked, but none the less expensive)" (*DM* 158). "Middlebrow" does not create a fictionalized reader, nor does it revise the power relationship between author and implied reader. In opposition, Portrait 8 is dialogic, spoken first by a fictive middlebrow before the speaking voice reverts to a denunciatory persona claiming that middlebrows are "infecting the sheep" (*CSF* 246). The fictive middlebrow is not distanced by inserted authorial devices such as physical or emotive descriptions, but parodies himself by calling Shakespeare and Wordsworth equally "Bill" (*CSF* 246).

Woolf utilizes a modernist pictorial syntax elements of which we can see in the penultimate paragraph of Portrait 8: "when one walks in the garden, what's that on the cabbage? Middle brow. Middle brow infecting the sheep. The moon too is under your sway: misted. You dull tarnish" (*CSF* 246). In some ways these

---

[10]See Humm n5.

lines are overtly modernist. The formal simplification is achieved by a repression of narrative and descriptive linkages in favor of Woolf's focus on images and on differing perspectives, from a close up on the cabbage to a long shot of the moon. The series of photographic perspectives is joined by the common theme of the imagined effect of middle brow culture on landscape in general. Woolf's visual hyperbole in the Portrait combines with an attention to detail in photographic images. Like her contemporary American modernist photographers Paul Strand and Aaron Siskind in the 1920s and 1930s, Woolf similarly attends to surface textures in close up to make the commonplace into something much more than a mere object. Part of Paul Strand's assault on pictorialism was to seek the essence of photography in "absolute unqualified objectivity" (Eisinger 56). Strand and Siskind photographed objects in the city and country, such as cars, shoes and windows, like Woolf emphasizing texture, pattern and shadow to make everyday detritus into something significant (Clarke 177).

Graham Clarke points out in *The Photograph*, "the literal nature of so much photography would seem to place it at the opposite end of modernist aesthetics and philosophical inquiry" (110). Clarke suggests that modernist novels such as Henry James's *Portrait of a Lady* abandoned literal forms of representation while the photograph "insisted on the principle of representation and the depiction of space that modernism rejected" (111). But the paradox remains that modernism was also a response to technological innovation, and film and photography plays a major role in modernism's symptomatic response to Western modernity. Montage was a means of bringing hidden relations into discursive view and many modernist writers, including H. D. and James Joyce as well as Woolf, wrote about the new visual experiences of cinema, advertising and photography.

Photography's ways of looking impact on Woolf's structures. Associations are focused by means of each character's close-up engagement with objects, faces or food. Fragmentary elements of personal histories are remembered in single frames. Woolf includes a number of perspectives, both male and female, bourgeois and highbrow, as if capturing these in a family album. After visiting her sister Vanessa Bell's show in 1928, Woolf admired Bell's elaborate optical representations in terms very similar to those of the later Portraits:

> I am greatly tempted to write "Variations on a Picture by Vanessa Bell" for Desmond's paper—I should run the three women and the pot of flowers on a chair into one phantasmagoria. I think you are a most remarkable painter. But I maintain you are into the bargain, a satirist, a conveyor of impressions about human life: a short story writer of great wit and able to bring off a situation in a way that rouses my envy. I wonder if I could write the Three Women in prose. (*L3* 498)

By introducing architectonic elements into her painting, Bell was free to explore the emotions of color just as Woolf uses photographic elements to explore gendered memories. "Portraits" fairly resonate with camera shots as Woolf turns from object to object, facial details to physiognomy. In short, "Portraits" exhibit a fundamental tenet of modernist writing: the significance of the fragmentary and the provisional shaped by a powerful investment in the capacity of photography to provide a memorial and gendered optics.

Special appreciation goes to my two anonymous readers for their astute and critical comments.

Works Cited

Armstrong, Nancy. *Fiction in the Age of Photography*. Cambridge: Harvard U P, 1999.
Barthes, Roland. "The Photographic Message" in *A Barthes Reader* ed. S. Sontag. London: Jonathan Cape, 1982. 194-210.
Clarke, Graham. *The Photograph*. Oxford: Oxford U P, 1997.
Cohen, Phil. "Laboring Under Whiteness" in *Displacing Whiteness: Essays in Social and Cultural Criticism*, ed. R. Frankenberg. Durham, NC: Duke U P, 1997.
Davidov, Judith F. *Women's Camera Work: Self/Body/Other in American Visual Culture*. Durham, NC: Duke U P, 1998.
Dick, Susan, Ed. *The Complete Shorter Fiction of Virginia Woolf*. 2nd edition. London: Hogarth Press, 1989.
Eisinger, Joel. *Trace and Transformation: American Criticism of Photography in the Modernist Period*. Albuquerque: U of New Mexico P, 1995.
Elliott, Bridget and Wallace, Jo-Ann. *Women Artists and Writers*. London: Routledge, 1994.
Evans, Jessica. ed. *The Camerawork Essays: Context and Meaning in Photography*. London: Rivers Oram Press, 1997.
Farwell, Beatrice. *The Cult of Images: Baudelaire and the 19th Century Media Explosion*. Santa Barbara: USCB Art Museum, 1977.
Freud, Sigmund. *The Standard Edition of the Complete Psychological Works of Sigmund Freud Vol 4 and 5*. Trans. J. Strachey. London: Hogarth Press, 1953.
Gillespie, Diane F. *The Sisters' Arts: The Writing and Painting of Virginia Woolf and Vanessa Bell*. Syracuse: Syracuse U P, 1988.
——. "'Her Kodak Pointed at His Head': Virginia Woolf and Photography," in *The Multiple Muses of Virginia Woolf*. ed. D. F. Gillespie. Columbia: U of Missouri P, 1993.

Gover, Jane C. *The Positive Image: Women Photographers in Turn of the Century America*. Albany: State U of New York P, 1988.
Harrison, Charles. "Degas' *Bathers* and Other People." *Modernism and Modernity* 6, 3 (September 1999): 57-91.
Hertz, Neil. "Dora's Secrets, Freud's Techniques," in *Dora's Case: Freud, Hysteria, Feminism*. Eds. C. Bernheimer and C. Kahane. London: Virago, 1985.
Hirsch, Marianne. *Family Frames: Photography, Narrative and Postmemory*. Cambridge MA: Harvard U P, 1997.
Humm, Maggie. "Virginia Woolf's Photography and the Monk's House Albums," in *Virginia Woolf in the Age of Mechanical Reproduction*. Ed. P. Caughie. NY: Garland, 2000.
Lichtenberg Ettinger, Bracha. *The Matrixial Gaze*. Leeds: Feminist Arts and Histories Network, 1995.
Moore, G. E. "The Refutation of Idealism." *Mind* (October 1903): 433-53.
Morphet, Richard. "Image and Theme in Bloomsbury Art," in *The Art of Bloomsbury*. Ed. R. Shone. London: The Tate Gallery, 1999.
Orton, Fred and Pollock, Griselda. *Avant-Gardes and Partisans Reviewed*. Manchester: Manchester U P, 1996.
Parsons, Deborah C. *Streetwalking the Metropolis*. Oxford: Oxford U P, 2000.
Pollock, Griselda. *Vision and Difference*. London: Routledge, 1988.
——. *Differencing the Canon: Feminist Desire and the Writing of Art Histories*. London: Routledge, 1999.
Roberts, John. *The Art of Interruption: Realism, Photography and the Everyday*. Manchester: Manchester U P, 1998.
Rugg, Linda. *Picturing Ourselves: Photography and Autobiography*. Chicago: U of Chicago P, 1997.
Proust, Marcel. *Swann's Way*. Vol. 1 *In Search of Lost Time*. New York: Vintage, 1996.
Smith, Lindsay. *The Politics of Focus: Women, Children and Nineteenth-Century Photography*. Manchester: Manchester U P, 1998.
Wilson, Elizabeth. *The Contradictions of Culture: Cities, Culture, Women*. London: Sage, 2001.
Woolf, Virginia. *Walter Sickert: A Conversation*. London: The Hogarth Press, 1934.
——. *The Death of the Moth and Other Essays*. Harmondsworth: Penguin, 1961.
——. *The Letters of Virginia Woolf. Volume Two 1912-1922*. New York: Harcourt Brace Jovanovich, 1976.
——. *A Change of Perspective: Collected Letters 3 1923-28* New York: Harcourt Brace Jovanovich, 1977.
——. *The Diary of Virginia Woolf 5 1936-41*. New York: Harcourt Brace Jovanovich, 1985.

———. "Portraits" in *The Complete Shorter Fiction of Virginia Woolf.* Ed. S. Dick. New York: Harcourt Inc; 1989.
———. *A Passionate Apprentice: The Early Journals 1897-1909.* Ed. Mitchell A. Leaska. San Diego: Harcourt Brace Jovanovich, 1990.

"Vanished, Like Leaves": The Military, Elegy and Italy in *Mrs Dalloway*

David Bradshaw

While there is universal agreement that *Mrs Dalloway*, among other things, is an eloquent condemnation of militarism and war in which the official foci of national mourning—the Cenotaph and the Tomb of the Unknown Warrior—are treated with anything but straightforward veneration, Woolf's fourth novel is nevertheless a commemorative text which memorializes the dead of the First World War in a variety of ways even as it dissents from the necrolatry of the state. In fact, at one point or another, just about every aspect of the formal culture of remembrance is evoked in the novel and on each occasion the narrative mood is much closer to solemnity than mischief. Indeed, there are moments of observance in the text which are almost ceremonial in their reverence and dignity.

Before going on to scrutinize *Mrs Dalloway*'s memorial moments and monumental features, however, I shall examine afresh Peter Walsh's encounter with a contingent of boy soldiers in Whitehall. Two things, in particular, are clear: Woolf's language in this passage is more resonant with anti-militarist (and, possibly, even personal) animus than has so far been acknowledged; and by deploying (here and elsewhere in the novel) the ancient topos of falling or fallen leaves, an age-old simile for the numberless dead (see, for example, Isaiah 34:4), Woolf plainly encourages the reader to conceive of her book as an elegy. The final part of the essay will offer an explanation of Woolf's unusual choice of the Italian front for the war service of Septimus Warren Smith and his friend Evans, as well as suggesting that she borrowed facets of both characters from two young men of her acquaintance.

A temporary cenotaph was erected in Whitehall to coincide with the Peace Day celebrations of July 19, 1919, and on the same day that the Unknown Warrior was interred in Westminster Abbey (November 11, 1920) Sir Edwin Lutyens' permanent Cenotaph was unveiled by King George V: four days later, the queue of those waiting to lay wreaths still stretched for seven miles through the streets of London (Gregory 26). Some years later, Woolf recalled "going down the Strand the night of the Cenotaph; such a lurid scene, like one in Hell. A soundless street; no traffic; but people marching. Clear, cold and windless... women crying Remember the Glorious Dead, and holding out chrysanthemums. Always the sound of feet on the pavement" (*D2* 79-80).

By the early 1920s two distinct responses to the War had emerged. At the same time as statues, crosses and memorials in stone, bronze and brick went up in villages, towns and cities throughout the Mother Country and her dominions,

> another, alternative version of the war's meaning was also taking form, a version that we might call collectively the anti-monuments. These were not buildings or statues or soldiers' graves, of course: those belonged to the state, or were the public gestures of private mourners. They were, rather, all the other forms in which judgements and conclusions about war could be expressed: paintings, poems, novels, histories, plays, music. These were works that rendered the war without the value-bearing abstractions, without the glory, and without the large-scale grandeur. Often they were conscious, aggressive rejections of the monument-making principles; they turned away from celebration, in search of war's reality. (Hynes 283)

Woolf was one of many intellectuals on the left who reacted with cynicism to the state's orchestration of the nation's grief and joy, and it is obvious that *Jacob's Room*, *Mrs Dalloway* and *To the Lighthouse* are primarily "anti-monument[al]" in tone and design. These novels, after all, are the work of a writer who wrote in her diary on July 19, 1919:

> One ought to say something about Peace day, I suppose, though whether its worth taking a new nib for that purpose I dont know. I'm sitting wedged into the window, & so catch almost on my head the steady drip of rain which is pattering on the leaves. In ten minutes or so the Richmond procession begins . . . I've a sense of holland covers on the chairs; of being left behind when everyone's in the country. I'm desolate, dusty & disillusioned. Of course we did not see the procession . . . it seems to me a servants festival; some thing got up to pacify and placate "the people"—& now the rain's spoiling it; & perhaps some extra treat will have to be devised for them. Thats the reason of my disillusionment I think. There's something calculated & politic & insincere about these peace rejoicings . . . (*D*1 292)

This type of reaction was very common in certain circles, where the Peace Day celebrations (and the Government's other commemorative initiatives) tended to be viewed not just as integral to the state's campaign to legitimize the War, but also as part of its attempt to defuse post-War social and political tensions. In the wake of the Russian Revolution, with the extreme left and right appearing an equal danger to state in Germany, and with mutinies in France, the British Government was conscious of the urgent need to instil a sense of national unity: "If ever there was a time when rituals of integration and unity appeared to be required it was in the autumn of 1919" (Gregory 10).

Yet although the left was suspicious of the Government's motives—"the journalist Francis Meynell . . . condemned the burial of the Unknown Warrior in Westminster Abbey as a 'pageant' organised by those responsible for the war in the first place" (King 7)—no one could gainsay the intense outpourings of emotion which the interment of the Warrior, Peace Day and the unveiling of the Cenotaph occasioned. Similarly, it is interesting to note that on July 20, 1919, the day after Peace Day, Woolf wrote another entry in her diary which highlights her ambivalence towards the official apparatus of thanksgiving and remembrance: "What herd animals we are after all!—even the most disillusioned. At any rate, after sitting through the procession & the peace bells unmoved, I began after dinner, to feel that if something was going on, perhaps one had better be in it" (*D*1 294). She and Leonard then went out to watch fireworks, etc. Six years later, recording a bus journey through central London which she made with Leonard, Woolf noted that the two of them "crossed Westminster Bridge; admired the Houses of Parliament & their fretted lacy look; passed the Cenotaph, which L. compromised by sitting with his hat off all the way up Whitehall" (*D*3 23). Like her husband, Woolf undoubtedly felt alienated from the mass culture of memorialization, but also like Leonard she felt something of a need to "compromise" with the rest of the "herd" and "be in it."

Not surprisingly, this "compromise" seeded itself in *Mrs Dalloway*, generally regarded as one of the most consummate products of Hynes' "counter-culture, rooted in rejection of war and its principles" (Hynes 283). So although the War dead throng the text (see, for example, 15, 17, 56, 74, 93, 123, 125, 153), a victim of shell-shock is one of its central characters, and grief-stricken mothers are mentioned soon after the novel begins, ensuring that no reader can fail to apprehend *Mrs Dalloway* as a "rejection of war and its principles," less blatantly but just as scrupulously it also commemorates the fallen in ways which seem either to allude to, or parallel, the various "rituals of integration and unity" which the Government had instituted.

In my Introduction to the new Oxford World's Classics edition of *Mrs Dalloway*, I stress that the reader of Woolf must be extremely attentive to what she or he might be tempted to dismiss as the "small print" of her texts, ever alert to what some readers might gloss over as the minutiae of her novels, in order to be fully alive to the range of her meanings: we must close with Woolf's texts through the closest of close readings. For instance, I point out that when a young woman's cloak blows out as she walks past "Dent's shop in Cockspur Street" (45) it is not disarranged outside any old retail outlet but the premises founded by E. J. Dent, "the man who built both Big Ben's clock for the Palace of Westminster and the primary Standard Timekeeper of the United Kingdom at the Royal Observatory, Greenwich" (xxxiv). So-called "minor" details (like the name of the shop) and Woolf's major themes (like time) form part of the same continuum in *Mrs Dalloway*, and this is no less true of her work as a whole.

Yet another example of Woolf's tendency to punctuate her fiction with apparently unimportant names, words or descriptive terms which turn out to be loaded with significance once they are investigated is the reference to "Finsbury Pavement" in *Mrs Dalloway* (a place-name, I regret to say, which I failed to investigate sufficiently for my edition of the novel). Walking up Whitehall, Walsh is overtaken by a detachment of young soldiers who, having placed against the Cenotaph "the wreath which they had fetched from Finsbury Pavement to the empty tomb" (43), are now, presumably, on their way back there. More specifically, it may be surmised, the soldiers are returning to 39 Finsbury Square, Finsbury Pavement, London, E.C.2, the headquarters of the Territorial Army Association of the City of London (*Post Office London Directory* 355, 2829).

Established as the Territorial Force in 1908 (it changed its name in 1921), the Territorial Army, like the British Expeditionary Force, its extra-territorial counterpart, was the brainchild of Richard Burdon Haldane (1856-1928), Viscount Haldane of Cloan, Secretary of State for War 1905-12, and Lord High Chancellor 1912-15 and 1924. Haldane was a tireless reformer who also created the Imperial General Staff and the Officer Training Corps in schools; Field Marshal Haig called him "the greatest Secretary of State for War England has ever had" (Haldane 288). In a key memorandum of April 25, 1906 Haldane outlined his "scheme by which boys would be gradually prepared for service in the Territorial Army . . . On leaving school all boys would have the opportunity of joining a cadet corps or miniature rifle club where they could be thoroughly trained . . . Thereafter they would be able, at the age of 19, to enrol in the Territorial Army" (Spiers 96). It is such a corps or club ("boys of sixteen" [43]) which marches past Walsh in Whitehall.

Educated at Edinburgh and Göttingen, Haldane, in addition to being a distinguished lawyer and statesman, was a prominent idealist philosopher, deeply read in German metaphysics. In envisaging the Territorial Army, he told the Army Council that he wished to form an "Hegelian Army" (Haldane 185), and in the words of one historian:

> He wanted, in short, to establish a clear idea of the Army, with all its reserves, as a *Ding an Sich*, and this went far beyond the more usual approach of asking what the Army was *for* . . . He visualised an entire Nation in Arms . . . [where] . . . the military training and indoctrination of the Nation should be undertaken by a new Territorial Army and by associated training corps at schools and universities (Howard 9).

Woolf's treatment of the boy soldiers indicates that their "military training and indoctrination" in the Territorial Army have been successful. As they approach him, Walsh hears "a rustling, regular thudding sound, which as it overtook him drummed his thoughts, strict in step, up Whitehall, without his doing. Boys in uniform, carrying guns, marched with their eyes ahead of them, marched, their arms stiff, and on their faces an expression like the letters of a legend written round the base of a statue praising duty, gratitude, fidelity, love of England" (43). It is as if Walsh, too, has been militarized, "indoctrinat[ed]" and recruited to their well-drilled ranks, and the Indian civil servant feels the "Hegelian" pull of the soldiers even more strongly as they march on past him "in their steady way, as if *one will* worked legs and arms uniformly, and life, with its varieties, its irreticences, had been laid under a pavement of monuments and wreaths and drugged into a stiff yet staring corpse by discipline" (44; emphasis added). In its ideological thrust, this passage in *Mrs Dalloway* is of a piece with Woolf's description of the Mediterranean Fleet sailing past the *Euphrosyne* in *The Voyage Out*, an event which triggers a dipping of the merchant ship's flag, the raising of Richard Dalloway's hat, the squeezing of Rachel's hand "[c]onvulsively" by Clarissa, and the "casting [of] a curious effect of discipline and sadness on the waters" (60); Richard Dalloway's conviction in the same novel that "if the meanest screw fails in its task, the proper working of the whole is imperilled" (57); the young sailors in *Jacob's Room* who "descend with composed faces into the depths of the sea; and there impassively . . . suffocate uncomplainingly together"; the doomed "tin soldiers" of the army on the same page of that novel, and the "smoothly sculptured" and "impassive" traffic policeman whose "face is stiff from force of will and lean from the effort of keeping it so" (216-17). Like the young soldiers in Whitehall, "one will" is working the limbs of all these dutiful British citizens and they have all been "drugged . . . stiff" with an "Hegelian" sense of duty and national purpose. The ubiquity of the "Hegelian" spirit is brought home a few pages further on when Walsh, out of the blue, reflects on the world in a way which would have been second nature to a Neo-Hegelian idealist like R.B. Haldane: "Nothing exists outside us except a state of mind, he thinks . . . But if he can conceive of her, then in some sort she exists, he thinks . . . " (48). So closely was Haldane identified with Germany and German thought, that no sooner had the War been declared than wild rumors began to circulate calling his loyalty into question. He was maligned as "a Teutonic windbag" and it was even alleged that he was the illegitimate son of the Kaiser (Hall and Martin 256; see also 253-60). By May 1915 Haldane's position in the cabinet had become so untenable that he had to leave the Government, but when Woolf was at work on *Mrs Dalloway* he was once again in the public eye as Lord Chancellor in Ramsay MacDonald's short-lived Labour administration of 1924.

 The allusion to "Finsbury Pavement," therefore, is not a mere geographical filler, an area of London plucked at random from a gazetteer, but yet another signpost which alerts the reader to the all-encompassing nature of the novel's critique of war and militarism. And that is not the end of the matter. A response to "the evident need for urgent military reform which had been made clear by the virtual breakdown of Army administration during the Boer War" (Howard 4), Haldane's Territorial and Reserve Forces Act of 1907 was to go a long way to delivering this new model army—in many ways it did offer what Walsh calls "a very fine training" (43)—but Woolf also implies that the same public health and social problems remain in place in 1923 as in the late 1890s. The physical feebleness of many urban recruits was one of the main reasons cited for Britain's initial poor showing against the Boers, but the boy soldiers Walsh observes do "not look robust. They were weedy for the most part, boys of sixteen, who might, tomorrow, stand behind bowls of rice, cakes of soap on counters" (43).

Haldane was a friend of Leslie Stephen (*L*1 111) and twenty years previously, on February 23, 1904, the day after Stephen's death, he had written to Woolf and described her father as being "like Socrates in the calmness of his wisdom. One cannot hope to look on such another again in the course of life, and it is good to have been permitted to be near him. But for you the blank and the numbing reaction will presently be hard to bear" (Maitland 490). These words must have given Woolf some succor, but the following Christmas "was to some extent marred for Virginia by . . . Mr Haldane, the Liberal statesman, who wrote unenthusiastically to Violet Dickinson about Virginia's Haworth article [see *E*1, 5-8]. It was Virginia's first taste of literary adversity and she did not like it" (Bell 94). On December 30, 1904 Woolf wrote to Dickinson:

> I can't think why you condemn me to suffer so needlessly. Mightn't you have saved me 2 *sleepless* nights—if not 3—by telling me straight out *what* Mr Haldane said of Haworth? Anyhow, you needn't have told me he was very severe . . . Really I think I shall give up writing, or at any rate showing my things to other people; I only get criticism and abuse . . . After all I didnt ask Haldane to criticise me—and yet he thinks he has a right to be very severe' (*L*1 170; see also 171).

"What news of the Lord Chancellor?" (*L*1 190) Woolf asked Dickinson in May 1905, with Haldane in mind—a full seven years before he was promoted to that office and in a way which suggests that she was possibly still irked by his criticism of her work. It is even conceivable that Woolf still felt a sense of personal grievance towards Haldane when writing *Mrs Dalloway*, but she undoubtedly abhorred the militarism which his reforms cemented.

This is made absolutely clear through the manner in which the boy soldiers enter Walsh's consciousness. The preceding paragraph ends with these words (Walsh has been thinking about the idealism of his youth): "The future lies in the hands of young men like that, he thought" (43). Yet the next begins with: "A patter like the patter of leaves in a wood" (43). This unexpectedly autumnal phrase attracts the reader's eye because *Mrs Dalloway* is set on a very hot summer's day: "June had drawn out every leaf on the trees" (6), we read, while later on, en route to Clarissa's party, Walsh notes "the thick foliage of squares" (137). More resoundingly, Woolf's simile catches the reader's ear: falling or fallen leaves are an ancient literary topos for the dead. In effect, the marching boy soldiers are preceded by a figurative march past of "the fallen," the dead soldiers of the War whose ranks they are being trained to fill. Tentatively, we might note how the words Woolf uses to describe the arrival of the young Territorials recall the rain "pattering on the leaves" just above her head as she made her diary entry on Peace Day 1919. More assuredly, we can pinpoint this "patter of leaves" passage as an inter-textual hot spot where Woolf brings into play a wide range of elegiac literature.

The comparison of successive generations to the fall of leaves in autumn is a poetical commonplace in classical literature. In the *Iliad* (VI, 146-50) we find:

> As is the generation of leaves, so is that of humanity.
> The wind scatters the leaves on the ground, but the live timber
> burgeons with leaves again in the season of spring returning.
> So one generation of men will grow while another dies (Homer 157).[1]

We encounter a similar idea in the work of the seventh-century elegiac poet Mimnermus, Aristophanes' *Birds* (I, 685), and most influentially of all, perhaps, in the *Aeneid* (VI, 305-10):

> huc omnis turba ad ripas effusa ruebat,
> matres atque viri, defunctaque corpora vita
> magnanimum heroum, pueri innuptaeque puellae
> impositique rogis iuvenes ante ora parentum:
> quam multa in silvis autumni frigore primo
> lapsa cadunt folia . . .

["Hither rushed all the throng, streaming to the banks; mothers and men and bodies of high-souled heroes, their life now done, boys and unwedded girls, and sons placed on the pyre before their fathers' eyes; thick as the leaves of the forest that at autumn's first frost drop and fall . . . "] (Virgil 554-5).

---

[1] With both this passage and *Iliad*, XXI, ll.464-6 in mind we should heed G. S. Kirk: "The likening of human generations to the fall of leaves in autumn and their growing again in spring carries no suggestion of rebirth, but means that life is transient and one generation succeeds another" (Kirk 176).

There is a passing reference to Septimus reading the *Inferno* in *Mrs Dalloway* (75) and these lines from *Aeneid* VI lie directly behind Canto III, ll.112-14 of Dante's poem, where the dead gather on the banks of the Styx to be ferried across by Charon:

> Come d'autunno si levan le foglie
>   l'una appresso dell'altra, fin che 'l ramo
>   vede alla terra tutte le sue spoglie,
> similemente il mal seme d'Adamo
>   gittansi di quel lito ad una ad una,
>   per cenni come augel per suo richiamo.

["As in autumn the leaves drop off one after the other till the branch sees all its spoils on the ground, so the wicked seed of Adam fling themselves from that shore one by one at the signal, as a falcon at its recall."] (Alighieri 52-3). Milton, too, imitates the *Aeneid* passage in *Paradise Lost*, (I, ll.302-3)—"Thick as autumnal leaves that strew the brooks/ In Vallombrosa"—and, in turn, Arnold imitates both Virgil and Milton in "Balder Dead" ("Then must he not regard the wailful ghosts/ Who all will flit, like eddying leaves, around," ll.176-7). The fallen leaves topos informs the "Ode to the West Wind," especially the opening stanza, and it is also employed by Shelley in "Adonais" (stanza xvi), by Byron in "The Destruction of Sennacherib" (stanza ii), by Tennyson in *In Memoriam A.H.H.* (stanza xcv), and by A. E. Housman in *A Shropshire Lad* (XXXI), significantly, "one of the poems AEH gave Walter Raleigh permission to print in one of *The Times Broadsheets* for the trenches" in 1915 (Housman 342). Moreover, Donald Davie has argued that "the original eighteen poems of . . . the Hardy sequence [*Poems of 1912-13*, that is "The Going" to "The Phantom Horsewoman"] . . . tell a story of the poet's pilgrimage to his and Emma's early haunts, matching the stages of the journey there and back to specific stages of Aeneas's journey, in *Aeneid* 6, to the abode of the blest" (Davie 137) and, if Davie is correct, the Hardy poem which most obviously corresponds to Virgil's fallen leaves passage is "The Voice." In other words, even if Woolf did not know her Virgil and her Dante, which she did, there are numerous applications of the fallen leaves topos in English literature with which she was familiar.

As further indication of the universality of the topos, Woolf's linking of dead leaves and dead soldiers is paralleled in the work of two American poets, Wallace Stevens and Allan Tate. Stevens makes striking use of the leaves theme in a number of poems from 1915-18, such as "Domination of Black," "Tea," "Sunday Morning," which, James Longenbach contends, "employs the topos precisely because it is situated in a time of war: the world of 1915 made the music of the

"VANISHED, LIKE LEAVES"

leaves more meaningful" (Longenbach 78), and "The Death of a Soldier," the first stanza of which both enunciates and enacts the topos:

> Life contracts and death is expected,
> As in a season of autumn.
> The soldier falls.

Likewise, Tate's "Ode to the Confederate Dead" uses the topos in its varied refrain, a device which intensifies the elegiac *gravitas* of the poem, while a more recent poet, Seamus Heaney, also draws on the theme in his deeply Virgilian *Seeing Things* (1991).[2]

In exploiting the fallen leaves topos at the Cenotaph, then, Woolf not only problematizes the boy soldiers' presence in Whitehall by presaging their deaths in battle, but also, in a sense, like Walsh, joins in their act of remembrance. As if to reinforce this commemorative strain in the novel, the topos reappears a little further on when the "battered woman" opposite Regent's Park tube station is likened to "a wind-beaten tree for ever barren of leaves which lets the wind run up and down its branches singing." The old woman laments lost love at both a personal level and in terms of the nation's collective sense of loss in the early 1920s, after "death's enormous sickle had swept those tremendous hills" (69). As Walsh gives the woman a coin, "the passing generations . . . vanished, like leaves, to be trodden under, to be soaked and steeped and made mould of by that eternal spring . . . " (70). Here again, an awareness of the fallen leaves topos imbues the narrative with a commemorative sonority. Such knowledge also, incidentally, makes us all the more sensible of Kaiser Wilhelm II's unfortunate turn of phrase when he assured his departing troops in August 1914 that they would "be home before the leaves have fallen from the trees" (Tuchman 123).

Virgil had previously conjured up the same "throng" of the dead which was to feature in *Aeneid* VI ("matres atque viri . . . parentum") in the *Georgics* (IV, 471-77), where he says there were:

> quam multa in foliis avium se milia condunt,
> Vesper ubi aut hibernis agit de montibus imber (ll.473-4)

["as many as the myriads of birds that shelter among the leaves when evening or a wintry shower drives them from the hills"] (Virgil 252-3). Woolf first read the *Georgics* in February 1905 (*PA* 238), and this second Virgilian source almost cer-

---

[2] I would like to express my gratitude to colleagues with whom I discussed the fallen leaves topos: Peta Fowler, John Fuller, Stephen Gill, Tony Nuttall, Nick Shrimpton, Fiona Stafford and Edward Wilson deserve thanking by name.

tainly helps to explain why, sitting in Regent's Park, the bereaved Septimus becomes ever more convinced that "leaves were alive, trees were alive . . . the leaves being connected by millions of fibres with his own body . . . " (19). It also explains why he believes "Men must not cut down trees," and why the sparrows of central London sing to him "in voices prolonged and piercing in Greek words, from trees in the meadow of life beyond a river where the dead walk, how there is no death" (21). "The supreme secret must be told to the Cabinet," Septimus insists further on in the novel, "that trees are alive" (57; see, also 125), while in "The Hours" Septimus recalls: "'. . .I went on to Brindisi' through the fields of Italy. the plains of Italy. ~~Here the bird chorus sang with him imitated the rustling of leaves, & the flowing of a river~~" (Woolf, *"The Hours"* 66). In its pervasive imagery of leaves, trees and birds, *Mrs Dalloway* soughs with Virgilian allusion and once we attend to these echoes the novel's elegiac temper is powerfully enriched.

Its arboreal imagery may also be rooted in a non-literary tradition. In June 1919 a "Roads of Remembrance Association" was formed, dedicated to "'the adornment of suitable highways and the precincts of schools and institutions with trees in memory of those who gave their lives in the war,'" (King 73), and in a leader of October 1922, entitled "Trees for Remembrance," *The Times* described how:

> In an Essex village oak trees have been planted as memorials to men who died in the war. They bear attached to them the names which they severally commemorate, and the hope has been expressed that other villages will follow the same idea. It is one which should appeal to pious sentiment.[3]

Who knows, it may also have appealed to the congenitally impious Virginia Woolf.

When Evans comes out of one of the trees in Regent's Park, the scene is described thus:

> . . . the branches parted. A man in grey was actually walking towards them. It was Evans! But no mud was on him; no wounds; he was not changed. I must tell the whole world, Septimus cried . . . raising his hand like some colossal figure who has lamented the fate of man for ages in the desert alone with his hands pressed to his forehead . . . and with legions of men prostrate behind him he, the giant mourner. (59-60)

Like the description of the "battered old woman" opposite the tube station, this is another of the novel's statuary moments, in which characters bring to mind (or are themselves described as) monumental figures cast in attitudes of grief or

---

[3] "Trees for Remembrance," *The Times* (26 Oct 1922), 13.

lamentation. In the literature and iconography of the early 1920s the bereaved were invariably represented as women, and this convention, surely, lies behind the third statuary moment in the novel, when Walsh has a sudden, inner-city vision of a "solitary traveller" leaving a wood:

> and there, coming to the door with shaded eyes... with hands raised, with white apron blowing, is an elderly woman who seems... to seek, over the desert, a lost son, to search for a rider destroyed; to be the figure of the mother whose sons have been killed in the battles of the world. So, as the solitary traveller advances down the village street where the women stand knitting and the men dig in the garden, the evening seems ominous; the figures still; as if some august fate... were about to sweep them into complete annihilation. (49)

Walsh envisages a kind of alternative war memorial, one representing not a gallant soldier in action, but the women and men who wait endlessly for his return, mothers and fathers immortalized in pitiful attitudes of hope.

In addition, all three of these statuary figures and their several references to "death's enormous sickle," "legions of men" laid out in death, and "complete annihilation," should be considered alongside the "smashed... plaster cast of Ceres" in Mr. Brewer's garden, like his cook's nerves, a victim of the "fingers of the European War" (73), and Elizabeth Dalloway riding up Whitehall on the top deck of an omnibus "like the figure-head of a ship... her cheeks the pallor of white painted wood; and her fine eyes, having no eyes to meet, gazed ahead, blank, bright, with the staring, incredible innocence of sculpture" (115). This description of Elizabeth is one of a number of curious depictions of the living in *Mrs Dalloway* as though they are dead or inanimate. Mrs. Coates's baby, "lying stiff and white in her arms" (17), as if shrouded in death, is another case in point, while Clarissa sees herself as a kind of corpse in a field after Peter Walsh's visit, "so that anyone can stroll in and have a look at her where she lies with the brambles curving over her" (37).

At 11 o'clock on Tuesday, November 11, 1919, the Government introduced a two-minute "Silence" to commemorate the first anniversary of the Armistice. It was a tremendous success and universally respected. In its account of the event, "*The Nation* compared the abrupt halt in London to 'the mechanical scene in a Swiss toy show after the penny in the slot had done its work'" (Gregory 16). The Silence became an annual act of remembrance from then on, and a common way in which it was signalled in the early 1920s was by letting off a maroon. This practice may well be echoed in the "violent explosion" which, along with the grand grey car, brings Bond Street to a Silence-like "standstill" (12). But the most widespread way "of signalling the silence was the use of bells, particularly church bells" (Gregory 13). When Richard Dalloway calls in on Clarissa on his way back to the House of Commons from Lady Bruton's, a clock strikes three and "the sound of the bell flooded the room with its melancholy wave" (100), and when Big Ben sounds half past three a little further on, it makes "the moment solemn" (108). The bells which resonate throughout *Mrs Dalloway* in the summer of 1923 are the same bells which will herald the autumnal Silence five months later, and the bell marking half past eleven in the novel enters Walsh's consciousness in a similar manner to the way the bells of Armistice Day will bring London to silent and pensive halt: "the sudden loudness of the final stroke tolled for death that surprised in the midst of life" (43). It is quite possible that Woolf hoped the reader would hear both the striking of the hour and the tolling of the Silence simultaneously.

But without doubt the most poignant act of observance in the whole novel occurs as the sky-writing airplane circles overhead:

> All down the Mall people were standing and looking up into the sky. As they looked the whole world became perfectly silent, and a flight of gulls crossed the sky, first one gull leading, then another, and in this extraordinary silence and peace, in this pallor, in this purity, bells struck eleven times, the sound fading up there among the gulls. (18)

Mrs Dalloway's 11 am silence is surely the fictional counterpart of the annual 11 am Silence. In the mind of Sir Percy Fitzpatrick, the man who conceived it, the emphasis of the Silence was not on mourning, but on togetherness, "to remind us of the greater things we hold in common" (Gregory 9), and this also seems to be Woolf's purpose at this point in a novel which is more generally concerned with exposing divisions, exclusions and inequalities. A little further on, the novel's eleven o'clock silence is reprised when Big Ben strikes the half hour and Walsh looks back to his meeting with Clarissa thirty minutes earlier:

> As a cloud crosses the sun, silence falls on London; and falls on the mind. Effort ceases. Time flaps on the mast. There we stop; there we stand. Rigid, the skeleton of habit alone upholds the human frame. Where there is nothing, Peter Walsh said to himself; feeling hollowed out, utterly empty within (42).

As with so many words, phrases and descriptive passages in *Mrs Dalloway*, this excerpt, which calls forth both the official Silence *and* the Cenotaph ("hollowed out, utterly empty within"), lends itself to a commemorative interpretation. Nor can it be entirely coincidental that Walsh is overwhelmed with a sense of being "utterly empty within" just before he walks past the Cenotaph proper.

Mrs Dalloway, therefore, not only opposes the official memorialization of the dead—Doris Kilman's experience at the Tomb of the Unknown Warrior in Westminster Abbey alone makes that plain enough (113-14)—but also contributes to the culture of remembrance. The reader of the novel, like so many of its characters, is not allowed to forget the war—on his way to see his wife and disposed to romance, Richard Dalloway suddenly recalls "the war, and thousands of poor chaps, with all their lives before them, shovelled together, already half forgotten" (98)—and this may be sufficient in itself to account for Woolf's choice of northern Italy, the front over which Major Robert Gregory was shot down by accident on January 23, 1918 and the front on which Hemingway's work as an ambulance driver led to *A Farewell to Arms* (1929), as the location of Evans' and Septimus's war service. George Cassar's study of the British campaign in Italy is called *The Forgotten Front* and in the same year that this book appeared, 1998, another work about the war in Italy was published with a similar title: Jan F. Triska's *The Great War's Forgotten Front*. Both titles reflect the comparative obscurity of the Italian front for a modern audience and even in the 1920s there was a perceived need to remind the country that an Italian front had actually existed. In his "Preface" to *With the 48th Division in Italy* (1923), for example, Lieutenant-Colonel G. H. Barnett justified his book in this way: "My excuse for writing it is that in the first place very little has been written concerning the part played by British troops in the Italian campaign, and the general public is somewhat ignorant of this phase of the war, and inclined to treat it as an unimportant side-show" (Barnett v-vi). By selecting Italy as the scene of Evans' death and Septimus's shell-shock, Woolf asks her readers, almost as pointedly in the mid-1920s as today, to remember a forgotten front. In addition, since Book VI of the *Aeneid*, the focal point of Virgil's epic, describes how the Trojans finally reach Italy at Cumae, and the remaining six Books centre on war in Italy of one kind or another, Woolf's choice of the Italian front may also point to her desire to further amplify the Virgilian/Dantean ring of the novel.

As Cassar explains, "Britain's involvement on the Italian front was the culmination of Lloyd George's relentless effort to find a cheap and quick way to end the war" (Cassar ix).[4] Faced with stalemate on the western front, Lloyd George thought the British should switch some of their resources to attacking Germany's weaker allies. Matters came to a head in October 1917 when "the Austrians, reinforced by handpicked German units, mounted a large-scale offensive in the Julian Alps, breaching the front at Caporetto and sending the Italians reeling back in total disarray" (Cassar ix-x). British and French troops were rushed south "to restore Italian morale and stabilise a new defensive line. British forces remained in Italy until the end of the war, playing a pivotal role in two battles that had a major influence on the course of the war" (Cassar x), the Battle of Asiago (June 15-16, 1918) and the Battle of Vittorio Veneto in late October, early

---

[4]For further information about the British Army's role in the conflict in northern Italy, see John and Eileen Wilks, *The British Army in Italy 1917-18* (Barnsley: Leo Cooper, 1998) and Sir James E. Edmonds and H. R. Davies, *Military Operations Italy 1915-1919* (London: HMSO, 1949).

November 1918. Six French, and two British Divisions were sent to Italy after Caporetto, the British reinforcements being the 7th and the 48th Divisions. Interestingly, in view of those "weedy" Territorials from Finsbury Pavement, the 48th Division formed part of the Territorial Army and among the regiments it comprised was the Gloucestershires (Cassar 93), the county regiment a Stroud boy (72) like Septimus is likely to have joined.

Septimus's friend Evans, who "was killed, just before the Armistice, in Italy" (73), must have been a casualty of the Battle of Vittorio Veneto, and the tragedy of his death and Septimus's grief is only heightened if the reader is aware that this battle was almost wholly unnecessary, with the War already won. By the time the battle commenced on October 24, 1918, the "Austrian government was close to collapse . . . Turkey had been defeated in Palestine and Syria. The Allies [had] pierced the Hindenberg Line on 26 September and continued to roll back the Germans. In late September an Allied force, marching north from its base in Salonika, cut the Bulgarian army in two and forced its retreat" (Cassar 185). On October 4 the Germans and the Austrians appealed to President Wilson for an armistice but still the war continued in northern Italy: the Italians could not accept that "Habsburg armies still entrenched on Italian soil" (Cassar 185) and Austrian military leaders were determined to fight on, despite what was happening at home, on the assumption that when an armistice was declared, the further south they had penetrated, the stronger their bargaining position would be at the ensuing peace conference. When the Battle of Vittorio Veneto finally came to an end, at 3 pm on November 4, 1918, the total number of British soldiers either killed or wounded since October 24 was 1662 (Cassar 215). Among the diverse meaningless deaths of the War, it is possible that Woolf regarded the fatalities of Vittorio Veneto as especially fatuous.

At the beginning of *The War in the Mountains*, Kipling describes the moment when he first looked at the northern Italian horizon from the "great Venetian plain" and was confronted by "one sheer rampart of brooding mountains." Observing the Trentino front more closely through field-glasses, Kipling recounts how it was composed of:

> tangled crosschains of worsted hillocks, hollow-flanked peaks cleft by black or grey ravines, stretches of no-coloured rock gashed and niched with white, savage thumbnails of hard snow thrust up above cockscombs of splinters, and behind everything an agony of tortured crags against the farthest sky (Kipling 4).

The Battle of Vittorio Veneto was fought over precisely this terrain and this helps to explain why, "alone with the sideboard and the bananas" in the Bloomsbury of 1923, Septimus reflects that he is "not on a hill-top; not on a crag; [but] on

Mrs Filmer's sitting-room sofa . . . Where he had once seen mountains . . . there was a screen" (123). And we can also see that when Clarissa asks herself, just after thinking her party will be a failure, "Why, after all, did she do these things? Why seek pinnacles and stand drenched in fire?" (142) her most peculiar turn of phrase is drawn directly from the mountain warfare of the Italian front and is another of the numerous thoughts and experiences she shares with Septimus in the novel (see xxxiv-xxxviii of my edition of the novel). Certainly, an awareness of the Battle of Vittorio Veneto brings new meaning to Rezia Warren Smith's recollection of "a flag slowly rippling out from a mast when she stayed with her aunt at Venice. Men killed in battle were thus saluted . . . "(127). Venice is only about fifty miles due south of Vittorio Veneto, and this Venetian flag and mast, and time "flap[ping] on the mast" (42) during the 11 am silence earlier on in the novel, are thematically even closer together.

"Found at the back of a small book containing Woolf's reading notes and partial translation of the *Choephori* of Aeschylus" in the Berg Collection of the New York Public Library are some holograph notes dated from November 9, 1922 to August 2, 1923" (*"The Hours"* 413). Among musings Woolf wrote down on November 19, 1922 are these: "Question of S's character. founded on R.? His face. eyes far apart—not degenerate. not wholly an intellectual. Had been in the war . . . Why not have something of G.B. in him?" (*"The Hours"* 417-19). I believe Septimus was indeed "founded on R.," at least in part: that is, on Ralph Partridge, born in 1894 and, by 1918, a major on the Italian front and a holder of the Military Cross (and bar) and the Croce de Guerra (Brenan 217; Fielding 3). It also seems likely that Woolf did decide to endow Septimus with "something of G.B.," that is Partridge's great friend Gerald Brenan, also born in 1894 and himself the holder of the Military Cross and the Croix de Guerre (Brenan 234; Gathorne-Hardy 125) and much closer to Septimus in build than the physically imposing Partridge. Woolf, we should not forget, tells us specifically that Septimus "had won crosses" (75) in the War, not simply medals or decorations (see also xiv-xv of my edition).

Brenan did not fight in Italy, but he did join up, like Septimus, at the beginning of the War. He was commissioned in the 5th Gloucestershires, and in December 1914 he was seconded to the 48th Divisional Cyclists' Company (Gathorne-Hardy 98-9)—that is, the same Division of the Territorial Army which would be involved in the mountain warfare of Vittorio Veneto four years later— where he first met Partridge early in 1915. Brenan grew very attached to Partridge—"The only man out here I like," he wrote from the western front—and "looked up to him as a hero, supremely good at many things that I should have liked to be good at" (Gathorne-Hardy 105-6). Xan Fielding has written: "There was an element of hero-worship in Gerald's liking for [Ralph]: 'I admired his sexual prowess and . . . found his rollicking high spirits and zest for life irresistible . . . A Roman rather than a Greek by temperament, he called up—or so I then thought—Plutarch's portrait of Mark Antony'" (Fielding 3; Brenan 197-8). Woolf could have heard about Brenan's war on the western front and Ralph Partridge's Italian campaign from a number of people, chief among whom are Lytton Strachey, Carrington and the two men themselves.

Partridge worked for the Hogarth Press from August 1920 until March 1923. At first the Woolfs liked him but their relationship with him soured, and although Hermione Lee may well be correct in her assertion that Woolf, in time, "disliked having [Partridge's] bullying male sexuality thrust at her" and once referred to him as "the gawkish boor" (Lee 464), that does not preclude the possibility of her being intrigued by his tales of army life on the Italian front and his friendship with Brenan. Alternatively, Woolf may have been inspired by the reminiscences of Brenan, whom she met "in May 1922 and liked . . . immediately" (Lee 464), about his life and friendship with Ralph Partridge on the western front and about Partridge's experiences in Italy. In April 1923, the Woolfs visited Brenan in Granada. As Lee notes, "they talked all day and night," at Yegen, "—about *Ulysses*, about Ralph and Carrington, about their lives. 'Our tongues wag—mine like a vipers, his like a trusty farmyard dogs.' She found [Brenan] 'a sympathetic but slightly blurred figure, who owing to solitude and multitudes of books has some phantasmagoric resemblance to Shelley'" (Lee 465).

Though they had the occasional row and periods of coolness, Partridge was "for forty-five years [Brenan's] closest friend" (Brenan 187) and even in their post-First World War correspondence there is a distinct sense of "two dogs playing on a hearth-rug," like Septimus and Evans, "one [Septimus/Brenan] worrying a paper screw, snarling, snapping, giving a pinch, now and then, at the old dog's ear; the other [Evans/Partridge] lying somnolent, blinking at the fire, raising a paw, turning and growling good-temperedly. They had to be together, share with each other, fight with each other, quarrel with each other" (73). It would be going much too far to suggest that Woolf simply winched the friendship of Partridge and Brenan into *Mrs Dalloway* lock, stock and barrel, but it seems very likely that she picked up and utilized aspects of it: Partridge's Italian front, the military crosses of both men, some of their physical attributes (for example, the "sturdy"-ness (73) of Partridge/Evans), their friendship and the emotional dynamics of their relationship.[5]

Gillian Beer has written persuasively about the elegiac tenor of Woolf's next novel in "Hume, Stephen, and Elegy in *To the Lighthouse*" (Beer 29-47), and Alex Zwerdling has described *Jacob's Room* as an "elegiac novel [which is] persistently small-scaled, mischievous and ironic. [Woolf] . . . had an instinctive distrust for reverence of any kind, treating it as a fundamentally dishonest mental habit that made symbols out of flesh-and-blood human beings. She was no more interested in a cult of war heroes than she had been in a religion of eminent Victorians" (Zwerdling 73). This is perfectly true as far as *Jacob's Room* is concerned, but, as we have seen, there is a reverential attitude discernible in *Mrs Dalloway* as well as a "distrust for reverence." "Several of Virginia Woolf's books compose themselves about an absence," Beer notes. "Jacob's absence from his room, Mrs Ramsay's in the second half of *To the Lighthouse*, and in *The Waves* Percival's in India and in death" (Beer 29). *Mrs Dalloway*, this essay has argued, is "compose[d] about [the] absence" of the fallen of both the western and Italian fronts, and perhaps this is why on June 27, 1925, Woolf wrote in her diary "I have an idea that I will invent a new name for my books to supplant 'novel.' A new —— by Virginia Woolf. But what? Elegy?" (*D*3 34). Given that she wrote this only a month after the publication of *Mrs Dalloway*, the second of her three elegies of the 1920s, it is not surprising that "elegy" is the first word that sprang to her mind.

[5]When asked to comment on this possibility, Frances Partridge agreed that Septimus has "something" of Gerald Brenan in him (to borrow Woolf's word from *"The Hours"*) and she concurred with Xan Fielding's view that "There was an element of hero-worship in Gerald's liking for [Ralph]." Mrs. Partridge was sent a draft of this essay and she returned it to the author with a check of assent against this statement: "Ralph Partridge and Gerald Brenan were, I feel certain, the model for Woolf's fictional soldiers" (this sentence did not make it into the final version of the essay). Annotated copy of my letter to Frances Partridge of September 17, 2001, returned to me undated [on September 29, 2001]. In the possession of the author.

Works Cited

Alighieri, Dante. *The Divine Comedy*. Vol.1: "Inferno." Trans. John D. Sinclair. New York: Oxford U P, 1939.
Barnett, George Henry. *With the 48th Division in Italy*. Edinburgh and London: William Blackwood, 1923.
Beer, Gillian. *Virginia Woolf: The Common Ground*. Edinburgh: Edinburgh UP, 1996.
Bell, Quentin. *Virginia Woolf: A Biography*. Vol. 1: "Virginia Stephen 1882-1912." London: Hogarth Press, 1972.
Brenan, Gerald. *A Life of One's Own: Childhood and Youth*. London: Hamish Hamilton, 1962.
Davie, Donald. "Virgil's Presence in Ezra Pound and Others." *Virgil in a Cultural Tradition: Essays to Celebrate the Bimillennium*. Ed. Richard A. Cardwell and Janet Hamilton. Nottingham: University of Nottingham Monographs in the Humanities IV, 1986. 134-46.
Fielding, Xan. ed. *Best of Friends: The Brenan-Partridge Letters*. London: Chatto and Windus, 1986.
Gathorne-Hardy, Jonathan. *The Interior Castle: A Life of Gerald Brenan*. London: Sinclair-Stevenson, 1992.
Gregory, Adrian. *The Silence of Memory: Armistice Day 1919-1946*. Oxford and Providence, Rhode Island: Berg, 1994.
Haldane, R. B. *Autobiography*. London: Hodder and Stoughton, 1931.
Hall, Jean Graham and Douglas F. Martin. *Haldane: Statesman, Lawyer and Philosopher*. Chichester: Barry Rose Law, 1996.
Homer. *The Iliad*. Trans. Richard Lattimore. London: Routledge and Kegan Paul, 1951.
Housman, A. E. *The Poems of A. E. Houseman*. Ed. Archie Burnett. Oxford: Clarendon Press, 1997.
Howard, M. E. *Lord Haldane and the Territorial Army*. London: Birkbeck College, London, 1967.
Hynes, Samuel. *A War Imagined: The First World War and English Culture*. London: The Bodley Head, 1990.
King, Alex. *Memorials of the Great War in Britain: The Symbolism and Politics of Remembrance*. Oxford and New York: Berg, 1998.
Kipling, Rudyard. *The War in the Mountains*. Garden City, New York: Doubleday, Page and Co., 1917.
Kirk, G. S. *The Iliad: A Commentary*. Vol 2: Books 5-8. Cambridge: Cambridge UP, 1990.
Lee, Hermione. *Virginia Woolf*. London: Chatto and Windus, 1996.
Longenbach, James. *Wallace Stevens: The Plain Sense of Things*. New York and Oxford: Oxford UP, 1991.
Maitland, Frederic William. *The Life and Letters of Leslie Stephen*. London: Duckworth, 1906.

The Post Office London Directory with County Suburbs for 1924. London: Kelly's Directories, 1924.
Spiers, Edward M. *Haldane: An Army Reformer.* Edinburgh and London: Edinburgh UP, 1980.
Tuchman, Barbara W. *August 1914.* London: Constable, 1993.
Virgil. *Eclogues, Georgics, Aeneid I-VI.* Trans. H. Rushton Fairclough. Rev. G. P. Goold. Cambridge, MA and London: Harvard UP, 1999.
Woolf, Virginia. *"The Hours": The British Museum Manuscript of* Mrs Dalloway. Transcribed and Ed. Helen M. Wussow. New York: Pace UP, 1996.
——. *Jacob's Room.* Ed. Kate Flint. Oxford: Oxford UP, 1992.
——. *Mrs Dalloway.* Ed. David Bradshaw. Oxford: Oxford UP, 2000.
——. *A Passionate Apprentice: The Early Journals 1897-1909.* Ed. Mitchell A. Leaska. London: Hogarth Press, 1990.
——. *The Voyage Out.* Ed. Jane Wheare. Harmondsworth, Middlesex: Penguin Books, 1992.
Zwerdling, Alex. *Virginia Woolf and the Real World.* Berkeley: University of California Press, 1986.

Suggestions of Other Worlds:
The Art of Sound in *The Years*
Rishona Zimring

> *Self-control is minimally stressed in an oral milieu where most of the data important for survival and understanding are channeled into the individual through the open conduits of his senses, particularly his sense of sound, in a continuous interaction linking him with the world outside him.*
> —Anne Carson, *Eros the Bittersweet* (43-4)

> *Possessiveness is the devil.*
> —Martin in *The Years* (245)

During the party in the "Present Day" section of *The Years*, Peggy's thoughts capture something of what it feels like to be modern, that is, unmoored, isolated, and apprehensive. When the dance music pauses, Peggy listens to the sounds outside.

> Far away she heard the sounds of the London night; a horn hooted; a siren wailed on the river. The far-away sounds, the suggestion they brought in of other worlds, indifferent to this world, of people toiling, grinding, in the heart of darkness, in the depths of night, made her say over Eleanor's words, Happy in this world, happy with living people. But how can one be "happy," she asked herself, in a world bursting with misery? On every placard at every street corner was Death; or worse—tyranny; brutality; torture; the fall of civilisation; the end of freedom. We here, she thought, are only sheltering under a leaf, which will be destroyed. (388)

That Peggy thinks of the decline of western civilization and freedom shadowed by tyranny is not surprising, given the context of *The Years*' publication: the rise of fascism, economic depression, Hunger Marchers, a despondent, if radicalized, intelligentsia, and war on the horizon.[1] The passage's resonances reach past the late thirties. Woolf's allusion to Conrad reminds us of a paradigmatic modernist disposition toward empire: a consciousness of its lies, failures, crimes, and perhaps imminent collapse. The fearful sensibility—"we . . . are only sheltering

---

[1] Bradshaw, in "The Socio-Political Vision of the Novels," quotes this same passage and points to its echoes of *The Voyage Out*, Woolf's most Conradian novel. To view *The Years* as Woolf's portrayal of London as a sepulchral city would also support an interpretation of it as Conradian.

under a leaf"—recalls Eliot's Fisher King shoring fragments against his ruins, and suggests the poet of Auden's "Spain," who "whispers, startled among the pines . . . on the crags by the leaning tower." Like her brother North, Peggy despairs over the experience of modernity, feeling the pain of living in a "fractured world" (390). Juxtaposing the poetic allusions of Woolf's language are the unmistakably suggestive sounds of a horn hooting and a siren wailing. They echo previous and insistent horns and sirens in the text which belong to a cacophony of urban and other sounds that resonate throughout *The Years*. Open your ears, Woolf's novel seems to say to its readers: to the "here and now," the novel's original title, and to suggestions of other worlds that can't be shut out of "this" one. In *The Years*, sound fragments bring to mind disintegration, barriers toppling, and the juxtaposition of worlds crowding up against one another: not only the "rupture" and "fragmentation" with which many literary critics characterize modernism itself, but also the "continuous interaction" of my epigraph.[2]

Woolf's insistent use of sounds to emphasize the porosity of boundaries (between here and far away, this world and others) hints at both the utopian and dystopian possibilities latent in a modernist sensibility of change and disintegration. As well as feeling alienated and alone, Peggy, after all, should seem modern in a liberating sense: she's a professional, emancipated woman; as a doctor, she's a representative of science; non-domestic, she wears lipstick and smokes. *The Years* has recently been described as a saga of progress and emancipation (Briggs 80), but Peggy is just one of several characters who experience progress negatively. Having entered the machine age, Peggy feels like the gramophone is simply "cutting grooves in her mind" (388).[3] Repeatedly complaining that she is in a groove and can't get out (354, 356), Peggy joins North in bemoaning the present day's paucity of authenticity and beauty, its ruts and repetitions, its stagnancy. "Round and round they go in a circle," she observes of the habitual conversations and relationships of her companions (359). Both North and Peggy feel trapped, not liberated, by the technological "present day," with its cars, innovative shower-baths, telephones, aeroplanes, wireless, cinemas, make-up, electric light, sirens, vacuum cleaners, and, of course, gramophones (all of which are mentioned in this section). But whereas Woolf uses sounds to insist upon the alienating *noise* of a modern, urban existence (and its ideologies of progress), she also uses the omnipresence of sounds to challenge one common

---

[2]For a recent survey of the critical terminology for modernism, see Friedman.

[3]The metaphor repeats that of *Three Guineas*, in which the gramophone's stuck needle is a figure for human nature in the thrall of ideology.

reaction to modernization: the retreat to an isolated, interior, closed-off and strictly private refuge.⁴

A typical reaction, after all, to the experience of being modern is to fashion a retreat to art.⁵ In the terms with which we familiarly converse about cultural modernism, this often entails a withdrawal from "low" forms of culture to "high"; from popular to elite; the middle and upper classes sheltering under a leaf to protect themselves from the lower; a cultural and aesthetic purism seeking refuge from various social and cultural pollutions. Peggy's despair does *not* result in retreat or purism; the hooting and wailing that infiltrate her mind prompt an awakening of consciousness that upsets and unsettles her, but gets her out of her "groove." By contrast, there is the young male poet whose face is "knit up; nerve-drawn; fixed" (360) and whose tiresome egocentrism, his "I, I, I," sounds to Peggy like "a vulture's beak pecking, or a vacuum-cleaner sucking, or a telephone bell ringing" (361). Peggy's ironic similes imply that "I, I, I"—the loud insistence on the autonomous self—is a fictional byproduct of the machine age, a defense mechanism against all those destabilizing, democratizing technologies that threaten an established order. The apprehensive experience of the world as a fragile, fractured place, an openness to the suggestions of other worlds brought in by horns and sirens, is a pointed challenge to the poet's retreat to a monologic position. To retreat, consolidation, fixity, limitation, and pure "I," all of which offer the illusion of protection from modernization, the sounds of *The Years* pose the deliberate aesthetic threat of noise pollution whose political and cultural significance is, precisely, their suggestion of *other* worlds.

The Years is strewn with references not just to horns and sirens, but intrusive voices, street music, pigeons cooing, bells booming, clocks striking, the din of traffic, dance music, neighbors shouting, children crying, hawkers yelling, drays roaring, lorries crashing, hammering, the clangour of shunting carriages, trombones wailing . . . and the "babbling—babbling" of human patter, all ending up with the incomprehensible song of the caretakers' children, "so shrill, so discordant, so meaningless" (430). The "hideous noise" (430) of the children's song could be taken as a synecdoche for the text's overall cacophony. The song's listeners, Eleanor and Maggie, describe it as "extraordinarily beautiful," an

---

⁴The interior can be taken as a literal and metaphorical space in the case of both Benjamin's "bourgeois interior" and Woolf's "room of one's own." See Hankins (12) for a cogent discussion of both authors' ambivalence about such spaces.

⁵Blair provides a particularly cogent summary of how the modernist aesthetic programme to "make it new" "could simultaneously mean the open embrace of modernity's opportunities and the defensive rejection of its challenges" (166), explaining modernism's most hermetic and organicist impulses as reactions to modernity's "worst excesses," including the "perversion of 'true' cultural (or racial) characters, histories, ideals" (160).

indication that the text's cacophony is artful, an aesthetic strategy and an important element of *The Years*' experimentation and lyricism. The sounds of *The Years* are not just a politically and culturally significant intrusion of the "lower" upon the cloistered interiors of the middle and upper, although that is an important part of their function. These sounds also call for an appreciation of linguistic creativity as a struggle with fleeting, incoherent noises and voices. What results is an art of fragmentation and heterogeneity, not synthesis and unity. As I shall argue, it is especially through Woolf's artist figure, Sara Pargiter, that the text foregrounds linguistic creativity as a struggle between solitude and intrusive sound.

The text's urgent sounds provide an important counterpoint to a vein in Woolf criticism that stresses the silences, gaps, and pauses in Woolf's texts. Such criticism tends to privilege silence as a kind of aesthetic minimalism, a deconstructive agreement with the inadequacy and betrayal of language. One explanation for such minimalism is that it is a desirable cultivation of interiority in retaliation against the "real" world's crowdedness. "The subject of silence has particular appeal in the word-clogged reality of the twentieth century, a time when we are bombarded with words from the public spaces of advertising, public relations, and journalism," writes Patricia Ondek Laurence (4). Woolf is likened to other modernists who "also employ indirection and silence . . . to dramatize the limitations of language and withdrawal from a fragmented culture into an interior world" (6). While *The Years* certainly depicts many instances of attempted withdrawal, its overall impression is of the futility of escaping from "public spaces" into purely private ones. Everywhere, the superabundant sounds of *The Years* mitigate the construction of a closed world of intimacy. Thus, my reading of *The Years* is in sympathy with Lucio Ruotolo's emphasis on interruption in Woolf's work; interruption undermines stasis and "an outdated expectation of artistic fulfillment" (10). Far from withdrawing from a fragmented culture, *The Years* is an attempt to negotiate and inhabit one in spite of the silence and solitude that beckon with illusions of unity and coherence. Part of *The Years*' distinction is its unusual struggle, dramatized particularly through Sara, with inwardness.[6]

While Sara is a sensitive listener, the fragmented sounds of *The Years* do not constitute an incompleteness that challenges the reader to hear unsayable traumas, although psychoanalytic interpretations such as Judith Greenberg's of reverberations and "resonant fragments" add an important conceptual framework

[6]To say that *The Years* conveys a struggle with inwardness is to recast Woolf's famous difficulty with the composition of this work. Radin, for example, characterizes Woolf's struggle as her "fear of becoming shrill and one-sided, of allowing her ideas to destroy her art" (xvii). Separating her project into two parts, *The Years* and *Three Guineas*, allowed

to Laurence's of silence, and Ruotolo's of interruption. Most of the urgent urban sounds that constantly interrupt in *The Years* do not point towards hidden meanings or secret, unspoken traumas. Rather, they are often obnoxiously obvious. Horns hooting, traffic roaring, clocks striking—"The air over London seemed a rough sea of sound" (224). These "gallant and strident" noises are not fragments of past traumas returning and demanding representation (Greenberg, "When Ears Are Deaf" 51). It makes more sense to think of them as the present knocking quite loudly on the door, even as signs of the future: "they seemed to be whirring a preliminary warning" (227). Less incomplete than overflowing, these sounds represent a rush of progress, more than they do repressed pasts bubbling to the surface.

Several recent interpretations of Woolf's late work have focused on acoustic disruptions, but primarily with reference to the use of the gramophone in *Between the Acts*, rather than to the human and technological urban soundscape in *The Years*. Jane De Gay writes that Woolf "characterized the developing political crisis in terms of auditory disturbance or interruption . . . which . . . called for artists to prove their social and political usefulness" (39. Scott regards the gramophone as bestowing upon Miss La Trobe some of the "revolutionary potential" of the cyborg (105). Pridmore-Brown finds the gramophone in *Between the Acts* to be a feminized instrument of play, communication, dialogue and multiplicity in a world that threatens a masculinist solidity (420). Cuddy-Keane considers a wider range of texts in her formulation of a "new aurality" that emerges in the context of new sound technologies such as the gramophone and wireless, calling attention to the "use of the full field of sound, the emphasis on a participatory audience, and the indeterminacy and openness of signification" as models for community (93); her essay's focus on diffusion, however, does not consider *The Years*. Each of these critics, as well as Beer in her discussion of Woolf's deployment of metaphors from the new physics, interprets sound or sound waves as figures for freedom, resistance, play. Cuddy-Keane's "diffusion," Pridmore-Brown's "static" and "noise," Scott's "subversion": all celebrate

---

Woolf to distinguish between the "shrill" (loud, public) voice and her "art" (or inward voice). However, my reading of *The Years* may suggest that the separation was not entirely successful; this is to imply that the critical agenda of *Three Guineas* knocks at art's door in Woolf's novel, loudly. The turn away from inwardness also provides a counterpoint to readings which posit emptiness and loss as preconditions for creativity: Abel's Kleinian reading of Woolf (with its emphasis on Lily Briscoe's preeminence as Woolf's stand-in) is exemplary of such interpretations. My insistence upon Sara's importance as an artist figure in Woolf's work implies that it is crowding (in this case, acoustic) that produces the crucial friction that inspires creativity. This can be better explained by the Kleinian idea of aggression, rather than the notion of reparation ("Infantile Anxiety Situations") which is key to Abel's important study.

the liberatory possibilities of the gramophone in the mode of Benjamin at his most populist, as an aura-destroying technology of reproduction.[7] The sounds of *The Years* are so aggressively intrusive, and felt as such by several characters, that they cannot simply be taken straightforwardly as redemptive signals of mobility or expansion, the embrace of new or other worlds. Perhaps the most controversial sound of *The Years*, after all, is that of the Jew taking a bath in the apartment next to Sara's. A crucial, problematic nodal point of the text (to which I shall return), this moment is one of many in which sounds signal social, cultural, and linguistic friction. Such friction carries with it an aesthetic of dissonance that can be heard throughout the text.

The Years is a novel *about* urban heterogeneity, including the metaphorical pollution of lower-class foreigners in an English world preoccupied with cleanliness.[8] There are several pointed references to the presence of foreigners in England, most (in)famously the Jew, but also Nicholas the Pole, Mrs. Fripp (the American who visits Oxford), the exotic Eugenie, the Levy's (Eleanor's charity case), Patrick (Delia's Irish husband), and the Belgian *arriviste* who employs Crosby, the Pargiters' former housekeeper.[9] If Woolf's novel "anatomises the 'deformed' culture of which she was both a product and a victim" (Bradshaw 179), I suggest that "deformity" can be heard in the text's use of exterior sounds to create a dissonance that threatens, as well as potentially liberates, a protective culture of privacy and inwardness. Think of an analogy from that youthful art form, film: at the time Woolf was composing *The Years*, other modernists were decrying the advent of synchronized sound in cinema. One of the most famous

---

[7]The studies I cite all situate Woolf's work in the context of new sound technologies or theories of sound waves. They should be considered along with theorizations of voice in modernist narrative such as Kahane's and Stewart's.

[8]In "The Socio-Political Vision of the Novels," Bradshaw remarks on the pollutedness of *The Years*, that is, its preoccupation with smears, smudges, and stains (205). The stains can be interpreted as the characters tainted by the "abominable system of family life"(*TY* 212; Bradshaw 206). From the "unreal cleanliness" (22) of the "1880" sick-room, and all the many references to washing in the opening section, to the "untidy" house of Eugenie and Digby, to Crosby's disgust with the Belgian whose bath she must clean of spittle (303), to Sara's and North's discussion of the Jew in the bath, Eleanor's new shower-bath that she brags about to North (308), and Peggy's derisive mention of an advertisement for sanitary towels (336), there is throughout *The Years* a remarkable preoccupation with cleanliness and dirt. Meisel also comments on the many references to deformity and mutilation, such as Sara's uneven shoulders, the Colonel's missing fingers, and the noseless violet-seller. While Meisel writes of a general "fear of fragmentation and deformity" in the novel (210), my reading suggests rather than fear, an ambivalent attraction played out in Sara's and others' acoustic contact with other worlds.

[9]Blair ("Real Space, Real Time") has provided useful information on the actual demographics of Bloomsbury of Woolf's time.

detractors of synchronized sound, Dorothy Richardson, bemoaned the loss of silent cinema as solitude:

> Life's 'great moments' are silent. Related to them, the soundful moments may be compared to the falling of the crest of a wave that has stood poised in light, translucent, for its great moment before the crash and dispersal. To this peculiar intensity of being, to each man's individual intensity of being, the silent film, with musical accompaniment, can translate him. All other forms are, relatively, diversions. . . . Perhaps the silent film is solitude and the others association. (200)

The Years uses sound to foreground association, ultimately to distance the reader from solitude and from the desire for it. The sounds of *The Years* belong to Woolf's critique of the private/public divide and remind readers of the noisy heterogeneity that is modern, urban life. The disruptive crowd of sounds inspires creativity at a time when isolation and exclusion were great temptations. Challenging readers not to retreat to a room of one's own, the sounds of *The Years* provide access to streets which fall short of a "classless utopian vision" but which remain potentially "fertile, teeming spaces of art in process" (Hankins 18) with all the fragility and loss of control that implies.

Sight, Sound, and the City

In "Oxford Street Tide" Woolf wrote, "The charm of modern London is that it is not meant to last; it is built to pass. . . . We knock down and rebuild as we expect to be knocked down and rebuilt. It is an impulse that makes for creation and fertility" (19-20). In this apparently cheerful paean to London's great shopping street, Woolf uses sound to disrupt the sight of all that glitters and is gay. Incorporating the voices of a middle-class woman who shops on a limited budget, and a thief who nabs a customer's purse, Woolf reaches the end of her essay with: "A thousand such voices are always crying aloud in Oxford Street. All are tense, all are real, all are urged out of their speakers by the pressure of making a living, finding a bed, somehow keeping afloat on the bounding, careless, remorseless tide of the street" (21). Even in an essay that purports to celebrate the fragility of modern life, Woolf was acutely conscious of the price of flimsiness, no matter how creative and fertile its impulse. The use of "a thousand such voices" partakes of a consistent pattern in Woolf's texts whereby the aural sense, rather than the visual, links the reader to multiple worlds.

The urban soundscape often involves release, rather than "pressure." When Eleanor Pargiter, Peggy's aunt, walks out onto London's streets in the "1891" section of *The Years*, the "London roar" brings relief and a new sense of openness to a woman just emerging from the Victorian home. "[S]he heard the dull

London roar with pleasure . . . The uproar, the confusion, the space of the Strand came upon her with a shock of relief. She felt herself expand" (112). On her walk, she hears "the voices of men crying, 'any old iron to sell, any old iron'" from the East End (91); near Trafalgar Square, she hears birds chattering shrilly (113), the sound of traffic, paper-boys crying, and pigeons cooing (115). From 1880, with its stifling death-bed scene and claustral domesticity, we shift to a newfound sense of agency and freedom experienced by a woman of the crowd, surrounded by "women . . . swarming in and out of shops with their shopping baskets" (94). Eleanor's consciousness expands with her freedom to walk anonymously, the "roar" and "uproar" affording her pleasure. Here and elsewhere in Woolf's work, *flânerie* arouses the sense of sound.

More often than not, critics have tended to view Woolf's urban texts as celebratory of "the dissolution of self" that characterizes *flânerie*, with its shock experience of perceptual confusion, disintegration, freedom of movement, and open passivity that is a precondition for creativity (Minow-Pinkney 162-5). Critics such as Rachel Bowlby, Susan Merill Squier, Makiko Minow-Pinkney, Leslie Hankins, Bill Brown, Jane Garrity, and Jennifer Wicke have all situated Woolf's work within *flânerie*'s terminology for such modernist preoccupations as anonymous wandering (whether by foot or car), shopping, bricolage, and fashion-consciousness.[10] To focus upon the figure of the *flâneur* (or *flâneuse*) in Woolf's work tends to privilege sight over sound. In "Street Haunting," Woolf writes about venturing onto London's streets to become a "central oyster of perceptiveness, an enormous eye." To stroll is to see; to see is to build pearls from the grit of perception, a metaphor for art. Following in the footsteps of Baudelaire, for whom the *flâneur* was both observer and painter, the source of creativity appears to be the exhilarating access to intense visual stimulation in the vast array of stuff that offers itself up to the consuming gaze.[11]

The concentration on visual stimulation as the core experience of creative *flânerie* obscures the importance of sounds in Woolf's version of urban wandering. In "Street Haunting," no sooner does Woolf introduce the metaphor of the treasure-bearing oyster and the eye, than she undermines the authority of the gaze. She links sight with surfaces, and hearing with depth. The eye perceives many painterly treasures: islands of pale light, the "glossy brilliance" of

[10] Their studies of Woolf's *flânerie* are part of the larger historical project on women and the turn of the century city that refers to both Baudelaire and Benjamin. See Bowlby, *Just Looking*, Felski, Nord, Parsons, Walkowitz, and Wolff.

[11] Baudelaire's *flâneur* is, of course, a voraciously visual creature. "He goes and watches the river of life flow past him in all its splendour and majesty . . . He gazes upon the landscapes of the great city . . . if waists have been raised and skirts have become fuller, be very sure that his eagle eye will already have spotted it from however great a distance" (11).

omnibuses, the "carnal splendour" of butchers' shops, flowers "burning" through the glass of florists' windows. But "we are gliding smoothly on the surface. The eye is not a miner, not a diver, not a seeker after buried treasure . . ." (22). A sound disrupts the introductory paragraphs' catalogue of sights. Evocative of the pivotal pistol-shot noise that explodes in *Mrs. Dalloway*, an ambiguous ring causes an interruption. A Prufrockian woman is "measuring out the precise number of spoons of tea which—She looks at the door as if she heard a ring downstairs and somebody asking, is she in?" (23) In this break, the essay's narrator develops the tensions between sight and sound: "here we must stop peremptorily. We are in danger of digging deeper than the eye approves. . . At any moment, the sleeping army may stir itself and wake in us a thousand violins and trumpets in response; the army of human beings may rouse itself and assert all its oddities and sufferings and sordidities" (23). Sight excludes humanity's variety and mutes the musicality of emotional response. Implying an opposition between vision and intellect, on the one hand, and hearing and feeling, on the other, Woolf uses sound to reveal the limitations of the visual. Suppose that a visually-oriented *flânerie* diminishes empathy; sound counters the hegemony of the image and the gaze, inspiring the literary imagination anew. While vision lends itself to notions of secrecy and mastery (the oyster hoards its treasure, the eye is "enormous"), the ambiguous "ring" prompts a description of openness and potential engagement. In the activity of digging deeper, the passage evokes Woolf's famous "tunneling process" (*D2* 272), bringing one to recesses of responsiveness conveyed in musical metaphors. If the city is a text, this implies, sound is its subtext and its rich subconscious, a world to which the creative writer seeks access.

    Woolf often represented the city's acoustic inspiration in terms of its musicality. In her early essay, "Street Music," Woolf expressed a utopian hope for the socially redemptive power of urban musicians, envisioning a crimeless, harmonious society in which "at each street corner the melodies of Beethoven and Brahms and Mozart could be heard" (Squier 42). Similarly, the battered woman's song in *Mrs. Dalloway* is arguably the signal moment of redemption in Woolf's portrait of London. Interrupting Peter Walsh's disgruntled thoughts about women lacking passion (thoughts goaded by his aggressively *visual flânerie*), the woman's song is first heard simply as "a voice bubbling up without direction . . . with an absence of all human meaning . . . the voice of an ancient spring spouting from the earth" (80). The song serves the same function as the skywriting airplane and the lugubrious motorcar, urban nexes of attention that allow Woolf to practice the art of roving narration. The battered woman's song is also an instance of urban sound that interrupts and disrupts. Not just music, but more random sounds undermine unity and liberate selves from static *tableaux* which threaten to still the urban life that Woolf insistently portrays as fragmented and unstable.

There is, for example, the famous "pistol shot" sound on the street that interrupts Clarissa as she chooses flowers at Miss Pym's. Clarissa is at first one with a visual extravaganza, a twilight moment when "every flower—roses, carnations, irises, lilac—glows; white, violet, red, deep orange" (13). Breaking up this fusion of colors which Clarissa experiences as a "wave" flowing over her, the sound of the explosion outside fragments the scene, rendering individuals and objects once again distinct from one another. When the aural sense is violently awakened, the scene suddenly and refreshingly shifts to "rumours . . . at once in circulation" (14), successfully marking a transition from painterly still-life to acoustic stimulation, variety of characters (it is here that Rezia and Septimus are introduced), and the commotion of mobile traffic and multiple consciousnesses. Sound disrupts unity; it helps to instigate and foreground the multiplicity for which Woolf's fiction is justifiably celebrated.[12]

The city's acoustic disorder provides relief from rigidity and static *tableaux*, leading away from unity to multiplicity, from static coherence to dynamic fragmentation, from private to public. This is nowhere more obvious than in young Elizabeth Dalloway's experience of London's uproar. Elizabeth is the real *flâneuse* of Woolf's novel when she enjoys her freedom on the omnibus like an "eel-like" pirate and a "pioneer" (133-4). Feeling the urgency to move away from maternal infantilization, she views her patriarchal inheritance of public service as a form of emancipation.[13] In keeping with the pattern whereby urban sound relieves, Woolf marks Elizabeth's sense of liberation from maternal bondage with extravagant urban noise. As the omnibus moves her, and she thinks of public service, she *listens* to the city:

> She liked the geniality, sisterhood, motherhood, brotherhood of this uproar. It seemed to her good. The noise was tremendous; and suddenly there were trumpets (the unemployed) blaring, rattling about in the uproar; military music; as if

---

[12] Auerbach's is the classic defense of Woolf's democratic style in his analysis of the realist detail and multiple, roving consciousnesses of *To the Lighthouse*; a more recent celebration of Woolf's multiplicity, in this case a weapon against fascism, can be found in Pridmore-Brown's essay, in which the gramophone's potential for shaping herd mentality can be challenged by exploiting noise and privileging the act of listening. While Beer, Pridmore-Brown, Scott and Cuddy-Keane read the emphasis on sound in Woolf's late work as progressive, Stonebridge reads it as a regression compatible with, rather than resistant to, fascist tendencies.

[13] Squier contrasts Elizabeth's experience of the city with Clarissa's: "Clarissa feels herself as background and spends her time giving parties; Elizabeth, rebelling against 'whatever her mother might say,' feels an important figure in society and contemplates a profession" (103).

> people were marching; yet had they been dying—had some woman breathed her last and whoever was watching, opening the window of the room where she had just brought off that act of supreme dignity, looked down on Fleet Street, that uproar, that military music would have come triumphing up to him, consolatory, indifferent.
> ... Forgetfulness in people might wound, their ingratitude corrode, but this voice, pouring endlessly, year in year out, would take whatever it might be; this vow; this van; this life; this procession, would wrap them all about and carry them on, as in the rough stream of a glacier the ice holds a splinter of bone, a blue petal, some oak trees, and rolls them on. (138)

The final image of this passage is a natural collage, the bringing together of fragments which, importantly, retain their distinctiveness: they are not unified, but are preserved, rolled on through time, as disparate elements. Woolf's masterful geological metaphor brings home the importance of the city's din. Like the glacial ice, it displays and preserves fragments; such fragments are the individual voices or sounds Elizabeth hears amidst the general din. That din is "consolatory" even while it remains indifferent; not quite elegiac, it nevertheless possesses the capacity to compensate in the wake of death and wounding. The uproar is "good" and connotes a universalist vision of the human family, resounding with Elizabeth's desire to become part of the public. Elizabeth's absorption in the urban uproar is a paradigmatic moment of the most liberatory aspects of Woolf's acoustic *flânerie*.

By contrast, *flânerie* is only a partial, problematic source of redemption and release in *The Years*. Midway through the novel, in the "1914" section, Martin's and Sara's walk from St. Paul's to Hyde Park provides an aesthetically pleasing urban soundscape in which the self has a chance to dissolve. Bombarded by a cacophony of urban sounds while they wind their way through public spaces, Sara and Martin experience "shock." Yet in this section, with its obvious reference to the beginning of the war, fragmentation is as ominous as it is relieving. On the one hand, the urban soundscape's incoherence signals a redemptive insubstantiality, a dispersal whereby selves dissolve into sounds and a "primal innocence" (242) triumphs. On the other hand, the litter of broken sentences and floating voices amounts to a disturbing breakdown of communication.

After meeting at St. Paul's and dining in a restaurant, Martin and Sara make their way to Hyde Park where Martin experiences the "dissolution of self" characteristic of *flânerie*. His feeling is described in terms of visual and aural impressionism, the emphasis on auras of light and sound. In this way, the urban experience of fragmentation comes across as a modernist release of revolutionary energies just before the war. Martin looks at a woman eating an ice: "The sun dappled the table and gave her a curious look of transparency, as if she were caught in a net of light; as if she were composed of lozenges of floating colours

... The sun dappling the leaves gave everything a curious look of insubstantiality as if it were broken into separate points of light. He too, himself, seemed dispersed. His mind for a moment was blank" (241-2). To accompany this visual break-up, there is an aura of sound: "The birds made a fitful sweet chirping in the branches; the roar of London encircled the open space in a ring of distant but complete sound" (242). The sound of adult voices, which have dominated the section as fragments of aborted conversation and shouted oratory, now dissolve into the inarticulate sounds of children and dogs: "The size of the human figure seemed to have shrunk. Instead of full-grown people, children were now in the majority. Dogs of all sorts abounded. The air was full of barking and sudden shrill cries" (242). Martin thinks of this as a scene of "primal innocence"; to the reader, the scene's innocence must seem ironic and melancholy, given the section's historic date. Yet it is important to recall, this scene seems to say, the feeling of exciting change and rejuvenating innocence that can attend a walk in Hyde Park, replacing an anxiety over incompleteness and disintegration with a sense of possible coherence: "a ring of distant but *complete* sound." Poised to go to war, Europe at leisure is still innocent, and Martin's experience of "the world ... without an 'I' in it" (242) echoes other moments (140, 330) where characters explore the world without a self.[14] Kitty Lasswade, escaping her London party for the country up north, also experiences a primal innocence. Outdoors in a place "uncultivated, uninhabited," she listens as a "deep murmur sang in her ears—the land itself, singing to itself, a chorus, alone. She lay there listening. She was happy, completely. Time had ceased" (278).

Still, Kitty's and Martin's absorption into soundscapes that provide the synesthetic feeling of eternity, completeness, and innocence are temporary interludes in a section that urges upon the reader a consciousness of the self in the world of history, politics, and violence. At the outset, there are telltale sounds of strife. "The air over London seemed a rough sea of sound through which circles traveled. But the clocks were irregular as if the saints themselves were divided. There were pauses, silences. . . The great clock, all the clocks of the city, seemed to be gathering their forces together; they seemed to be whirring a preliminary warning. . . . even the pigeons were frightened" (224-7). The "rough" sea of sound and its "warning" point to the more alarming aspects of fragmentation in this chapter's *flânerie*. Most strikingly, Sara's and Martin's urban walk is characterized by an anxiety-provoking inability to communicate, on the one hand, and the ease with which politically charged speech speeds its way towards unwitting listeners, on the other. In addition, the party scene from which Kitty departs to the "uncultivated" country is marked by political talk and symbolic violence.

---

[14]Naremore's treatment of Woolf's fiction remains one of the most helpful guides to this idea.

Through its carefully orchestrated fragmentation of sound and voices, the "1914" section conveys an urban world in which the experience of "disintegration" indicates violence and conflict as well as regeneration, destruction as well as creativity.

The prevailing feeling in "1914" is not a liberatory dissolution of self, but a constraining difficulty of speech and lack of privacy. Fragmentation means frustration, not freedom. When Martin and Sara walk, the urban shock experience of being bombarded with stimuli annoys them. Martin wants Sara to "'Say something . . . very profound'" (236); three times in rapid succession we are told that "he wanted her to speak" (236). But the desire for meaning and depth, as well as for Sara's peculiar eloquence, is constantly frustrated by the noise of London. "Fragments of other people's talk reached them in broken sentences" (231). "[I]t was impossible to talk. Too many people were listening." (232). "Conversation was impossible" (233). "It was impossible to talk because of the crowd" (234). "It was impossible to talk" because of the roar of traffic (235). "It was difficult to concentrate" (236) in the presence of an omnibus. In the restaurant, "[t]oo many people were listening" (232). Although eventually Martin rejoices in the dissolution of self and constructs the noise around him as an enveloping halo of sound and illusion of completeness, the scene of walking and talking marvelously captures the street's impingement upon private conversation. To amplify the sense of disconnection, there are pointed references to speakers with no listeners. When Martin first comes upon Sara, she is talking to herself (229). In Hyde Park, there are several parkgoers who talk to themselves: a middle-aged woman, a young man "in a closely buttoned up coat as if he had no shirt," and a lady who whistles as though she had a dog (237-9). Adrift and isolated, they are one step removed from the Hyde Park orators whose audiences shift and mingle, listening partially or not at all to the speeches. Weakest of the orators is an "old lady, hardly audible, saying something about sparrows" to whom nobody listens. Most threatening are the male orators, one of whom beckons to passersby with "'Don't be afraid . . . Do I look like a Jew'" (240), and another who speaks about "joostice and liberty" to a "crowd of loafers, errand-boys and nursemaids [who] gaped up at him with their mouths falling open and their eyes gazing blankly" (240). Threatening to Martin, who sees in this spectacle the death of beauty in the uprising of labor, this and the other speech fragments convey a world unpleasantly fractured and incoherent, a site of destruction and tension. Xenophobia, class hatred, and severe alienation characterize the London world, and to be bombarded by its stimuli is to experience its violence. These are the conditions for the desire to be enclosed in a "circle of privacy" where one can turn from violent disintegration to "the potency, the fecundity of spring" (245).

Kitty's party provides the other circle of privacy, a partial refuge from London's rough sea of sound. Yet here too, talk is shaped by history and politics, and symbolic violence renders the party a place from which Kitty flees to the refuge of the land singing its chorus in the country. Wishing for erotic talk with a young woman at the party, Martin finds himself listening "to the sounds in the street. He could just hear the cars hooting; but they had gone far away; they made a continuous rushing noise" (251); their sounds grow more distant as Martin's senses become suffused with wine. His desire for escape into wine and intimacy is derailed, however, by talk of politics. During a discussion of Ireland, a man arranges "crusts of bread by the side of his plate . . . as if they were fragments of human destiny, not crusts, that he held in his fingers" (253); soon thereafter, a footman spills wine on a lady's dress, while one of the younger girls speaks of Nijinsky and the Russian dancers. Worlds collide, and there is really no refuge from the perceptual confusion of London traffic in the private houses of the upper class; with the sound of horns hooting, the "rushing noise" of progress just outside, inside Ireland and Russia, political violence, cultural upheaval, and revolution all jar up against one another. This is the "fractured world" Peggy will inherit, and the "preliminary warning" struck by the clocks at the beginning of "1914" signals not only the unmentioned war, but the gathering forces of revolutions in "other" worlds. The world of "1914" will give way to that of "1917", with its air-raid scene and unfinished conversation about a "new" world, its bombs and sirens; and finally we arrive at the "Present Day" where the violence symbolized by wine spilt upon a dress will reappear as thirteen broken glasses at the Pargiters' party, and as the intrusive noise that so threatens North, the silence-seeker of the next generation.

However intrusive and antagonizing the noises become, Woolf's novel does not promote silence and solitude as a relief. Rather, in the struggle with acoustic crowding, machine-age noise, and sound fragments Woolf eschews the defensive rejection of heterogeneity and an aesthetic linked to ideals of purity. Instead she fashions a poetic speech corrupted by London's "rough sea of sounds" whose value lies in its power to defamiliarize. Through the novel's artist figure, Sara Pargiter, Woolf dramatizes the conflict between urban cacophony and silent inwardness. The struggle itself inspires linguistic creativity and a distinctive mode of speech in which frictions resonate, instead of being shut out or plastered over ("pargeted").

Strange Speech: The Struggle with Sounds

As exotic "Elvira" in Woolf's manuscript, the eventually massively edited Sara represented, according to Grace Radin, "the repudiation of society." In

January of 1935, Woolf decided to have her sing, "'and so lyricise the argument'" (*D4* 276, Radin 63). Writing of the "whimsical way Sara speaks, moving from one image to another with the rhythm of music," Radin (among other critics) views Sara as Woolf's stand-in, a character for whom "everything she experiences in the present is inextricably mingled with everything she has read, seen or heard" (43). Sara has inspired a startling range of interpretations, from Bradshaw's characterization of her virulence as cryptofascist, to Nelson-McDermott's description of her as parodic, to Caserio's championing of her as the "muse of . . . haphazardness . . . given to a deranged form of speaking," and "antic artist-parodist" who provides "hope" (77-9). Consistently over the years, critics have remarked that Sara is poetic.[15] While other characters notice urban sounds, of course, Sara is the most vulnerable and her exposure to urban sounds the most dramatic in the novel. She recollects other figures from Woolf's writing who are depicted as audience of the urban cacophony, but her exposure to noise is not simply an occasion for celebration of freedom and public life, as it is for Eleanor Pargiter or Elizabeth Dalloway. Nor does she experience a delicious passivity in the joy of dispersal, as does Martin. Rather, Sara engages in a continuous set of conflicts when worlds collide through sounds, and the friction produces her "deranged form of speaking."

Frequently described as a family chronicle, a return to realist fiction, and a particularly political novel (bound up with the composition of *Three Guineas*), *The Years* has been categorized in such a way as to minimize the effects first promoted by its initial reviewers, who extolled its virtues as an experimental work, a "long poem," "long-drawn-out lyricism in the form of a novel," and not to be read as one reads *Pride and Prejudice*, but rather as one reads *The Prelude*.[16] Many readings have marginalized *The Years* (Woolf's bestselling novel, in her own time) from Woolf's lyricism or have excluded it from considerations of her experimentation.[17] Yet how realist is this text? *The Years* foregrounds Sara as a poet-orator. It contains many dreamlike descriptions in the interludes that open every chapter ("where the moonlight fell on solid objects it gave them a burnish

---

[15]Fleishman refers to Sara as especially expansive and imaginative, and also as a depressive (183, 185); van Buren Kelly compares the "poetic Sara," whom she also describes as a "visionary outsider," to Bernard of *The Waves* (214-15); Montefiore describes Sara as a "poet manqué" (64); Marder designates her "the poetic Pargiter cousin" (220); Richard Church quotes Sara's "water" speech (her recollection of the bridge) and writes that at moments such as these, "the poet flashes out"; see Majumdar and McLaurin 381.

[16]See Church's review, 379, and David Garnett, "Review" in *New Statesman and Nation* 20 March 1937, in Majumdar and McLaurin 389, 384.

[17]Furthermore, appropriated by some feminist critics as an anti-fascist argument in line with *Three Guineas*, the text's allusion to Antigone has been taken to have less literary than political significance. To amplify the significance of the allusion *qua* literary allu-

and a silver plating, so that even the leaves in country roads seemed polished . . . even the cobbles were frilled as with some celestial laundry" [129]). It employs strategies of surreal juxtaposition (the people huddling inside during the air raid look "cadaverous and unreal in the blue light" while outside an old man with twinkling eyes munches on "a hunk of bread on which was laid a slice of cold meat or sausage" [301]). Throughout, it alludes to Eliot's poetry (the violets [174]; the game of chess [153]; the polluted city; nightingales; the rain in "1880"; hollow men [406]; the "full fathom five" speech from *The Tempest* [186]; the problematic Jew; Woolf's reading of Dante while working on *The Years*). And it is rife with symbolism (the thirteen broken glasses in the "Present Day"; exactly seventeen uses of the word "silence" or "silent" in "1917"; the wine spilt on the dress; the myriad references to mutilation and deformity in a mutilated and deformed world; the use of sound itself). *The Years* is the lyrical half of the project that initially combined novel and essay, art and ideas. Presenting Woolf with agonies in its composition, its references to broken bodies could be taken as a figure for the text itself (an amputation), and Sara's voice as its struggling lyricism. While the argument became *Three Guineas*, *The Years* could be understood in the terms with which Adorno describes lyric's relation to society. Ideally remaining "unaffected by bustle and commotion," opposed to society and the weight of material existence, lyric must inevitably be social as well: "only one who hears the voice of humankind in the poem's solitude can understand what the poem is saying." Lyric speech redeems "the voice of human beings between whom the barriers have fallen" (37-8, 54). In Sara, the novel dramatizes both opposition to social "commotion" and the associations with other worlds made known in lyric speech.[18]

Throughout *The Years*, Sara is an isolated, strange figure constantly warding off noise from her world of private reverie. In "1907" she reads in her bedroom while dance music and a "confused babble of sound" (133) interrupt. Later her mother returns from the party and, while relating her experience as a kind of bedtime story, is interrupted by the girls' father. An idealized moment of storytelling

---

sion, introducing the reader to Sara's literariness, does not, however, lessen its subversive implications. Through Antigone, the text amplifies Sara's gifts, her power to give voice to the "litter" around her. George Steiner's discussion of post-WWI versions of *Antigone* is relevant here. Emphasizing the nakedness of the dead and citing among his examples *The Years*, Steiner writes of the "unimaginable condition" of between a quarter and a third of a million men being left unburied during the battle of Verdun. See Steiner 141.

[18]Sara's gender is significant. Think of *The Years* in proximity to Woolf's essays on the situation of poetry in the 1930s, "The Leaning Tower" and "Letter to a Young Poet," in which she allows, quite simply, no cultural place for female poets; Woolf addresses herself to an entirely male establishment of contemporary voices carrying a certain burden of guilt to speak publicly to the situation of contemporary politics. The only female poets of

in a female sanctuary is rudely interrupted by the sound of footsteps and the father's voice.[19] In "1910," outside noises penetrate Sara's and Maggie's rooms on a shabby street: "[t]he swarm of sound, the rush of traffic, the shouts of the hawkers, the single cries and the general cries, came into the room ... where Sara Pargiter sat at the piano" (163). The swarm of sounds suggests an urban orchestra, juxtaposed with the solo instrument, the piano. When Maggie reminds Sara that their cousin Rose is about to visit for lunch, "Sara stopped. Her face fell." When she hears Rose's footsteps, Sara retreats melodramatically: "'This is the worst torture . . .' Sara began, screwing her hands together and clinging to her sister, 'that life . . .'" (164). When she and Maggie are alone again, Sara watches a pub from the window, and listens to "a sound of brawling . . . a scuffling and trampling . . . . Voices jeered and shouted." As she listens, "her face in the mixed light looked cadaverous and worn, as if she were no longer a girl, but an old woman worn out by a life of childbirth, debauchery and crime. She stood there hunched up, with her hands clenched together . . . ." (189). In "1914," as we have seen, she and Martin are besieged by traffic that prevents their conversation.

Sara's peculiar sensitivity to urban sounds is part of her linguistic creativity. Early on, Woolf lays the groundwork for Sara's emergence as a poetic recluse who composes from fragments. In the "1907" section, when she reads alone in resistance to the street noise outside, her reading material is *Antigone*, translated by her cousin Edward. As many critics have noted, her empathetic response to the text stands in marked contrast to Edward's own when he reads from it earlier.[20] This episode shows Sara as a creator of scenes out of verbal fragments. After having imagined the obviously traditional poetic trope of two nightingales calling to each other in the moonlight, the reverie that the dance music had interrupted, Sara becomes one with Sophocles' play, in a kind of descent with the dead.

> At first she read a line or two at random; then, from the litter of broken words, scenes rose. . . . The unburied body of a murdered man lay like a fallen tree-trunk. . . . She glanced at the tree outside in the garden. The unburied body of the murdered man lay on the sand. Antigone? She came whirling out of the dust-cloud to where the vultures were reeling and flung white sand over the blackened foot. She stood there letting fall white dust over the blackened foot.

Woolf's generation anthologized by Untermeyer are Anna Wickham, Edith Sitwell, and Sylvia Townsend Warner; the only woman included by Skelton is Anne Ridler. None of these women, of course, are included in the exclusively male rubric of the "Auden generation."

[19]This scene suggests itself to a biographical interpretation, recalling as it does the sisterly sanctuary of Virginia and Vanessa in their night nursery. See Moran, *Word of Mouth*, 166 n. 19.

[20]See for example Montefiore, 63; Joseph 28; Comstock 275; Marcus 287.

> Then behold! . . . she was seized; her wrists were bound with withies; and they bore her, thus bound—where? (136).

Especially significant here is the notion of the "litter of broken words" from which Sara composes vivid scenes, the word "litter" suggesting at once debris, decay, and offspring. Sara's acute empathy is triggered by the presence of decayed words, mere fragments. Like the fragmentary sounds that intrude on Sara's private reveries, these are her raw material. Out of broken words, Sara composes two bodies, the dead one itself a kind of debris, the other "bound." The dead and deadened bodies starkly contrast the harmonious nightingales she had initially created. She moves from a lyric wholeness to a discordant shattering and a blurring of boundaries between the text and her actual surroundings, the melding of body-as-tree and the tree outside in the garden. This shattering pronounces the modernist vein of Sara's artistic work, the collage-like shards and repetitions of her later speeches.

Reminding us of the urban sources for much modernist collage, Sara repeatedly composes out of the city's own "litter of broken words." Sara's voice unmistakably resonates not only with literary precursors but with the living sounds surrounding her. Remember that Sara's withdrawal into Sophocles' text is preceded by her frustration with the intrusion of dance music, party chattering, "a confused babble of sound" (133) into her solitude and private reverie. Her reading of *Antigone* focuses on the decaying body and its pollution; we are at the scene of vultures swirling above a carcass, a fantasy that incorporates the babble, or "litter," of social life from outside. We see a similar composition again when Sara returns from a journey with Rose through London, and relates her day to Maggie.[21] Maggie asks Sara to sing, and Sara begins to play the piano, "but her voice was reedy and thin. Her voice broke. . . . 'What's the good of singing if one hasn't any voice?'" (186). Maggie continues to sew, and soon Sara resumes. At this point, she becomes unusually eloquent. Again, we find Sara composing a scene out of contrasting fragments of urban noise and visions of a garden, another enchanted episode of strange transformation that defamiliarizes the city and makes it surreal. Sara's description begins with a trope of poetic reverie: she tells Maggie that she "'Stood on the bridge and looked into the water,'" a phrase she immediately repeats. Humming in time to the music, she continues: "'Running water; flowing water. May my bones turn to coral; and fish light their lanthorns; fish light their green lanthorns in my eyes . . .'" (186). Sara echoes the "Full fathom five" speech from *The Tempest*, and we can connect her words

---

[21]This scene, in both published and especially the unrevised manuscript versions, is treated extensively by Squier in *Virginia Woolf and London*, a discussion to which the present essay owes much, but which differs in its emphasis on Eleanor, not Sara, as the city's protagonist, and in its suggestion of the city as "devouring mother" (155).

with both the *Antigone* episode (descent with the dead), and with the fecund bath that later, in the "Present Day," provides Sara with a sort of raw material for verbally "composing" the city. Evoking both Narcissus and Milton's Eve, Sara's moment on the bridge suggests above all her role as reflector, or echoer; her talent for imitation is mentioned with remarkable frequency (127, 141, 168, 174, 187, 189, 238, 315, 323).[22] As she continues with her description of the day, she uses rich language to express what might otherwise be banal observations; a woman enters a room, for example, "'clothed in starlight'" (187), and Sara describes Rose, crying, as "'withered Rose, spiky Rose, tawny Rose, thorny Rose'" (188). The verbal efflorescence and musicality with which Sara speaks makes things strange, recasting as dreamlike her experience of public spaces, both literal (the streets) and figurative (Rose's political activism).

The most conspicuous episode of Sara's struggle with intrusive sounds comes, of course, in the "Present Day" section, when she is visited by her cousin North. Here we get the full force of sound's significance as the sign of urban heterogeneity corrupting an intimate, private world. After being described twice as having a smudge on her face (324, 327), Sara is drawn into conflict with the "other world" close at hand. She constructs with North a contemplative moment in which he quotes lines from Marvell's "The Garden" ("Society is all but rude— / To this delicious solitude"). During their shared poetic reverie, a sound interferes. It is, Sara says, "'The Jew having a bath . . . . And tomorrow there'll be a line of grease round the bath'" (339). At first, North reacts with disgust, and Sara with indifference. She repeats the Marvell lines (poetry about isolation as a challenge to noise pollution) and informs North that the man is named Abrahamson, is in the tallow trade, and is engaged to a pretty girl in a tailor's shop. He does, she adds, leave hairs in the bath Sara shares with him. North voices his disgust with "a noise like 'Pah!'" At this point Sara begins to speak vehemently, and with peculiar eloquence. She creates a striking urban scene by using a poetic language distinctly reminiscent of *The Waste Land*, the most conspicuous of many instances where *The Years* seems to allude to Eliot.[23] She mixes the language of compressed images and metaphor, an oratorical register, unattributed quotations and mundane facts. The passage is worth quoting at length:

[22]Greenberg's discussion of Echo as representing "the possibility of turning fragmented and incomplete voice into signification" ("Echo of Trauma" 321) is relevant here; my emphasis is less upon the structures of listening and speaking than upon the significance of Sara's responsive speech in a heterogeneous urban context and a climate of anxiety about art's social role.
[23]In addition to the many possible references in *The Years* to *The Waste Land* and "The Hollow Men," this passage is taken by Ruotolo to allude in particular to "Gerontion."

'And then,' she said, sipping her coffee, 'I came back into the sitting-room. And breakfast was waiting. Fried eggs and a bit of toast. Lydia with her blouse torn and her hair down. The unemployed singing hymns under the window. And I said to myself—' She flung her hand out, '"Polluted city, unbelieving city, city of dead fish and worn-out frying-pans"—thinking of a river's bank, when the tide's out. . . . So I put on my hat and coat and rushed out in a rage . . . and stood on the bridge, and said, "Am I a weed, carried this way, that way, on a tide that comes twice a day without meaning?" . . . And there were people passing; the strutting, the tiptoeing; the pasty; the ferret-eyed; the bowler-hatted, servile innumerable army of workers. And I said, "Must I join your conspiracy? Stain the hand, the unstained hand,"'—he could see her hand gleam as she waved it in the half-light of the sitting-room, '"—and sign on, and serve a master; all because of a Jew in my bath, all because of a Jew?"'

She sat up and laughed, excited by the sound of her own voice which had run into a jog-trot rhythm. (341)

Sara goes on to relate, almost as a fairy tale in which she is the protagonist, her trip to a newspaper office in search of a job, carrying with her a letter of introduction ('"I had a talisman, a glowing gem, a lucent emerald . . . a letter of introduction"'[p. 341]). As she trails off into silence, North interprets her narration as meaning "that she was poor; that she must earn her living, but the excitement with which she had spoken, due to wine perhaps, had created yet another person; another semblance, which one must solidify into one whole" (342). North's observation recalls Woolf's description of poets at the end of *Three Guineas* who "overflow boundaries and make unity out of multiplicity" (143); Sara seems to be *in* this process, at a point where "multiplicity" is foremost. If the role of sounds is to dissolve the self into the urban soundscape, Sara's delirious aspect is entirely in keeping with the pattern of urban sound's power in Woolf's work. In an ecstasy of poetic derangement, Sara's strange speech is a key moment of transformation in which a conventional poetic solitude is interrupted and subverted by an invasive sound. The result is a new kind of poetic speech—Marvell replaced by Eliot.[24]

In this passage, Sara gives expression to the city's jumble of sound fragments. Out of the urban pollution (which we have heard repeatedly as the intrusion of street noise into Sara's states of private reverie) arises Sara's ambivalent articulation of both resistance and participation, her feeling of being a weed tossed in currents of meaninglessness, her reluctance to "join your conspiracy," and her rejection (while her own hand gleams) of the "stained" hand which signs on to serve a master. She is, however, on her way to join the workers. Sara's rec-

---

[24]My emphasis on Eliot should not be taken as an insistence that Eliot's influence on Woolf is monolithic. Indeed, a fruitful line of thinking would replace *The Waste Land* with Mirrlees' "Paris" as a modernist ur-text for acoustic *flânerie*.

ollection contains its own episode of noise and response; the unemployed sing outside, and Sara responds with an Eliot-esque speech from inside. We listen to a dialogue, a collaboration of sorts between inside and outside, public and private, the anonymous worker and the economically "fallen," physically deformed daughter of a distinguished bourgeois family. Sara's verbal composition of this scenario of urban turbulence and of overcrowding is fraught with the urban social tensions between haves and have-nots, natives and foreigners. She stands apart from the "servile innumerable army of workers" by virtue of a magic talisman, the letter of introduction that betokens a family connection gaining her entrée into the world of writing, permitting her to rise above others into an enchanted world where dirt is transformed into print. She describes the press: "The great machines went round; and little boys popped in with elongated sheets; black sheets; smudged; damp with printer's ink" (342). What began with Sara's smudged face and with grease and hair in a bath has become a world of smudges and wetness, no less than the daily world of words on pages. She has listened to various urban sounds, and now finds her voice as she composes an urban prose poem out of fragments.

What prompts her creativity is the residue (like the hairs in the bath) of urban noise, the sounds out of which she composes a verbal collage. She translates the ugly "Pah!" into a strange fairy-tale, mixing *The Waste Land*'s alienated despair over urban pollution and poverty with a transformative vision of ink on pages, a mystified world to which one gains entry by means of a "lucent emerald." Sara has a gift: an enigmatic, excited voice in which heterogeneous urban sound fragments are amplified without being synthesized. Failing to achieve solitude and silence, Sara becomes instead "another semblance," un-whole, through contact with sound's suggestion of other worlds. Significantly, Sara's very last appearance in the novel, after she dances with Nicholas at the party, is as nothing *but* an interrupting "voice." There, while Nicholas gives a speech, during his pause "a head popped up over the edge of the table; a hand swept up a fistful of flower petals and a voice cried: 'Red Rose, thorny Rose, brave Rose, tawny Rose!'" (419). The insistently trochaic and dactylic voice is never identified, but it is plausibly Sara's, given the fact that she has uttered nearly identical adjectival variations on the theme of Rose several times before in the novel (164, 188, 231). In her ultimate speech, Sara performs much like the poet Woolf describes as filling in the gaps left by prose: "can prose say the simple things which are so tremendous? Give the sudden emotions which are so surprising? Can it chant the elegy, or hymn the love, or shriek in terror, or praise the rose, the nightingale, or the beauty of the night? Can it spring at the heart of its subject as the poet does? I think not" ("The Narrow Bridge," 20). In her praise of Rose and her startling speeches on the city, Sara provides Woolf's novel with the poet's capacity to surprise.

The History of Sound: From Victorian Lullaby to Modern Noise

Julia Briggs describes the narrative of *The Years* (which is, of course, chronologically ordered) as linear and progressive: the novel "records the gradual release of its closely constrained young women into freedom and even self-determination"; it "documents the Pargiters' progression from the oppressive atmosphere of life at Abercorn Terrace to a much more open existence"; it "echoes and enlarges upon the movement first outlined in *To the Lighthouse*, from the warmth and oppression of the Edwardian family . . . to the much more open relationships of post-war society" (80-81). If it is an emancipation narrative, however, *The Years* is a deeply problematic one, for we may, on some accounts, come full circle, back to the "tyranny of the patriarchal Victorian family" which has an "umbilical connection [to] the fascist oppression of the late 1930s"; according to David Bradshaw, it is not openness and enlargement, but "pessimism and anxiety" which hold sway in Woolf's penultimate novel ("Socio-Political Vision," 204-5). Do sounds change over the course of the years, or do they come around in a circle? Do they support those readings of Woolfian *flânerie* which champion the dissolution of self in the metropolitan shock experience as emancipatory? Or do they underscore the incomplete project of emancipation, a project under fire in the 1930s whose difficulty causes the "anxiety" Bradshaw observes? Is Sara's art of sound redemptive and consoling, or strangely terrifying?

Some things remain the same from 1880 to the "present day." In the 1880 scene, exterior sounds that penetrate the thick walls of the curtained Victorian edifice include "musicians [who] doled out their frail and for the most part melancholy pipe of sound," a "barrel-organ," children in the street, an elderly street singer, a beggar singing, and pigeons shuffling (3-84); the music and birds singing constitute a "lullaby that was always interrupted" (3). In the "Present Day" section, some fifty years later, we hear almost identical sounds. An old man cries "'Old chairs and baskets to mend,'" a woman sings scales, children scream in the street, a trombone wails "lugubriously" with a doleful sound, and a barrel-organ plays (307-317). The similarities are striking, suggestive of a circular, rather than linear, movement. Class divisions and urban poverty remain. The "lullaby" persists, with all its implications of passive, sleeping, perhaps deluded citizens, a particularly chilling idea in the 1930s. If the "present day" has a lulled populace, Peggy's feeling of desolation is warranted, and she is right to dwell upon the image of "faces mobbed at the door of a picture palace; apathetic, passive faces; the faces of people drugged with cheap pleasures" (388).

The noise of London is not just repetition, however. There are distinctly new sounds, of course: the sounds of cars hooting, for example, mentioned repeatedly (308, 310, 311). Intruding upon North's consciousness, as he undergoes the culture shock of returning to London from years spent farming in Africa, "[t]he noise of London still seemed to him deafening . . . Everywhere there was profusion, plenty" (308). North's feeling of being jangled by new technologies is joined by Eleanor's: she complains to Peggy about the nuisance of hearing the wireless (333). The telephone is also an audible presence in this section (ringing at Sara's), as is the gramophone to which the party-goers dance and which, in the end, plays "God save the King" (433). As realist details, the sounds of new technologies are certainly a key component of Woolf's rendering of the contemporary context: her society's progress is audible.

One response to the "profusion, plenty" is Eleanor's sense of optimism and expectation about the present. Eleanor embraces the here and now in terms that recall Martin's feeling of exhilarating dispersal and primal innocence in "1914." Eleanor feels "that they were all young, with the future before them. Nothing was fixed; nothing was known; life was open and free before them" (382). Suffused with an expectant hope that the present moment might shine "whole, bright, deep with understanding" (427), Eleanor's desire for a meaningful order (and her optimism that it lies close at hand) is couched in a musical metaphor: "Does everything then come over again a little differently? she thought. If so, is there a pattern; a theme, recurring, like music; half remembered, half foreseen? . . . The thought gave her extreme pleasure" (369). Her "pleasure" in repetition contrasts Peggy's and North's frustration with progress, and her faith in musical recurrence opposes their apprehensive sense of living in a broken world without meaning.

Eleanor's musical pattern would explain the fractured voices of the partygoers themselves: they repeat the "1917" discussion of a new society. But the predominant sense in the "Present Day" is of disorder. The noise of the present day is a jumble of exterior sounds (suggesting other worlds) mingling with the broken, sometimes incomprehensible speech of the family members who have gathered. In the context of instability foreshadowed by the opening description of "red brick villas on the high roads [that] had become porous, incandescent with light" (306), the "Present Day" displays a precarious world where nearly everything, including speech, seems to be broken or breaking apart. In addition to the thirteen broken glasses (426), partygoers stumble and fall (415). Eleanor spills coins, prompting Peggy to think "Directly something got together, it broke. She had a feeling of desolation. And then you have to pick up the pieces, and make something new, something different" (393). Eleanor, longing for understanding and pattern, thinks that this life is "too short, too broken" (428), and North, too, thinks of everything as fallen and broken (375). In this setting, the world Peggy thinks of as "fractured," speech disintegrates, nearly to complete incoherence. The voices at the party are repeatedly described as a "babble" (345, 350, 424); Peggy notices Delia "talking at random" and thinks of the guests as talking "such nonsense . . . such complete nonsense" (351), later hearing "scraps" of conversation (389) and a "roar" of voices (397). North thinks of Eleanor's questions as "damp falling patter" (374). There is a "buzz of talk . . . like the buzz of flies over sugar" (415). Peggy, North, and Nicholas try, and fail, to make toasts. And, of course, there is the song of the caretaker's children, "so shrill, so discordant, so meaningless" (430). The "Present Day" leaves the impression of a world where speech has broken down beyond meaning. Fragmentation, here, is not the liberating dissolution of self celebrated in certain versions of *flânerie*, but a disturbing breakdown of communication and coherence in a surreal cacophony, a sound collage juxtaposing machine noises, the singing, crying, and screams that waft in from outside, incomplete speeches, mere "buzz," "patter," and "babble," and an enigmatic song heard as "hideous noise" and as "extraordinarily beautiful." Does this surreal soundscape even reach its listeners or matter? At least two of the partygoers, we learn, are deaf (352, 358).

In the midst of this chaos there are two competing routes towards order. One is a nostalgic and purist retreat to silence and solitude associated with poetic tradition. The other is true to Peggy's sense that in the midst of that which is broken, "you have to pick up the pieces, and make something new, something different." The first is represented by North, Edward, and the "nerve-drawn" young male poet to whom Peggy speaks; its sounds are nightingales singing, quotations of Marvell and Sophocles, and "I, I, I." The second's representatives are Sara Pargiter and the singing children; their sounds are the strangest in the text, and can be explained as the picked-up pieces that make something new, something different. These new and different voices are so strange they run the risk of coming across as mere sound fragments rather than as meaningful speech. Keeping listeners on edge, they push readers towards an abyss beyond linguistic ambiguity and into the territory of sheer incoherence. Yet as poetic diction and as song, Sara's and the children's utterances are also among the text's examples of art, however strange. This is speech that threatens to dissolve into mere sound; as such, it has the power to defamiliarize, and thus to fulfill Woolf's idea of poetry, its capacity to surprise, where tradition is rendered weak.

Three male characters come to the fore as representatives of a poetic tradition challenged and corrupted by new, dissonant voices. In a corrupt modern world whose incessant talk about money and politics North deeply resents, poetry seems to hold out the promise of redemption. Despairing over the current conditions where ideology runs rampant, loudly proclaimed through "reverberating megaphones" (410), North regards Edward, the cold classics scholar who quotes the *Antigone* in untranslated Greek, as "a priest, a mystery monger . . . the guardian of beautiful words" who hides "the past and poetry" behind his mask, keeping clear of "this muddle" (408). North has all but lost his own past of correspondence with Sara, in which he wrote to her of "nightingales, singing in the moonlight" (319) in "purple passages" (322). The two had tried to revive their erstwhile poetic pastime by quoting Marvell's poem "The Garden," but it was a failed attempt to create an aestheticist garden in the crowded, noisy urban milieu. Similarly, Peggy is exhausted by a professional life she feels enslaves her to money interests, but when she confronts a young male poet at the party, he offers her nothing but a "pale, pasty" aspect, a "nerve-drawn egotist's face," incessant talk of "I, I, I," and the demeanor of someone who "could not free himself, could not detach himself" (360-1). In Edward's coldness, North's longing, and the pasty poet's egotism, Woolf presents a portrait of a male poetic establishment, those who inhabit the "leaning tower" with a highly problematic mixture of elitism, nostalgia, and self-regard.

One can think of the trajectory of *The Years* as linear, its sounds evolving from the Victorian lullaby to the modern sounds of cars hooting. Or one can imagine it as a dynamic motion and as porosity, disruptive urban sound fragments pulling outward from the bourgeois interior space of family intimacy towards the streets where strangers cry and sirens wail (Martin's experience of "dispersal").[25] The peculiar sound finale signals both the strange, unfamiliar newness of the present, and the collapse of the border between inside, and out. The caretaker's children, who look "fierce" (428), possess "harsh" voices (430), sing "fiercely" (430), and "attack" their verses (429), arrive at the party, and Peggy refers to them as the "younger generation" (429). Asked to "sing a song for sixpence," they burst into a song none of whose words is "recognizable"; their "unintelligible words ran themselves together almost into a shriek" (430). Their sounds are like the persistent chorus of sounds that have disturbed from the edges of the Pargiters' world throughout the fifty years of the story's span; here, though, the sounds come from inside, like a "heart of darkness" not far away, but right here, heretofore disavowed. Their song may be an eruption of nonsense in the middle of a social gathering where the guests have attempted and failed

---

[25] As Hankins points out, Woolf has sometimes been pigeonholed by the attraction of "a room of one's own." She notes however that Woolf regarded domestic space, even a space of private seclusion, as a trap, and her sequel to *A Room of One's Own* was alternatively titled "Opening the Door" or "A Knock at the Door." See Hankins 12.

repeatedly to make speeches about a new and better society, and so undermine the optimism Eleanor feels with the anarchic force of completely meaningless syllables; the younger generation's song may amount, in that case, to "hideous noise" (430). Yet Eleanor and Maggie put words together to describe what they hear as "'Beautiful?'" . . . "'Extraordinarily'" (431). Woolf's choice of words to describe the children's song as not only "horrible . . . noise" but also simply unrecognizable and unintelligible suggests, too, that their sounds are a language, but one unknown to its listeners. Readers have interpreted their strange, unrecognizable syllables as either Cockney or Italian; either interpretation implies that Woolf means to convey not a complete lack of meaning or intelligibility in the children's song, but a difficulty of foreignness, either of class or culture. Bradshaw takes the Italian-sounding syllables to be "a scrambled allusion to Dante's inclusive vision of mankind" ("Socio-Political Vision" 206); if so, they are redemptive, and the younger generation a harbinger of the utopian vision Eleanor fosters. Whether their song is in an unintelligible Cockney accent, a foreign language, or simply the as-yet incomprehensible language of the younger generation, its ambiguity, being noise, song, language, hideousness, and beauty all at once, possesses a powerful capacity to unsettle the reader: this is the point.

With the children's song and Sara's strange voice, Woolf presents the reader with new arts of sound that disrupt both the poetic tradition represented by a male trio and the futile attempts to achieve solitude and silent inwardness throughout. The guests pay for the children's song; they invite the art of noise into their midst in the form of a commodity, and thus, in one ingenious move, Woolf slyly reminds us that worlds continuously interact in economic transactions as well as resented economic disparities; all those hawkers' and beggars' voices, as well as the unemployed singing outside Sara's window, might be heard in the song of the caretakers' children. So too does Sara's final poetic speech incorporate the frictions between private and public. When she flings petals and proclaims "'Red Rose, thorny Rose, brave Rose, tawny Rose!'" she pays final tribute to Rose, the feminist whose rebellion extended beyond the family to political action, reminding us of the violence Rose both propagates and suffers (her brick-throwing, her experience of sexual danger in "1880," and her imprisonment and forced feeding). Sara's voice lends a vital significance to the function of roses in the novel's closing. Contrasting the cacophonous hooting horns, broken glasses, babbling voices, and faltering speeches is a potentially unifying visual image: Maggie's arrangement of roses. As though to counter noise pollution and disintegrating boundaries with the gentle art of interior decoration, the flowers beckon as a final symbol of coherence and wholeness. But connected with *Sara*'s "Roses," the arrangement dissolves into a reminder of the contemporary world's *de*rangement, its flux and tensions. While North, Edward, and the enervated male poet represent an exhausted tradition of inwardness, silence and solitude, Sara's pithy, sing-song reminder of social and political upheaval, together with the younger generation's "fierce" verses, defy convention with a mix of praise and aggression. The "hideous noise" together with Sara's peculiar speech do not exactly lift the reader out of a feeling of anxiety at the end. However, rather than pure meaninglessness, theirs and the text's sounds figure the as-yet unsynthesized energies and potential of broken, interacting worlds whose progress is uncertain.

Works Cited

Abel, Elizabeth. *Virginia Woolf and the Fictions of Psychoanalysis*. Chicago: U of Chicago P, 1989.

Adorno, Theodor W. "On Lyric Poetry and Society." *Notes to Literature*, vol. 1. Trans. Shierry Weber Nicholsen. New York: Columbia UP, 1991. 37-54.

Auerbach, Erich. *Mimesis: The Representation of Reality in Western Literature*. Trans. Willard R. Trask. New York: Doubleday, 1953.

Baudelaire, Charles. *The Painter of Modern Life and Other Essays*. Trans. Jonathan Mayne. London: Phaidon: 1964.

Beer, Gillian. "Physics, Sound, and Substance: Later Woolf." *Virginia Woolf: The Common Ground: Essays by Gillian Beer*. Ann Arbor: U of Michigan P, 1996. 112-124.

Benjamin, Walter. "On Some Motifs in Baudelaire." *Illuminations: Essays and Reflections*. Ed. Hannah Arendt. New York: Schocken, 1955. 155-200.

Blair, Sara. "Modernism and the Politics of Culture." *The Cambridge Companion to Modernism*. Ed. Michael Levenson. Cambridge: Cambridge UP, 1999.

———. "Real Space, Real Time: Virginia Woolf and the Geography of Bloomsbury." *Tenth Annual Conference on Virginia Woolf*, Baltimore, Maryland June 8-10, 2000.

Bowlby, Rachel. *Just Looking: Consumer Culture in Dreiser, Gissing, and Zola*. New York: Methuen, 1985.

———. "Walking, Women, and Writing: Virginia Woolf as *Flâneuse*." *Still Crazy After All These Years: Women, Writing, and Psychoanalysis*. London: Routledge, 1992. 1-33.

Bradshaw, David. "Hyams Place: *The Years*, the Jews and the British Union of Fascists." *Women Writers of the 1930s: Gender, Politics, and History*. Ed. Maroula Joannou. Edinburgh: Edinburgh U P, 1999. 179-191.

———. "The Socio-Political Vision of the Novels." *The Cambridge Companion to Virginia Woolf*. Ed. Sue Roe and Susan Sellers. Cambridge: Cambridge UP, 2000. 191-208.

Briggs, Julia. "The Novels of the 1930s and the Impact of History." *The Cambridge Companion to Virginia Woolf*. Ed. Sue Roe and Susan Sellers. Cambridge: Cambridge UP, 2000. 72-90.

Brown, Bill. "The Secret Life of Things (Virginia Woolf and the Matter of Modernism)." *Modernism/Modernity* 6.2: 1-28.

Carson, Anne. *Eros the Bittersweet*. Normal, Illinois: Dalkey Archive P, 1998.

Caserio, Robert L. *The Novel in England, 1900-1950: History and Theory*. New York: Twayne, 1999.

Church, Richard. "Review." *John O'London's Weekly* 19 March 1937. Robin Majumdar and Allen McLaurin, eds. *Virginia Woolf: The Critical Heritage*. London: Routledge, 1975.

Comstock, Margaret. "Politics and the Form of *The Years*." *Bulletin of the New York Public Library* 80.2: 252-275.

Cuddy-Keane, Melba. "Virginia Woolf, Sound Technologies, and the New Aurality." *Virginia Woolf in the Age of Mechanical Reproduction*. Ed. Pamela L. Caughie. New York: Garland, 2000. 69-96.

De Gay, Jane. "'The Bray of the Gramophones and the Voices of the Poets': Art and Political Crises in *Between the Acts*." *Critical Survey* 10.3: 39-47.

Felski, Rita. *The Gender of Modernity*. Cambridge: Harvard UP, 1995.

Fleishman, Avrom. *Virginia Woolf: A Critical Reading*. Baltimore: Johns Hopkins UP, 1975.

Friedman, Susan Stanford. "Definitional Excursions: The Meanings of Modern/Modernity/Modernism." *Modernism/Modernity* 8.3: 493-513.

Garnett, David. "Review." *New Statesman and Nation*. 20 March 1937. Majumdar and McLaurin, eds. *Virginia Woolf: The Critical Heritage*. London: Routledge, 1975.

Garrity, Jane. "Selling Culture to the 'Civilized': Bloomsbury, British *Vogue*, and the Marketing of National Identity." *Modernism/Modernity* 6.2: 29-58.

——. "Virginia Woolf, Intellectual Harlotry, and 1920s British *Vogue*." *Virginia Woolf in the Age of Mechanical Reproduction*. Ed. Pamela L. Caughie. New York: Garland, 2000. 185-218.

Greenberg, Judith. "The Echo of Trauma and the Trauma of Echo." *American Imago* 55.3: 319-347.

——. "'When Ears are Deaf and the Heart is Dry': Traumatic Reverberations in *Between the Acts*." *Woolf Studies Annual* 7: 49-74.

Hankins, Leslie Kathleen. "Virginia Woolf and Walter Benjamin Selling Out(Siders)." *Virginia Woolf in the Age of Mechanical Reproduction*. Ed. Pamela L. Caughie. New York, Garland: 2000. 3-35.

Joseph, Gerhard. "The *Antigone* as Cultural Touchstone: Matthew Arnold, Hegel, George Eliot, Virginia Woolf, and Margaret Drabble." *PMLA* 96.1 (1981): 22-35.

Kahane, Claire. *Passions of the Voice: Hysteria, Narrative, and the Figure of the Speaking Woman, 1850-1915*. Baltimore: Johns Hopkins UP, 1995.

Klein, Melanie. "Infantile Anxiety Situations Reflected in a Work of Art and in the Creative Impulse." Ed. Juliet Mitchell. *The Selected Melanie Klein*. New York: Free Press, 1986.

Laurence, Patricia Ondek. *The Reading of Silence: Virginia Woolf in the English Tradition*. Stanford: Stanford UP, 1991.

Marcus, Jane. "*The Years* as Greek Drama, Domestic Novel, and Gotterdammerung." *Bulletin of the New York Public Library*. 80.2: 276-301.

Marder, Herbert. *The Measure of Life: Virginia Woolf's Last Years*. Ithaca: Cornell UP, 2000.

Meisel, Perry. *The Absent Father: Virginia Woolf and Walter Pater*. New Haven: Yale UP, 1980.

Minow-Pinkney, Makiko. "Virginia Woolf and the Age of Motor Cars." *Virginia Woolf in the Age of Mechanical Reproduction*. Ed. Pamela L. Caughie. New York: Garland, 2000. 159-182.

Mirrlees, Hope. "Paris." *Virginia Woolf Quarterly* 1.2: 4-17.

Montefiore, Janet. *Men and Women Writers of the 1930s: The Dangerous Flood of History*. London: Routledge, 1996.

Moran, Patricia. *Word of Mouth: Body Language in Katherine Mansfield and Virginia Woolf*. Charlottesville: U P of Virginia, 1996.

Naremore, James. *The World Without a Self: Virginia Woolf and the Novel*. New Haven: Yale UP, 1973.

Nelson-McDermott, Catherine. "Disorderly Conduct: Parody and Coded Humor in *Jacob's Room* and *The Years*." *Woolf Studies Annual* 5: 79-95.

Nord, Deborah. *Walking the Victorian Streets: Women, Representation and the City*. Ithaca: Cornell UP, 1995.

Parsons, Deborah L. *Streetwalking the Metropolis: Women, the City and Modernity*. Oxford: Oxford UP, 2000.

Pridmore-Brown, Michelle. "1939-1940: Of Virginia Woolf, Gramophones, and Fascism." *PMLA* 113.3 1998: 408-421.

Radin, Grace. *Virginia Woolf's* The Years*: The Evolution of a Novel*. Knoxville: U of Tennessee P, 1981.

Richardson, Dorothy. "A Tear for Lycidas." *Close Up 1927-1933: Cinema and Modernism*. Ed. James Donald, Annie Friedberg, and Laura Marcus. Princeton: Princeton UP, 1998

Ruotolo, Lucio. *The Interrupted Moment: A View of Virginia Woolf's Novels*. Stanford: Stanford UP, 1986.

Scott, Bonnie Kime. "The Subversive Mechanics of Woolf's Gramophone in *Between the Acts*." *Virginia Woolf in the Age of Mechanical Reproduction*. Ed. Pamela L. Caughie. New York: Garland: 2000. 97-113.

Skelton, Robin, ed. *Poetry of the Thirties*. London: Penguin, 1964.

Squier, Susan Merrill. *Virginia Woolf and London: The Sexual Politics of the City*. Chapel Hill: U of North Carolina P, 1985.

Steiner, George. *Antigones*. New Haven: Yale UP, 1984.

Stewart, Garrett. *Reading Voices: Literature and the Phonotext.* Berkeley: U of California P, 1990.
Stonebridge, Lyndsey. *The Destructive Element: British Psychoanalysis and Modernism.* New York: Routledge, 1998.
Untermeyer, Louis, ed. *Modern British Poetry.* New York: Harcourt, Brace, 1958.
Van Buren Kelly, Alice. *The Novels of Virginia Woolf: Fact and Vision.* Chicago: U of Chicago P, 1971.
Walkowitz, Judith. *City of Dreadful Delight: Narratives of Sexual Danger in Late-Victorian London.* Chicago: U of Chicago P, 1992.
Wicke, Jennifer. "Coterie Consumption: Bloomsbury, Keynes, and Modernism as Marketing." *Marketing Modernisms.* Ed. Kevin J. H. Dettmar and Stephen Watt. Ann Arbor: U of Michigan P, 1996. 109-132.
Wolff, Janet. "The Invisible *Flâneuse*: Women and the Literature of Modernity." *Feminine Sentences: Essays on Women and Culture.* Berkeley: U of California P, 1990. 34-50.
Woolf, Virginia. *The Diary of Virginia Woolf.* Ed. Anne Olivier Bell and Andrew McNeillie. 5 vols. New York: Harcourt, 1982.
——. "The Leaning Tower." *Collected Essays.* Vol. II. New York: Harcourt, 1966. 162-181.
——. "Letter to a Young Poet." *The Death of the Moth and Other Essays.* New York: Harcourt, 1970. 208-226.
——. *Mrs. Dalloway.* New York: Harcourt, 1981.
——. "The Narrow Bridge of Art." *Granite and Rainbow.* New York: Harcourt, 1958. 11-23.
——. "Oxford Street Tide." *The London Scene.* New York: Random House, 1975. 16-22.
——. "Street Haunting." *The Death of the Moth and Other Essays.* New York: Harcourt, 1970. 20-36.
——. *Three Guineas.* New York: Harcourt, 1966.
——. *The Years.* New York: Harcourt, 1965.

Willing Epigone: Virginia Woolf's *Between the Acts* as Nietzschean Historiography

Stuart Christie

> *There is a degree of sleeplessness, of rumination, of the historical sense, which is harmful and ultimately fatal to the living thing*
> —Nietzsche ("Uses," 59)

I. Nietzschean Laughter

Woolf's radical distinction in *Between the Acts* (1941), between the fullness of a transhistorical present and the burden of the national past, owes much to Nietzsche.[1] La Trobe and her many performers refigure patriarchal time through subversive acts of skipping cue and the forgetting of lines (*BTA* 77). This selective forgetting of the past, including the national history that makes such a past monumental, links Woolf's text to the dictum the "oversaturation of an age with [its] history . . . the belief that one is a late-comer and epigone" to the historical process, paralyzes (and at last destroys) the power of life in the present (Nietzsche, "Uses" 83).

La Trobe's pageant play performs the fight against such an "oversaturated" national history by redeploying Nietzsche's concept of the emasculated epigone as a figure of female power and an effective instrument of historiographical critique. For Nietzsche, the figure of the epigone cannot

> draw about [itself] an image to which the future shall correspond, and forget the superstition that you are epigones. You will have enough to ponder and to invent when you reflect on the life of the future; but do not ask of history that it should show you the How? and the Wherewith? to this life. (94)

Yet La Trobe's persistent re-appearing acts embody the epigone, precisely because the locus of historical subjectivity she inhabits is *belated* relative to the scenes of national history she encounters and subsequently redirects, signs whose present mutations rupture the historical field of the past. As a late-comer

---

[1] Direct mention of Nietzsche in Woolf's correspondence and diaries is scarce, yet numerous scholars have noted Woolf's preoccupation with modernist historiography as the rejection of past uses and abuses of history under patriarchal custodianship. See Cramer, 166-68; Cuddy-Keane, 275; Laurence, 216-17; McWhirter, 799; L. Marcus, 79-80; Wiley, 4-5; Wirth-Nesher, 186-88.

to history, the epigone inhabits gaps and fissures within national consciousness. Her belatedness upon the scene of the historical field empowers the *retournement* of Nietzschean philosophy in Woolf's interest. An artful politics of remembering national past and national future differently, the epigone is mindful of the ideological work gender can perform in the interests of nationalism on behalf of what Yuval-Davis calls "nationed gender" in a time of war (21).

Specifically, I argue that the epigone's disavowal of "nationed gender" constitutes Woolf's modernist rearticulation of Nietzsche's rhetorical question: "Supposing truth is a woman—what then?" (Nietzsche, "Preface" 1) The notion of historical truth as woman—as both chide and challenge, Nietzsche's off-hand remark links a particular gender category ("woman") to a specific philosophical debate he had with the Hegelians—was axiomatic. As a historical woman, the epigone inhabits an embodied form (such as La Trobe or Isa) even as she defers the historical "truth" *of* woman signified by Nietzsche's laughter: recalcitrance towards the historical principle marks the epigone's signature in the belated text her subjectivity performs (including holding to question the binaristic logic behind the historical subject Nietzsche at once endorses and queries, with "truth" as woman and history as man).

Contra Nietzsche, Woolf's epigone attempts to sever the phenomenology of history from its masculinist narratology, the latter a patriarchal burden Woolf rejected in terms rather more idealist than nihilistic.[2] Yet also to some extent sharing Nietzsche's suspicions about the burdens of the past, Woolf's epigone moves well beyond the critique of patriarchy to reject the monumentalization of history ("events") in favor of the multiplicities of everyday use ("happenings"). Accordingly, *Between the Acts* ably uses and abuses Nietzschean historiography as well as radically levels any topographical valuation of historical greatness (such as nineteenth-century nationalism) in favor of subtlety [*feinheit*]: "Rather go away. Flee into concealment. And have your masks and subtlety that you may be mistaken for what you are not, or feared a little" (Nietzsche, *Beyond Good and Evil* 36). The *feinheit* La Trobe displays in *Between the Acts*, her performed duplicities within the conventional historical field, establishes Woolf's own bold response to the "what then?" prod of Nietzsche, the writer's challenge to express an unessential history via the instrument of an unessentialized woman.

---

[2]The Helen Zimmern translation of *Jenseits von Gut und Böse* in 1907 (translated as *Beyond Good and Evil*) sought to recuperate the philosopher's legacy after its repudiation in England on grounds of purported anti-Semitism, and was followed by subsequent readings of continental philosophy, notably by G. E. Moore and Bertrand Russell, which sought to soften Nietzschean iconoclasm in the interest of broader theorizations of aesthetics, including post-Impressionism and Imagism. See Bradbury, 176; Kaufmann, xiii-xiv.

Woolf's modernist historiography likewise contests the monumentality of the philosopher's legacy in terms he himself devised: both the "what" *and* the "then" of historical truth as woman, Woolf's epigone parades an alternative history before a patriarchal historiography, rendering the latter's operations bare and obsolete before she herself vanishes or, just as suddenly, reappears.

Embodying *feinheit*, La Trobe and her pageant play offer a politics of the performative for history's actors and readers alike, all epigones situated "between" historical events constituted by present context as well as the imposition of imagined readings. The very intractability of the epigone toward historical "truth" reclaims the sovereignty history imposes post priori upon all its subjects. As both body and figure of representation, the epigone wages a battle against history itself, and offers in its stead the less stable (yet just as conceivably pleasurable) contradictory field of historical representation. Thus the epigone's historiographical critique, her own appropriation of Nietzsche's historical truth as woman, is intimately linked to the sovereignty of the subject in a represented rather than present world: "an 'act' is not a momentary happening, but a certain nexus of temporal horizons, the condensation of iterability that exceeds the moment it occasions" (Butler, *Excitable Speech* 14). Judith Butler's radical turn towards an iterative (rather than historical) basis of gender experience, her "certain nexus" of horizons that exceeds history's monumentality of the moment, is salutary to Nietzsche's own marked emphasis upon truth as all too often the servant of history which "knows only how to *preserve* life, not how to engender it" ("Uses" 75).

Accordingly, Woolf's epigone engenders life not only through the rejection of what history preserves as inherently patriarchal, but by embracing the excitable sovereignty (the engendering of historical truth) Nietzsche acknowledges and subsequently dismisses as a simile of irrelevance: "as" woman. Both the embodiment of an experienced history and the excitable articulation of an excessive praxis beyond momentary experience, Woolf's epigone enjoins the dialogue between the temporality and body of individual being [*sein*] and the experience of the quality of being that exceeds the individual experience of time (what we typically call "history"). Strictly speaking, the epigone cannot therefore claim exceptionalism for the historical female (body) as such; rather, she claims sovereignty for its *representation* within a given historiographic field. In *Between the Acts*, this field is constituted through the symbolically rich and conceptual interdependence of nation and gender to which the epigone remains, in Chantal Mouffe's remarkable phrase, "effectively nonpertinent" (376). As a politics of the performance of history, the epigone's nonpertinence entails a very relevant purpose:

> [the] project of radical and plural democracy need[ing] . . . not a sexually differentiated model of citizenship in which the specific tasks of both men and women would be valued equally, but a truly different conception of what it is to be a citizen and to act as a member of a democratic political community. (377)

Mouffe's challenge to reconceive democracy beyond sexual difference compels reconsideration of Nietzsche's apparent dismissal of the relevance of "woman" to historiography: a dismissal, we should note, that nevertheless creates new potential for a "truly different conception" of the relationship of gender to historical truth. The epigone's effective nonpertinence toward the timeliness and being of the historical woman—for example, in England at the outbreak of World War Two—seemingly gives ground to a precarious universalism, even as it invites scrutiny of what such a concession might achieve: the sovereign citizenship of an historical subject beyond that of "nationed gender."

Thus far my reading of Woolf's epigone is indebted to bivalent readings of Nietzschean laughter, whereby historical truth is represented both "as" woman and an irreverent "so what" as the *response* of woman. In response to the interpretive tension such a Nietzschean reading offers, I have presented the epigone as a figure in the text that remains disrespectful of Nietzsche's authority but shares his iconoclastic bent toward the monumentalization of history operating at the expense of life. Significantly, both Nietzschean philosophy and Woolf's epigone hold themselves at a remove from nation and nationalism in order to refashion their respective performances of historical truth both "as" and beyond "woman."

Yet the degree to which the performance of gender necessarily entails a concurrent reconsideration of the performance of national identity only further complicates the question of the relation between these two terms. The epigone's impertinence toward the performance of nation might recast her performance of woman likewise, both occasioning occultist disturbances along the conceptual horizon of normativity: not merely that trouble for one is bound to spell trouble for the other, but that both categories are inherently troubled and, just as markedly, rely upon each other in their trouble. But need such a description of the intimacy between the performances of gender and nation (or even their conceivable incestuousness) be exhaustive or even inherently prescriptive? Deploying an artful fusillade of rhetorical questions whose answers need to be ceaselessly deferred in the interest of what she calls "the future uses of the sign," Butler asks:

> Can the visibility of [gendered] identity *suffice* as a political strategy, or can it only be the starting point for a strategic intervention . . . . not a call to return to silence or invisibility, but, rather, to make use of a category that can be called into question, made to account for what it excludes. ("Imitation" 19)

Butler's question explicitly addresses the "strategic intervention" of the epigone in *Between the Acts*. If we consider the epigone's "making use" of the category of national history as merely the "starting point" highlighting an agency and sovereignty given substance through exclusion, La Trobe clearly makes use of history as a concept that may be called into question in any context of parody and farce, where the ruff of the ages becomes unpinned, and "Great Eliza had forgotten her lines" (*BTA* 85). And even as the epigone calls the category of national history into question, La Trobe derives considerable agency by eschewing the temptation to codify alternative "truths" of history anew, to impose her own will toward compensatory *inclusion* in a particular form upon the historical text. Rather, the viewers of La Trobe's pageant witness the iteration of a history gone awry as all histories, being iterative re-enactments, must necessarily do; nor can La Trobe claim exclusive authorship or assert the viability of her play as an historical model. Her play, like her identity, will be "historical" only once.

This iterative, rather than teleological, basis for historiography ensures that Woolf's epigone is uniquely situated to contemplate the insufficiency of the historiographical operation as a gendered practice—how history is lived and remade through the everyday experience of being "man," "woman," or the engendering world arising from these figures. La Trobe is suspicious of history and is herself historically suspect. She is of unknown origin, and this constitutive lacuna within the villagers' knowledge creates instability in how La Trobe is perceived—not as a hollow narrative of self, but interestingly, as a narrative of engendering possibility. La Trobe is "not altogether a lady" (*BTA* 58). For her part, Mrs. Swithin admires La Trobe's energy and exoticism: the director's features seem from Tartary (or maybe Russia) but are certainly not "pure English" (*BTA* 57), and "very little was actually known" about her (*BTA* 58). Because she occupies an historical ellipsis within the local imagination, rhetorical understatements about La Trobe's mysterious origin attribute to her a measure of phallic power ("often with a whip in her hand; and used rather strong language" [*BTA* 28]). She embodies the latent unknowability of history in a particular form—that of a present but still elusive female power. As an epigone, La Trobe is therefore able to prophesy such misapprehension of historical subjects as "neither a nation nor a people but something impossible to define" (Wiley 19).

In such terms, Woolf's epigone produces a queer history of "practices, performances, repetitions, and mimes" (Butler, "Imitation" 23) specific to the novelist's own historical context, even as the expropriations of heterosexual norms to queer purposes, the "acts" La Trobe performs (with an eye to the policings of heterosexuality) draw her backward and forward through time.[3] However, La Trobe's very apparency as lesbian, her "swarthy, sturdy, and thickset" body, cuts against the novel's rather different project of coded sexual politics that, in the conspiratorial tones Jane Marcus attributes to the Bloomsbury circle generally, refuses to harden into a reified concept or period caricature (146-48). The engendering of historical disciplines and a creative presentation of the history of gender—these twinned projects take center stage in *Between the Acts*, and both constitute Woolf's participation in a broader, philosophical discourse about how historical actions confer gender "identity," and how identity, once trammeled within representation, becomes "history."

For Woolf, the complex patterning of "history" is not teleological but necessarily metaphorical. The notion of lived history as emergent metaphoricity at play, prior to its implicit institutionalization as cultural artifact, behavior, or performance is patently Nietzschean:

> To expose the illusions [of being (*sein*)] produced by what was, in the end, only a *linguistic* habit, to free consciousness from its own powers of illusion-making, so that the imagination could "frolic in images" without hardening those images into life-destroying "concepts"—these were Nietzsche's supreme goals. (White 335)

One must consider the "hardening" agent that Nietzsche, and subsequently Woolf, chose to target with their newer linguistic economies of dissolute and dissolving acts. For Woolf, I suggest that histories of nation and nationalism, in particular, offered illusory safe-haven for the very bourgeois morality both thinkers contested. The categorical rejection of normative print-culture *Between the Acts* orchestrates, alongside La Trobe's own abuse of monumental history as more or less metaphorical (and certainly beyond the patriarchal precipitate of "events"), threatens to dismiss historical signs from their present obligations to the materiality of 1939, such that the printed words might draw themselves defiantly up and off of the national page: "they rose, became menacing and shook their fists at you" (*BTA* 59). Woolf's words are printed, too; however, La Trobe's pageant is not, and it invites metaphorical readings of history that Giles cannot appreciate because he, himself, cannot command metaphor at all (*BTA* 53).

---

[3]Butler's focus on the performative elements of all gendered identities can be readily applied to La Trobe's performance of history as a gendered and engendering practice. The queer performance of history in *Between the Acts*, moreover, neither ensures nor refutes lesbian readings against the Nietzschean grain, even as Woolf's epigone willingly partakes of (and, just as conceivably, disavows) emergent discourses—queer, lesbian, and otherwise—to read history after the patriarchal "fact." See Cramer, "Introduction" 117-127.

As both the playing of national "events" and the metaphorical cross-talk that demonumentalizes them, the history of the epigone in *Between the Acts* requires a forgetfulness of the past as well as a remembering of the future that playing history "straight," in any period, is loath to concede. For her part, Woolf (like her epigones) never played history straight. Prolific as a literary historian, she borrowed and adapted historical materials with impunity, raiding historical archives effectively and achieving in her work a broad array of historical effects, none of them unified (Rosenberg 1112-15; Schwartz 723-25). The disassembly of the national past in service to the exigencies of the ruptured present urges Woolf's targeting of national consciousness: not primarily as the platform for rendering a specific homology between gender and nation visible, but to highlight the instability and contingencies occasioned by their performance in close proximity.

II. Willing Epigone

Benedict Anderson's celebrated redeployment of Walter Benjamin's notion of "empty, homogenous time" suggests that newspapers constitute national subjectivity via a "transverse, cross-time, marked not by prefiguring and fulfillment, but by temporal coincidence, and measured by clock and calendar" (24). The imagined community of the "nation" exists, Anderson suggests, because we empower a specific ontology of national time, the clock of the nation, which print culture (specifically newsprint) both constitutes and conveys (24).

Beyond her own sacrifices and anxieties as a consequence of the looming war, Woolf categorically rejected such an ontology of nation as in any way the giver of life or the incitement to newer forms of speech for the disenfranchised.[4] In *Between the Acts*, La Trobe enacts this rejection by attacking national history from within—she targets "national time" through subversive introductions of narrative arrhythmia. She cannot break the national clock, but she can toy with the technologies of its tempo (Pridmore-Brown, 408-10; Caughie 10-12). Using a phenomenological methodology, Paul Ricoeur's analysis of *Mrs. Dalloway* offers the most coherent application of Nietzsche to Woolf's modernism to date (101-112). In his analysis, Ricoeur targets the chronologizing impulse of monumental time, the clocks and bells ringing throughout that text, which are

---

[4]*Between the Acts* rejects an ontology of nationalism as in any way the just response to the problem of history consistent with Nietzsche's own denunciation of "the pathological estrangement which the insanity of nationalism has induced" (*Beyond Good and Evil*, 196). In a well-known rebuttal to Anderson, Mary Louise Pratt underscores the "estrangement" national consciousness produces: specifically, that the print-nation thesis excludes women readers of the national text as citizen-soldiers, even as it silences oral cultures (83-86).

transformed into asynchronous gaps and ruptures within the national time of *Between the Acts.* If, as Ricoeur suggests, *Mrs. Dalloway* registers the alarming repetitions of history and their damaging impact on individuals, *Between the Acts* strives to place print culture before an alternative and incredulous public who can disable its destructive periodicity through the agency of readership. Woolf herself read difference into national history in terms of her own dislocation from it: "I become steadily more feminist, owing to the *Times,* which I read at breakfast and wonder how this preposterous masculine fiction [the war] keeps going a day longer" (*L2* 76).

Specifically, Woolf's "feminist" text targets the "preposterous fiction" of national culture Benedict Anderson would theorize decades later, that of an imagined community cohering via print culture ("owing to the *Times*"). Embodied by La Trobe, the pageant play offers a programmatic redesigning of national history that owes nothing to the time *of the Times*—a stance that implicates not merely patriarchy, but a printable model of history, the freight of past onto present, against which Nietzsche warns. At different moments during La Trobe's pageant play disembodied voices in the audience can be heard to say, "D'you believe what the papers say?" (*BTA* 104). The welfare of Jews on the Continent in the years immediately following Munich and *Kristallnacht,* sardonically juxtaposed with print media reports of the Duke of Windsor and Queen Mary's vacation on the Sussex coast, are paraphrased by the play's chorus: "D'you believe what's in the papers?" (*BTA* 121). The newspaper emerges in Woolf's "novel-play" as merely another text, another performer in the cacophony of modernity *Between the Acts* represents, no doubt a measured and stern response to the newspaper's claim as imprimatur of truth, as privileged harbinger of even the most dire and intimate of news.[5]

In contrast to such a presumptive authority, Woolf presents Page, the local agent of a national print culture in *Between the Acts,* metonymically with fleeting signifiers—the new money, the "unattached floating residents" (*BTA* 75) in town who arrived with the car factory and aerodrome. The new money has brought with it news; more importantly, the "unattached" bourgeoisie will make news and buy news. As transcriber of local events, Page embodies the role of print-consciousness to constitute (hence delimit) "events" through bounding discourses of representation such as propriety, sensibility, dramatic standards, and

[5]Woolf's nephew, Julian Bell, was killed in Spain on July 18, 1937. Anxious to fight fascism, but persuaded by his mother (Vanessa Bell) not to join a combat unit, Bell had volunteered with an international ambulance brigade. Virginia Woolf and Vanessa Bell heard word of the death of Julian Bell on July 18, 1937, but lacked confirmation of the event until July 23, with Woolf writing to Philip Morrell [no. 3280]: "It was in the *Times* today" (*L6* 148).

the like. Page's paper creates social cohesion; his print culture moors "unattached floating" consciousness. Yet like all reporters and editors of a representable reality, Page decides what gets left in, and what left out; what floats and what does not. He takes the roll-call of a representable reality, even if his "reportage" of the play's spectators, for example, is only artful cobbling: "And Mr. Page, the reporter, noted, 'Ms. Swithin; Mr. B. Oliver,' then turning, added further, 'Lady Haslip, of Haslip Manor,' as he spied that old lady wheeled in her chair by her footman" (*BTA* 97). Accordingly Page's role in the pageant, while all-powerful and constitutive of the national narrative, is virtually invisible; absolute silence attends what appears to be his passive witness (like that of the observing "nation") of La Trobe's experiment.

Beyond the blank, disciplinary potential of the national Page, La Trobe's pageant dramatizes a more aggressive model of engagement with history. Directing her own version of a present past, La Trobe's pageant play affirms the dictum that "Forgetting is essential to action of any kind" (Nietzsche, "Uses" 62). Such a forgetting of the national history is necessary if La Trobe is to forestall any collusion of the epigone with patriarchy. Only by willfully forgetting the national history handed down to her may La Trobe re-envision it.[6] *Between the Acts*, perhaps Woolf's most successful expression of a willed forgetfulness of nationalism, remains saturated not with the past *per se*, but pleasurable eruptions of the present within an alienated past and vice-versa, a relation in time that Benjamin describes as messianic and which Anderson finds anachronistic to national time (223). Thus Woolf's project in *Between the Acts* may be linked not to a critical legacy that typically reinscribes her relationship to a specific historical moment, World War Two, but to those uses and abuses of history in her work provoking ruptures within any narration of national time.[7]

Beyond the category of "wartime text," *Between the Acts* treats the gender of history as a modality in flux, an unstable frame whose excess (*pace* Nietzsche, "an excess of history is harmful to the living man") emerges as nothing so much as a feminist "Outline" (*BTA* 8; 108). The epigone walks the margins of the historical "Outline," which produces not the remasculinizing narrative of nation, but an alternative vision Swithin and La Trobe have yet to experience as transhistorical women, of "rhododendron forests in the Strand; and mammoths in

---

[6]La Trobe's artistic process reclaims individual will in the interest of the epigone, sunk "down on the threshold of the moment . . . balanced like a goddess of victory without growing dizzy and afraid" (Nietzsche, "Uses and Disadvantages," 62).

[7]Alex Zwerdling uses the World War Two context to focus more global energies of Woolf's historiography at work in *Between the Acts* (*Real World,* 302-323). For additional, comprehensive treatments of Woolf's relationship to this particular war, see Hussey; Plain; and Schneider.

Piccadilly" (*BTA* 30). Outlying nationalism, the epigone resists any notion that time begins and ends with an implicitly masculine subject, an assumption which breeds passivity and defeatism—a history "born already gray-haired" (Nietzsche, "Uses" 101)—and recycles violence against women. Isa's rendering of the rape of an unidentified woman by "the guard at Whitehall" (*BTA* 20) appears in print, juxtaposing the unknown rape victim with the unknown soldier (perhaps rapist) in the national imagining. By contrast, on his train ride home Giles reads in the newspaper about another fate for the unknown soldier: "that sixteen men had been shot, others prisoned, just over there, across the gulf, in the flat land which divided them from the continent" (*BTA* 46). Both newspaper accounts impose a national frame of reference onto what otherwise remain merely the actions of men: actions that fail to circumscribe the proliferation of different spatio-temporal registers elsewhere in the text—Darwinian, primordial, pagan, alongside Ms. Swithin's Christian piety—readings of the epigone that refuse to privilege any one *telos* of history, especially a nationalist one.

Some seventy years prior to the writing of *Between the Acts*, Nietzsche describes vividly how such seemingly discrete registers of public war and private rape may be rendered equivalent as "facts" by a devouring and sensationalist national history:

> The war is not even over before it is transformed into a hundred thousand printed pages and set before the tired palates of the history-hungry as the latest delicacy. (Nietzsche, "Uses" 83)

As reported by the newspapers, Woolf's and Nietzsche's respective accounts of "the war" reintroduce precisely what Anderson's model excludes: the "tired palates" of a scripted, national history of facts; in Isa's case, such facts constrain her resistances within a presumably universal, national imagining. As one measure of such resistance, La Trobe contests a print-culture allegory of England by scripting intervals within its nationalist ontology. Ricoeur's alarms and bells are here presented as interruptions and iterations of irreducible meaning: the "chuff, chuff, chuff" (*BTA* 82) of the gramophone alternately emerges as "tut-tut-tut" (*BTA* 164), and again "tick, tick, tick" (*BTA* 82; 174). The skipping effect is both metonymic and metronymic: these are discernible moments within the messianic (rather than national) text, otherwise invisible to the characters, who merely apprehend its ruptures: "Perhaps [La Trobe will] reach the present . . . if she skips" (*BTA* 120). Outside the text of the newspaper, other (and often competing) constituents of history in *Between the Acts* appear as sound bites, paintings, smells, and sounds. Such a sensorium motivates the text's "talk producers" (*BTA* 36), including the portrait of the male ancestor at Pointz Hall, the manor located inside the "hollow" of history (*BTA* 10). With his interesting portrait, the long-dead, male ancestor produces "talk," pre-national noise, as chitchat: whether his painted dog is to be Colin or Buster, or any dog at all (*BTA* 36; 48). This ancestor's talk, this transhistorical banter (in remarkable riposte to the Foucauldian disciplinarity) is distinguished from the portrait of the lady in Pointz Hall. Hers is simply "a picture," (*BTA* 36) inviting all who gaze upon it, particularly the artist-cum-clerk William Dodge, "down the paths of silence" (*BTA* 45).

Rather tidily, both ancestors appear here as contrasting models for the textuality of the "nation" descending from them: one proto-discursive, the other allegorical. The mapping in gendered terms of these ancestors and their avatars, Giles and Isa—as talk-producer man and pictured woman—suggests that both couples share a discomfiting division of labor centuries apart. Subsequent to the ancestors, the "nation" emerges to refigure, rather than question, such a false dichotomy of gender. The absolutely silent (and silencing) representation of the lady ancestor provokes initially what seems to be the text's critique of the tradition equating national allegory and femininity—as if, in essentializing terms, the lady could not be a "talk producer." Yet the "talk producer" of the modern feminine, embodied by the garrulous Mrs. Manresa, conflates the latter's "over-sexed" (*BTA* 41) and "sensuous" (*BTA* 55) identity with the oddity of Isa's furtive, half-heard neoromantic ejaculations: the poetic and slightly self-conscious "talk" she hides from Giles in an account book (*BTA* 50).

The alternatively boisterous and chastened chatter of these respective women suggests their incremental advance into discourse—if anything, Manresa is merely LOUDER—compared with their female ancestor. Yet it seems Manresa, in particular, has gathered to herself the confidence of volume, and little more. That she speaks idly in the text, or is perhaps misperceived as doing so, likewise suggests how the still romanticized terms of the feminine allegory of "nation" constrain the women in the novel. In this regard, the portraiture in Pointz Hall, the founding and engendering fictions the pictures impose (and that frame expressiveness and artistry) emerge as the patriarchal underwriting, the illicit content, of Anderson's "empty, homogenous time" of nationalism. Both Manresa and Isa cannot but be viewed as victims of such foundational national fictions, in alternating modes both shrill and silenced: women either avoiding its history, on the one hand, or suffering unduly from its burdens on the other. In either case, La Trobe's countervailing example—as epigone—demonstrates how both Manresa and Isa are doomed to fail as subjects within the bounds of existing historical discourse, unless they can rethink their own complicity with it.

Contrasted with Anderson's model, the historiography of *Between the Acts* envelops women artists and talk producers within Nietzsche's historical "atmosphere" of an enlivening present ("all living things require an atmosphere around them, a mysterious, misty vapor" ["Uses" 97]) and asks them to slough off the patriarchal inheritance of print nationalism as well as muted protest (such as Isa's) masquerading as self-censorship:

> Objectivity and justice have nothing to do with one another. A historiography could be imagined which had in it not a drop of common empirical truth and yet could lay claim to the highest degree of objectivity. (Nietzsche, "Uses" 91)

Eschewing "common empirical truth" in the interest of "the highest degree of objectivity," La Trobe undertakes the challenge of a newer, more just, historical imagining for her spectators. Antiheroes in the struggle for a history beyond nationalism, the spectators in *Between the Acts* (including La Trobe herself) ultimately cast themselves positively as belated players in the pageant play of history, as a chorus of epigones:

> They stared at the view, as if something might happen in one of those fields to relieve them of the intolerable burden of sitting silent, doing nothing, in company. Their minds and bodies were too close, yet not close enough. We aren't free, each one of them felt separately, to feel or think separately, nor yet to fall asleep. We're too close; but not close enough. So they fidgeted. (*BTA* 67)

The burden of the past in the present propels the audience toward a dissenting restlessness, then thirst, and finally voice. Feeling separated, they nonetheless emerge collectively as subjects in the present that, as Lucy reminds Isabella, is the only temporality available to them (*BTA* 82). In protest against the silence of the lady ancestor, and with implicit criticism for the owners and managers of the British popular culture industry, the text confers semiosis upon these fidgeting women in the audience as "talk producers."[8] La Trobe does not have to speak national culture as, on the front of the newspaper, the rape and malign neglect of women by national culture speaks for itself. From their place of ostensible and objective remove, couched within "empty, homogenous time," the newspapers reinscribe the gender division of labor in what will be staged by La Trobe as the dirty business of nationalism. Somewhere between chitchat and silence the nation shuffles relentlessly on towards conflict. Faced with her audience's fidgeting, a wind that steals the words of her players, and the play to end all wars, Miss La Trobe can only cry, "Louder! Louder!" (*BTA* 139).

In his persuasive essay, McWhirter suggests that Woolf's "tragicomedy of history" in *Between the Acts* presents a contrapuntal, dialogic, and hybrid text of

[8]John Reith (the founding Director-General of the B. B. C.) was disparaged by Bloomsbury for ensuring that only his notoriously buttoned-down and conservative viewpoints, and they alone, were broadcast. In 1931, Reith provoked the resignation of Hilda Matheson, the popular Talks Director, citing her record of promoting eccentric, anarchical, and "subversive" viewpoints (Furbank 171). Reith's successors at the B. B. C. further suppressed freedom of speech during wartime.

literary genres that strives to dissolve the "historical cul-de-sac of 1939" (794). This tragicomedy refuses to impose a totalizing value, such as historical "content" or master narrative, on the text. McWhirter aptly suggests that *Between the Acts* offers a Bakhtinian pageant, "a representation of history and a history of representations within the English novel" rather than a specific historiographical platform (803). Here I've suggested, rather, that Woolf's text does indeed embody a particular theory of history, that of a Nietzschean critique of bourgeois historiography which, contra Hegel, criticizes events as crystallizations of truth (Nietzsche, "Uses" 104). Woolf's text, accordingly, represents not the carnivalesque refusal to choose among different theories of history as McWhirter suggests (808) but what such a refusal cannot concede: that the banality of modernity, emerging in the form of the newspaper, has already stripped contestatory modes (genres) of history of any effective difference from nationalism. "Events" like rape and execution by firing squad become enshrined in the vaults of national memory as merely accumulated facts, the clichéd ideological property of Isa's mantra that Giles "is the father of my children" (*BTA* 14), whatever his enduring faults. In criticism of such a seamless and presumptive reproduction of stillborn history, Woolf's critique of the male imagined community reintroduces a radical simultaneity of time and moment, of spatio-temporality, in messianic time: "1830 was true in 1939" (*BTA* 52).

Yet La Trobe's pumping up of historical volume recasts the issue of trans-historical simultaneity beyond the terms of a cross-genre aesthetic. Although hybridized, as McWhirter suggests, *Between the Acts* may nevertheless be held to account as potentially complicit, in printed form, to the stasis of the national text. Once inscribed, Woolf's text (or La Trobe's, by the reporter Page) cannot avoid the predicament of nationalist (indeed canonical) reinscription. But by drawing attention to the imposed silences, to the simmering injustices, heard and recognized nowhere along the rows and alleys of the print-nation dyad Nietszche first identified and Anderson theorized, Woolf can, with La Trobe's help, cry foul about the textualization of national consciousness as the privileged expression of historical truth.

In marking the time of "neither one thing nor the other; neither Victorians nor themselves" (*BTA* 178), *Between the Acts* thus consistently repositions the monuments of national history to produce occult disturbances (why not call it the variable English weather?) within the national text. Then and now, two temporalities unfold at once, in grating and contrapuntal irreducibility: " 'O,' Miss La Trobe growled behind her tree, 'the torture of these interruptions!'" (*BTA* 79). Linked together in the narrative, then-and-now confounds the narrative stream of the country: "After Vic.," La Trobe ponders, "Reality too strong" (*BTA* 179). At this point, rain imparts Nietzschean atmosphere to any post-structuralist gloss on a shattered history, the mirrored fragments of La Trobe's history "not whole by any means" (*BTA* 185), not historical, but still conveying truth.

Like the pocket watch silenced by a bullet at Waterloo, under glass at the landing of the stair in Pointz Hall, time can be suspended. The would-be diachronic reading of the text's history occasions a flurry of otherwise labile and proliferating interruptions, some engineered by La Trobe, some not: "Don't bother about the plot: the plot's nothing" (*BTA* 91). National time, like La Trobe's play, stops only when the audience (or the playwright herself) becomes aware of its own motivating force that set it ticking in the first place. The historiography of "nation" is not an ontology nor a thing unto itself: it is a creative and flawed composition of intervals in time.

If La Trobe attempts to deconstruct a prison house of historical consciousness in *Between the Acts* (*BTA* 94), the text likewise proffers Isa's "sleep haze" which, although she remains imprisoned within patriarchy, deflects and blunts the arrows shot for the love and hatred of men (*BTA* 66). Clearly, the Nietzschean metaphor of atmosphere, of a present mist obscuring the monuments of history, serves to empower La Trobe's vitality and magisterial reappearance on the stage of her own proper "nation." The eminence and vitality of La Trobe's own stage, the lesbian proscenium from which she directs her engaging performance, would seem to suggest that the terms lesbian and "nation" are mutually exclusive in *Between the Acts*. Yet La Trobe's metahistory is not merely reactionary, limited to the critique of the citizen-soldier subject, and leaving the emergent lesbian subject to the margins as a consequence. Unlike La Trobe, the male artist can "only represent through mimesis. He cannot represent what he has not imagined . . . the disappearing woman as the essence of (or excuse for) patriarchal aesthetics" (Wiley, "Unrepeatable" 6). La Trobe, by contrast, plays the role of iterative re-emergence in the disrupted national history the play performs. The ruptures within national time mark openings and opportunities for recuperated same-sexual discourses not entirely "lesbian" as yet: La Trobe's often unintended entrance upon different scenes of her pageant play are strategically comedic, farcical, and even clumsy, but suggest the agency of the epigone who dares to reframe Nietzsche's "old age of mankind" ("Uses" 83) as a newer *chronos* of womankind without strictly defining what the "truth" of this alternative *sexual* history might mean. The director's dogged reappearances, from behind a solitary tree or pacing at a distance (*BTA* 62; 79), constitute her belated witness to an interrupted nationalist narrative that refuses to monumentalize the past:

> As long as the past has to be described as worthy of imitation, as . . . possible for a second time, it of course incurs the danger of becoming somewhat distorted, beautified and coming close to free poetic invention. (Nietzsche, "Uses" 70)

La Trobe knows that not only must her play fail; it must fail triumphantly, in order that other renderings, other newer histories, the brilliant attack of starlings, may emerge (*BTA* 209). Nietzsche's "danger of distortion" here becomes La Trobe's greatest achievement as a historical poetics. Whatever valuation Nietzsche imputes to such a danger, the indisputable fact remains that the force of La Trobe's personality has scrawled subversion forever across the national text as in any meaningful sense an expression of history. Her play stands not as the monument to history, but its productive defacement.

On cue, starlings swirl and attack the tree behind which La Trobe had hidden, revealing her as a beleaguered monument to her metahistorical project: she can no longer hide from the historical process she has set in motion. Nor can La Trobe's uses and abuses of history in the play conjoin her lesbianism to Nietzsche's caricature of epigone based upon the failure of La Trobe's own private affair ("Since the row with the actress who had shared her bed . . . the need of drink had grown on her" [*BTA* 211]). Presumably, new "words without meaning—wonderful words" (*BTA* 212) will engender new discrepant acts of history and signal unanticipated events of passion. Inhabiting such terms of cryptohistorical possibility, nor does La Trobe embody within discourse the "Sapphist," whose sharp outlines in representation, like the "Outline" of History itself, Woolf deplored.[9] Both present and absent within national history, signifying both the lack and fullness of women's engagement, La Trobe's historiography creates a place for the embodied experience of the epigone—slipping in and out of printed and printable culture—on a staged production of national and sexual difference. An enunciation of historical plenitude beyond patriarchy, La Trobe's "failure" confirms nothing, if not Nietzsche's credo that "history can be borne only by strong personalities, weak ones are utterly extinguished by it" ("Uses" 86). With the conclusion of the pageant play, Miss La Trobe's failure triumphs, and just as likely disappoints her audience; for his part, Mr. Page files the final report on behalf of a more diffuse, less personable national history:

> With very limited means at her disposal, Miss La Trobe conveyed to the audience Civilization (the wall) in ruins; rebuilt (witness man with hod) by human effort; witness also woman handing bricks. Any fool could grasp that. Now issued black man in fuzzy wig; coffee-coloured ditto in silver turban; they signify presumably the League of . . . (*BTA* 181-82)

The three-beat ellipsis concludes Page's report but does not punctuate it; the print of the nation, and the trouble of the fools comprising it, will trail on. By Page's own report, La Trobe's play (and Woolf's text proper) condemns print culture

---

[9]For a comprehensive treatment of the constitutive relationship between prewar sexual discourses (such as Sapphism) and antifascist struggles, see Carlston, 1-18; Shattuck, 289.

and its relationship to nationalist consciousness with "very limited means": the tick, tick, tick of an inviting but always absent historical excess. Imperial signifiers ("black" and "coffee-coloured") parade along the ranks of the national page alike, representing in caricature La Trobe's accusation of Western imperialism as, with the invasion of the "new" Poland in 1939, merely the most recent of nationalist experiments in thrall to the historical principle.

For her part, the epigone would rather wait. She looks toward another venue better adapted to her effective impertinence toward historical truth: the sovereignty of representation. Dwelling one beat after Page's ellipsis, she will continue to exercise her own excitable sovereignty over the life principle invited by Nietzsche's laughter, both as the embodiment of the historical "woman" and the "what then" of historical truth exceeding the gender prescriptions of woman. A willing epigone, La Trobe will always be tardy (or contrapuntal) when reviewing the monuments of history and re-scripting their occurrences. Accordingly, *Between the Acts* redirects history away from the page towards the stage—no mean feat, as *Between the Acts* remains thoroughly ensconced within a narrative loosened, but not altogether abolished, by its protagonist's willingness to be a late-comer to Anderson's imagined community.

Positioning her writing between the acts of modern historiography, Woolf addresses what Gramsci called "the diversity of morbid symptoms" of the interregnum—modernity as suspended "between" inevitable crises of global capitalism. Woolf's rewriting of Nietzsche responds to the impact of such perpetual crisis, of too-much-history upon the modernist text, as well as to the potential pitfalls attending any attempt of the individual will to impose an alternative "truth." Her willing epigone would vivify historical processes, and so seeks to avoid the paralysis imposed by an eternal past made present upon the historical stage, the "monstrous inversion" of a snake still alive, choking on a toad, still alive (*BTA* 99). By imparting to the epigone excitable speech—the added volume afforded by emergent discourse, whether lucid or inchoate—*Between the Acts* clearly counters the rhetoric of nationalist predicament silencing Woolf's historical women and enlivens their sovereignty in terms poignantly democratic, as historical subjects serving truth and life beyond national and gendered frames of history. The nation of the newspaper struggles unsuccessfully to be reborn, even as epigones cluster and disrupt the regimented lines of its printed text, their expressions arch in the knowledge that this news is servile, merely monumental, already old.

Works Cited

Anderson, Benedict. *Imagined Communities: Reflections on the Origin and Spread of Nationalism.* Rev. ed. New York: Verso, 1991.
Benjamin, Walter. *Illuminations.* Ed. Hannah Arendt. New York: Schocken, 1968.
Bradbury, Malcolm. "London 1890-1920." *Modernism.* Eds. Malcolm Bradbury and James McFarlane. London: Penguin, 1991. 172-190.
Butler, Judith. *Excitable Speech: A Politics of the Performative.* London: Routledge, 1997.
———. "Imitation and Gender Insubordination." *Inside/Out: Lesbian Theories, Gay Theories.* Ed. Diana Fuss. New York: Routledge, 1991.
Carlston, Erin G. *Thinking Fascism: Sapphic Modernism and Fascist Modernity.* Palo Alto, CA: Stanford UP, 1998.
Caughie, Pamela L. Ed. *Virginia Woolf in the Age of Mechanical Reproduction.* New York: Garland, 2000.
Cramer, Patricia. "Introduction." *Virginia Woolf: Lesbian Readings.* Eds. Eileen Barrett and Patricia Cramer. New York: New York University Press, 1997). 117-127.
———. "Virginia Woolf's Matriarchal Family of Origins in *Between the Acts.*" *Twentieth-Century Literature* 39.2 (Summer 1993): 166-184.
Cuddy-Keane, Melba. "The Politics of Comic Modes in Virginia Woolf's *Between the Acts.*" *PMLA* 105.2 (1990): 273-285.
Furbank, P. N. *E. M. Forster: A Life.* Vol. 2. New York: Harvest-Harcourt Brace, 1978.
Hussey, Mark Ed. *Virginia Woolf and War: Fiction, Reality, and Myth.* Syracuse, NY: Syracuse UP, 1991.
Kaufmann, Walter. "Translator's Preface." *Beyond Good and Evil: Prelude to a Philosophy of the Future.* 1885. Trans. Walter Kaufmann. New York: Vintage/Random, 1989.
Laurence, Patricia Ondek. *The Reading of Silence: Virginia Woolf in the English Tradition.* Palo Alto, CA: Stanford UP, 1991.
McWhirter, David. "Woolf and the Tragicomedy of History." *ELH* 60, 3 (Fall 1993): 787-813.
Marcus, Jane. "'Taking the Bull by the Udders': Sexual Difference in Virginia Woolf—a Conspiracy Theory." *Virginia Woolf and Bloomsbury: A Centenary Celebration.* Ed. Jane Marcus. Bloomington: Indiana UP, 1987. 146-169.
Marcus, Laura. *Virginia Woolf.* Plymouth, U.K.: Northcote House/British Council, 1997.
Mouffe, Chantal. "Feminism, Citizenship, and Radical Democratic Politics." *Feminists Theorize the Political.* Eds. Judith Butler and Joan W. Scott. London: Routledge, 1992. 369-384.

Nietzsche, Friedrich. "On the Uses and Disadvantages of History for Life." *Untimely Meditations*. Trans. R. J. Hollingdale. New York: Cambridge UP, 1983.
——. "Preface." *Beyond Good and Evil: Prelude to a Philosophy of the Future*. 1885. Trans. Walter Kaufmann. New York: Vintage/Random House, 1989.
Plain, Gill. *Women's Fiction of the Second World War: Gender, Power, and Resistance*. Edinburgh: Edinburgh UP, 1996.
Pratt, Mary-Louise. "Criticism in the Contact Zone: Decentering Community and Nation." *Critical Theory, Cultural Politics and Latin American Narrative*. Eds. S. Bell, Le May, and Orr. Notre Dame: U of Notre Dame P, 1993. 83-102.
Pridmore-Brown, Michele. "1939-40: Of Virginia Woolf, Gramophones, and Fascism." *PMLA* 113.3 (1998): 408-421.
Ricoeur, Paul. *Time and Narrative*. Vol. 2. Trans. Kathleen McLaughlin and David Pellauer. Chicago: U of Chicago P, 1984-1988.
Rosenberg, Beth Carole. "Virginia Woolf's Postmodern Literary History." *MLN* 115 (2000): 1112-1130.
Schneider, Karen. *Loving Arms: British Women Writing the Second World War*. Lexington: UP of Kentucky, 1997.
Schwartz, Beth C. "Thinking Back through Our Mothers: Virginia Woolf Reads Shakespeare." *ELH* 58.3 (1991): 721-46.
Shattuck, Sandra. "The Stage of Scholarship: Crossing the Bridge from Harrison to Woolf." *Virginia Woolf and Bloomsbury: A Centenary Celebration*. Ed. Jane Marcus. Bloomington: Indiana UP, 1987. 278-298.
White, Hayden. *Metahistory: The Historical Imagination in Nineteenth-Century Europe*. Baltimore: Johns Hopkins UP, 1973.
Wiley, Catherine. "Making History Unrepeatable." *CLIO* 25.1 (Fall 1995): 3-21.
Wirth-Nesher, Hana. "Final Curtain on the War: Figure and Ground in Virginia Woolf's *Between the Acts*." *Style* 28.2 (1994): 183-200.
Woolf, Virginia. *Between the Acts*. New York: Harcourt Brace, 1941.
——. *The Letters of Virginia Woolf*. Vols. 5–6. Ed. Nigel Nicolson. London: Hogarth Press, 1994-95.
Yuval-Davis, Nira. *Gender and Nation*. London: Sage, 1997.
Zwerdling, Alex. *Virginia Woolf and the Real World*. Berkeley: U of California P, 1986.
——. "*Between the Acts* and the Coming of War." *Novel* 10 (1977): 220-36.

Shufflings of Kristeva: The Choran Moment in Virginia Woolf

Emily M. Hinnov

> *I begin to long for some little language such as lovers use, broken words, inarticulate words, like the shuffling of feet on the pavement.*
> —Bernard in *The Waves* 341-2

The return to the maternal has been celebrated both by feminist theorists such as Elaine Showalter and Hélène Cixous,[1] and notably (and perhaps most exquisitely), I will argue, in the writings of Virginia Woolf. Her rendering of the choran technique creates a pregendered space for unspoken language hinted at in *A Room of One's Own* (1929). Through these "imaginary" moments of being, Woolf encourages the reader's visceral experience of the "symbolic" domain in her written texts, inventing plains of elevated "musicalit[y]" (Kristeva, "A Question of Subjectivity" 135) for the reader.[2] I will consider how Woolf's *Jacob's Room* (1922), *Mrs. Dalloway* (1925), *To the Lighthouse* (1927), in conjunction with her unpublished essay "Anon" as well as some of her later fiction, illustrate the choran experience. The chora, a pregendered space of unified existence[3] connected with the maternal core, offers a precursor to Woolf's concept of androgyny in which the "masculine" and "feminine" sides of our being are melded and become indistinguishable. Here I define "maternal" as not necessarily gendered; although we are symbiotic with the maternal body as we experience the chora, this encounter exists for both sexes and occurs before gender is even

---

[1] See Hélène Cixous, "Sorties." Phillip Rice and Patricia Waugh, eds., *Modern Literary Theory: A Reader* (New York: Arnold, 1996) 137-144, Elaine Showalter, *A Literature of Their Own: British Women Novelists from Brontë to Lessing* (Princeton, NJ: Princeton UP, 1977), and "Toward a Feminist Poetics," M. Jacobus, ed., *Women Writing About Women* (1979) 25-33; 34-6. Phillip Rice and Patricia Waugh, eds., *Modern Literary Theory: A Reader* (New York: Arnold, 1996) 99-108.

[2] Julia Kristeva, "A Question of Subjectivity—An Interview." *Women's Review* 12 (1986) 19-21, Phillip Rice and Patricia Waugh, eds., *Modern Literary Theory: A Reader* (New York: Arnold, 1996) 131-7. For a comprehensive collection of Kristeva's work, see Kelly Oliver, ed., *The Portable Kristeva* (New York: Columbia University Press, 1997).

[3] Some readers may wonder how I could use a phrase such as "unified existence" in light of postmodern theory. What I hope to suggest here is that this sense of wholeness exists before we are subjected to ideological constructs of gender difference. Perhaps these moments are temporary fantasies. I'll admit that we can never *literally* return to the chora of the past, but I argue that (at the very least) the choran moment is available in Woolf's fiction.

encoded by the symbolic realm of language. Since we are caught up in the constrictive binaries of gender difference once we reach the symbolic state of existence, we can only recapture the choran experience by striving toward androgyny. What I define as the choran moment as evidenced in the writings of Virginia Woolf encompasses pleasure, lyrical and even unspoken musicality, and an intimate re-connection with the maternal body that does not depend upon the construct of gender. I will argue that in the choran moments of being Virginia Woolf creates between those characters engaged in loving and sometimes erotic relationships, the voice of her fiction strives beyond a "feminine" orientation and toward an androgynous vision of absolute pleasure that merges, and finally transcends, binaries of gender distinction.

Julia Kristeva has subversively transformed Lacanian philosophy into feminist theory. Briefly stated, Jacques Lacan reappropriates Freud's Oedipal stage into his own theory for the process by which we acquire language.[4] Lacan maps our movement from the imaginary stage as an infant ecstatically unified with the maternal body, to a false but pleasurable sense of synthesis with his mirror image, and finally to the child who is thrust into the world of difference. Once "he" realizes that he is separate from his mother and his own reflection he must conform to the parameters of the symbolic order of language and greater society; language acquisition strives to restore (symbolically) the unity that has been lost. Julia Kristeva reinvents the imaginary realm of Lacan's mirror stage as the "chora," in which the infant's babblings to her mother and herself (which the child cannot yet distinguish between) are understood as a connection or return to the semiotic, prelanguage, pregendered and maternally bonded state of existence.

Out of this union comes the meaningful language of emotions, a "nonexpressive totality" (35) that is "nourishing and maternal" (Kristeva, *The Portable Kristeva* 36) and is apart from, yet equally as viable as the written language of the symbolic by which we are indoctrinated. In Kristeva's words, "Indifferent to language, enigmatic and feminine, this space underlying the written is rhythmic, unfettered, irreducible to its intelligible verbal translation; it is musical, anterior to judgment, but restrained by a single guarantee: syntax" (38). Kristeva does point out that the expression of this "recourse to the semiotic" ("A Question of Subjectivity" 137), or "state of disintegration in which patterns appear but . . . do not have a stable identity" (133), is in no way a monopoly of women. James Joyce incorporated this concept into his own work through use of a fluid, stream of consciousness narrative in which the speaker has no fixed identity; Joyce himself also had a particular affinity to a "feminine" version of language. Yet in her

---

[4]My discussion of the Lacanian origins of Kristeva's chora stems from Jacques Lacan, "The Mirror Stage as Formative of the Function of the I as revealed in Psychoanalytic Experience." Alan Sheridan, trans., *Ecrits, A Selection* (1949) 1-7.

reworking of Lacan, Kristeva lends credence to the power of a traditionally "female" realm of emotional language and expression similar to the "womanspeak" psychoanalyst Luce Irigaray[5] delineates as "decentered, irrational, and nonlinear, unlike the logocentric, hierarchal expression of patriarchy" (Haberstroh 125). Kristeva's emphasis on the magnificence of the chora even suggests that it is not important (as Freud and Lacan supposed in their blind phallocentrism) that the female infant could not properly delve into the male world of the symbolic.

Further, my assertion of the chora as a pregendered space that we can reach back to through the concept of androgyny resonates with Derrida's own sense of "khóra," which lies outside its Platonic origin of a feminine receptacle. According to Derrida, "in order to think *khóra*, it is necessary to go back to a beginning that is older than the beginning, namely, the birth of the cosmos" (126). He suggests the connection between androgyny and the chora in his determination of khóra as a space "beyond categories" (95), an "opening" (103) that originates before gender classifications in the "preoriginary, *before* and outside of all generation . . . [to] the dream [that] is between the two, neither one nor the other" (124-126). I also view the chora as a place of "neither this or that," a place where genders are preformed, intermingled, indistinguishable; thus gender here is fundamentally irrelevant.

In concurrence with Lisa Rado's *The Modern Androgyne Imagination: A Failed Sublime* (2000), I take the contemporary definition of androgyny; since the 1970s, androgyny has been referred to as a mixture of historically determined feminine and masculine characteristics within the same person. Similarly, Karen Kaivola draws upon Woolf and speaks of androgyny as an "intermix" (235) of the sexes and genders. While androgyny and Woolf's concept of it was initially popular in second wave feminism, it later came under heavy critique by scholars and social activists. For a brief time in the 1960s and '70s, critics such as Carolyn Heilbrun and Nancy Topping Bazin[6] admired Woolf's vision of androgyny's ability to provide men and women freedom from the constraints of gendered determinates of behavior. But by 1977, Elaine Showalter argued that Woolf's concept was a mere fantasy, one that necessitates the denial of a distinctly female literary tradition.[7] During the 1980s a new generation of critics began attacking androgyny as limiting; Toril Moi sought to "deconstruct the

---

[5]Margaret Whitford. ed. and intro., *The Irigaray Reader* (Oxford: Blackwell Publishers, 1992), provides a helpful anthology of her most well-known essays.

[6]Nancy Topping Bazin, *Virginia Woolf and the Androgynous Vision* (New Brunswick, NJ: Rutgers UP, 1973), and Carolyn Heilbrun, *Toward a Recognition of Androgyny* (New York: Knopf, 1973).

[7]For additional edification on the debate surrounding Showalter's critique of *A Room of One's Own*, as well as a useful guide on the development of feminist literary theory, see

metaphysical belief in two relatively fixed, immutable, complementary but opposing genders" (Kaivola 237), and argued instead for a "third" sexed position. By the 1990s the debate had become passé in the academy, but Kari Weil persisted with an argument that future discussions of androgyny should consider systems of difference other than gender. Weil asserts that we should include race, ethnicity and sexuality and to "envision a meeting rather than a joining across gulfs of difference" (Kaivola 238). Rado outlines how the phenomenon of androgyny represented the possibility of ultimate artistic genius for the Moderns:

> These writers present inspiration not as the incorporation of 'masculine' qualities but rather as generated by the precarious coexistence of female consciousness and a masculine other-self that goes beyond mere pseudonym . . . modernist literary men and women share the desire to embody the newly perceived strengths of both sexes and to transcend sexual and artistic limitation altogether. (13)

Freud suggests in "Psychology of Women" (1933) that "the proportions in which the masculine and feminine mingle in the individual are subject to quite extraordinary variations" (155; qtd. in Rado 18). He also notes that "what constitutes masculinity or femininity is an unknown element which is beyond the power of anatomy to grasp" (156). Certainly then, Modernists like Woolf grapple with the idea of a transcendent androgynous sublime. Further, I suggest a "meeting" place between genders, encapsulating an all-embracing sense of androgyny that does not regard gender as important, a kind of consciousness that originates from the time before we are inscribed by gender: the space of the chora. Virginia Woolf captures this essence in her art.

There is an immediacy in the moment and the emotion associated with the use of this otherlanguage, a kind of spontaneity that brings about the urgency and the authenticity of the imaginary experience I have long associated with Woolf's incandescent moments of being.[8] Although the chora has no stable identity and no traditional construction of language, Kristeva argues that it is the origin of

---

Mary Eagleton ed. and intro., *Feminist Literary Criticism* (London and New York: Longman Group UK, 1991).

[8]In an earlier draft of this paper, I utilize Cocteau Twins to illustrate the choran experience as it exists in music before examining the works of Virginia Woolf, thus providing a launching point with which to read similar choran moments in Woolf's writing. Cocteau Twins are an English trio, made up of vocalist Elizabeth Fraser, guitarist (and Fraser's husband) Robin Guthrie and bassist Simon Raymonde, who rarely use more than one short phrase of traditional language in their music. The "texts" of their songs abandon the symbolic realm of lyrics and embrace an atmospheric, primal soundscape of utterance that transforms the listener beyond the world of actual words into the intangible sphere of emotion. According to Cocteau Twins' web site, Fraser "thinks that people should take

poetry, and music and poetry are intimately linked. Kristeva indicates in the return to the maternal sphere of the semiotic that we are "searching for the inscriptions of language of the archaic contact with the maternal body which has never been forgotten . . . they are to be found in the tempo of the voice, in the rapidity of delivery . . . or in certain musicalities" ("A Question of Subjectivity" 135). Woolf realizes this orb of intuitive, orgasmic, expressionistic grace, and her work often strides beyond the realm of the feminine and on toward a transcendent space of gender-free rapture. I find that Woolf offers an intense, momentary, transcendent reading experience that illustrates this ideal, androgynous understanding that is the choran moment. As Pamela Caughie indicates, Woolf perhaps would not want her readers to approach her work without questioning it, blindly accepting that her texts will express human truths, but instead that we should as postmodern readers look for an opening up of possible readings (76). This is the task that I am striving to accomplish in my reader-response approach to Woolf. What I am arguing here is not only that "Woolf's narrative [is] a predecessor of Kristevan feminism" (Trotman 3), but that the spaces of genderlessness she creates bespeak the unspoken, and, often in a lyrical fashion, akin to the maternally-bound babblings of pleasure and emotion, Woolf's illuminated moments of harmonious connectedness are particularly choran.

Virginia Woolf mentions her concept of the need for a "female" voice in writing in chapter four of *A Room of One's Own*. Woolf notes that Jane Austen, like Shakespeare, did not become conscious of gender in her writing and she thus wrote in her own way (68). She then asserts that since women writers have no "common sentence ready to use" (76), they need to take on their own voice rather than adapt themselves to the public style established in the canon by male writers. In her essay "Women and Fiction" (1929), a precursor to *A Room of One's Own*, she addresses this necessity:

---

advantage of not being able to understand or decipher her lyrics." Bassist Simon Raymonde commented in an interview on how the experience of having his first child influenced the band's music: "I would say that it's inspiring the way Liz writes her lyrics. It's enlightening, having a child, and it's interesting to see how a child sees their world" (Suciu 2). Although he does not overtly declare the influence of this maternal connection on the music, he certainly implies the possibility that Fraser's "lyrics" represent a child's vision, thus bringing Cocteau Twins' music much closer to Kristeva's chora. Jas Morgan and Diana Trimble of *Mondo 2000* magazine agree: "We think it's all in the vowels. The pre-linguistic privatespeak of mother and child. The intimate conversations of pure emotion held before the acquisition of language. The lullaby. Lallation. The imitative sounds a child makes in the effort to infuse language with meaning" (1). For more on Cocteau Twins, see Cocteau Twins, *Otherness*. (London: Mercury Records, Ltd., 1995).

> The very form of the sentence does not fit her. It is a sentence made by men; it is too loose, too heavy, too pompous for a woman's use. Yet in a novel . . . an ordinary and usual type of sentence has to be found to carry the reader on easily and naturally from one end of the book to the other. And this a woman must make for herself, altering and adapting the current sentence until she writes one that takes the natural shape of her thought without crushing it or distorting it. (48)

From this rather brief yet important assertion she later develops her theory of the androgynous mind in *A Room of One's Own*, that which she believes all writers of genius possess. For Woolf, androgyny ultimately indicates a conjoining of our masculine and our feminine selves, an action that suggests the deconstruction of fixed concepts of masculinity and femininity because the two have become one as they step into the taxi: "It is when this fusion takes place that the mind is fully fertilized and uses all its faculties. Perhaps a mind that is purely masculine cannot create, any more than a mind that is purely feminine" (*AROO* 98). Again, it is this sense of a meeting and an intermixing of genders that seems to be the predecessor for the eventual goal of indifference to sex, to the preoriginary androgyny we all once possessed in the choran state.

Her concept of androgyny also depends upon the anonymity of the writer:

> The creative power differed, Woolf felt, from the creative power of men, but she insisted that the success and expression of that power depended on that impersonality or anonymity, that absence of special pleading, which lends to art 'that curious sexual quality which comes only when sex is unconscious of itself'. (DiBattista 17)

Although Woolf often appears to privilege the creative power of the female mind, thus calling for a female determination of language that can "break the sequence" (*AROO* 81), it is a sense of androgyny that frees the mind from societal constructions of gender (as well as biological constraints) that might otherwise impede the true voice of the artist in his or her work. As I have already hinted, I interpret Woolf's concept of androgyny as available through a reconnection with the chora; it is in the very unconsciousness of gender that the writer (and hence the reader) can embrace a true sense of an ecstatic unified, integrated self. At the same time this choran sense of androgyny opposes the patriarchy's rigid notions of gender Woolf so sought to eradicate. Kristeva explains that "Any creator necessarily moves through an identification with the maternal, which is why the resurgence of this semiotic dynamic is important in every act of creation" ("A Question of Subjectivity" 136), and Beth C. Schwartz states that "This anonymous world is, for Woolf, the locus of creation" (726). Thus Woolf's androgynous space of generative artistry falls in line with the Kristevan theory of the chora as the origin of creativity that transcends the binaries of gender.

Toril Moi picks up on what Elaine Showalter's *A Literature of Their Own* has missed in determining Woolf's androgyny as a failure to confront "her own painful femaleness" and a "denial of feeling." Like myself, Moi instead focuses on the Kristevan idea of the unitary self in Woolf's artistic vision, and arrives with Kristeva at a third realm of feminism "in which women are deconstructors of the very dichotomies upon which patriarchy is based, primarily the dichotomy of fixed gender identities" (Trotman 3). Thus, as Nat Trotman explains, a rupture between masculine and feminine is actualized, "creating a new space in which I find pleasure" (3). Since androgyny is placed outside the realm of "traditional, patriarchal discourse and its objective, rational, linear worldview, it must align itself with the subjective, the irrational, the realm of pleasure" (5), or the space of the chora. Marjorie Garber also builds upon Moi's concept of a third-sexed recognition of androgyny. For Garber, bisexuality, like androgyny, undercuts the seeming stability of the opposing poles of masculinity and femininity: "The 'third' is that which questions binary thinking and introduces crisis ... The 'third' is the mode of articulation, a way of describing a place of possibility" (qtd. in Kaivola 11). As in the work of Moi, Trotman, and my previous reference to Derrida, Homi K. Bhabha employs the concept of hybridity as a third designation to introduce the idea of the fundamental instability of the supposed pure forms of masculinity and femininity, and finally argues for a mixture of those terms. Bhabha characterizes the hybrid moment in quite similar terms as my reading of the chora, as one that rearticulates "elements that are neither the one . . . nor the Other . . . but something else besides which contests the terms and territories of both" ("The Commitment to Theory" 13; qtd. in Kaivola 258n). Here neither sexes nor genders can claim any significance. This choran rift allows for a freeing, personal interplay with Woolf's texts, producing pleasure for the reader in its intense, inspired, almost sacred moments of being. For Trotman, and for myself, here, "a tiny freedom is born" (7).

In Woolf's unfinished essay, "Anon," which she began in September of 1940, we find the most patent recognition of the choran experience. Here Woolf lays out her representation of the supremely androgynous mind, the Anonymous writer who is "sometimes man; sometimes woman" ("Anon" 382), standing between the inspiration for the art and the text, the imaginary and the symbolic. Beth C. Schwartz relevantly states that:

> We can still become anonymous: the anonymous world "still exists in us, deep sunk, savage, primitive, remembered." We can most readily recover [choran] anonymity through song, for song is "something very deep—primitive, not yet extinct" ("Anon." 398, 381, 377). And the "instinct of rhythm," she argues, is "the most profound and primitive of instincts," as deep-rooted as the "instinct of self-preservation" ("Anon." 403). (Schwartz 725)

Here we can reclaim the "original song," the "song beneath" ("Anon" 403-4), or "the world beneath our consciousness; the anonymous world to which we can still return" (385). This is the place that Kristeva notes emerges in the musicalities of the voice; the song of Anon is the song of the "mother tongue," that rapturous place of babbling interplay between mother and infant that excites a feeling of restored unity with the original self. Again, the return to the maternally connected experience is not essentially "feminine"; it offers every person the opportunity to re-embrace their own pregendered, amalgamated self.

Virginia Woolf's concern for form is expressed as follows, written in her diary in August of 1923 while she was working on *Jacob's Room*: "Suppose one can keep the quality of a sketch in a finished & completed work." Her solution is articulated when she discovered in late 1923 "how to dig beautiful caves behind my characters . . . The idea is that the caves shall connect, & each comes to daylight at the present moment" (*D2* 263). Part of this deeper connection between characters is represented by the children's voices in her novels, which in turn emulate the lost fusion with the maternal body in the symbolic order. When Jacob's brother Archer calls for him on the beach in the opening pages of *Jacob's Room*, we are told that "the voice had an extraordinary sadness. Pure from all body, pure from all passion, going out into the world, solitary, unanswered, breaking against rocks—so it sounded" (8-9). Clearly here, Archer's calls take on a lament for this destroyed connection from "body" and "passion." The forlorn quality of his voice can be associated with the jangling sounds of the child singers who appear at the end of *The Years*:

> Etho passo tanno hai . . .
> That was what it sounded like. Not a word was recognisable. The distorted sounds rose and sank as if they followed a tune . . . the unintelligible words ran themselves together almost into a shriek. The grown-up people did not know whether to laugh or cry. Their voices were so harsh; the accent was so hideous . . . It was so shrill, so discordant, and so meaningless. (429-30)

Here Woolf creates a curious and dramatic juxtaposition with the otherwise positively (or at least neutrally) rendered depictions of children's voices in the remainder of her fiction. She writes of *The Waves* in June of 1929 that " . . . this shall be Childhood; but it must not be *my* childhood; & boats on the pond; the sense of children; unreality; things oddly proportioned" (*D3* 236). Perhaps it is that the disparate, uneven and horrid song echoes the sorrow of that fundamental disconnect between the maternal body and our inevitable wrenching into the social order, or that sudden and disorienting "unreality . . . [of] things oddly proportioned" that she strives to eradicate through intense moments of wholeness in her fiction.

Yet ultimately in *The Years,* Eleanor, arguably the protagonist, rather uncertainly calls the song "Beautiful?" just before she takes in the "air of ethereal calm and simplicity [that] lay over everything" (434) and embraces the future. Eleanor is able to find the beauty in the incoherent voices the other adults could not truly comprehend. As Susan Squier argues, "*The Years* ends . . . [with a] vision of an affirmative response to otherness and change enacted by Eleanor Pargiter's final words to her brother Morris. 'And now?' she asked, holding out her hands to him'" (Squier 234; *TY* 435). Eleanor represents the individual who has both made peace with her separation from the glorious, maternally-secured past, and adjusted well enough in the process to take on whatever the future may hold. She has realized an open, more androgynous and thus all-inclusive vision, and can therefore find her way (metaphorically) back to the chora. This brash acceptance of loss could even be seen as a prerequisite for recapturing the choran experience. The choran voice is reestablished in *Jacob's Room,* however, in a picture of paramount motherhood: "The two women murmured over the spirit lamp, plotting the eternal conspiracy of hush and clean bottles while the wind raged and gave a sudden wrench at the cheap fastenings" (13). As Mrs. Flanders and Rebecca ruminate over the sleeping children who must "shut [their] eyes, and think of the fairies, fast asleep, under the flowers" (12), their echoing, soothing, murmuring tones bathe the children in a womb-like space of restful fluidity, reconnecting them with that preexistent space of unified infancy.

The mother-child bond is also masterfully accomplished throughout *To the Lighthouse* in the interactions between Mrs. Ramsay and her children. As Mrs. Ramsay knits while caressing her son James, she simultaneously creates a balm-like, supportive, life-giving energy. As she senses that her husband is "demanding sympathy" she shores up her feminine verve for the task at hand:

> Mrs. Ramsay, who had been sitting loosely, folding her son in her arm, braced herself, and, half turning, seemed to raise herself with an effort, and at once to pour erect into the air a rain of energy, a column of spray, looking at the same time animated and alive as if all her energies were being fused into force, burning and illuminating (quietly though she sat, taking up her stocking again) . . . [with] this delicious fecundity, this fountain and spray of life. (37)

This extraordinary, fluid force is surely "her capacity to surround and protect" (38), her ability to "combine" (39) and create permanence with her supreme motherly energy. Its associations with "rain" and the "spray" of water once again tie the expression of what I would call a choran moment with the associated amniotic fluid and the chamber of protection and bliss. This space is echoed in *The Waves* when Susan watches over her newborn baby. "Sleep, sleep, I croon . . . Sleep I sing . . . I sing a song by the fire like an old shell murmuring on the beach . . . wrapping in a cocoon made of my own blood the delicate limbs of my baby . . . making my own body a hollow, a warm shelter for my child to sleep in" (294-5). Clearly the image of the sheltering maternal space is an important metaphor for Woolf, who lost her own mother at the age of thirteen.[9] In a letter to Ethel Smyth in April 1931, she writes "What you give me is protection, so far as I am capable of it. I look at you and . . . think if Ethel can be so downright and plainspoken and on the spot, I need not fear . . . Its the child crying for the nurses hand in the dark . . . we all cry for nurses hand" (*L4* 302). This longing for reconnection with the maternal body is one that resounds with the choran realm Kristeva articulates over forty years later.

Joseph Allen Boone's discussion of the mythical place of Elvedon in *The Waves* offers another example of this child-like world of fantasy. Although he does not evoke Kristeva's chora, he argues that "Woolf suggests that Bernard's story records a vestigial memory, part of his preconscious history *preceding* identity; his telling of it thus becomes a process of recovering an original status buried beneath layers of the meaning of Elvedon's memory" (633). Bernard's "search for permanence" (636) here also links with the character of Mrs. Ramsay, a maternal, artistic force that "combines" and creates moments of wholeness. Only for Bernard, the recognition of this vision can be made in the symbolic realm of written language, rather than the choran imaginary space. He finds in Elvedon "that which is *symbolic*, and thus perhaps permanent, if there is any permanence in our sleeping, eating, breathing, so animal, so spiritual and tumultuous lives" (*TW* 349; italics mine). Yet even though Bernard might doubt the notion of permanence in *The Waves*, Woolf continually strives to "let . . . her imagination sweep unchecked round every rock and cranny of the world that lies submerged in the depths of our unconscious being" ("Professions for Women" 61) in her subsequent writing, and thereby reestablishes our common subconscious world.

In *To the Lighthouse*, Mrs. Ramsay imagines a child's state of mind as she interrupts her daughter Cam daydreaming: "What was she dreaming about? . . . seeing her engrossed . . . so that she had to repeat the message twice . . . The words seemed to be dropped into a well, where, if the waters were clear, they were also so extraordinarily distorting that, even as they descended, one saw them twisting about to make Heaven knows what pattern on the floor of a child's mind" (54). She later worries that James "was thinking, we are not going to the lighthouse tomorrow; and she thought, he will remember that all his life" (62). Not only does Woolf here, through the thoughts of Mrs. Ramsay, assert the importance of childhood experience in developing our adult sensibilities, she

---

[9]See Jane Marcus, "Virginia Woolf and Her Violin: Mothering, Madness, and Music" *Virginia Woolf and the Languages of Patriarchy* (Bloomington: Indiana University Press, 1987).

also expresses a kind of uterine solace in the "limitless" moments tied with Mrs. Ramsay and her children. Mrs. Ramsay feels at these moments, while James plays at cutting out magazine pictures, that "she could be herself, by herself" (62). The space we can return to enables us:

> To be silent; to be alone. All the being and the doing, expansive, glittering, vocal, evaporated; and one shrunk, with a sense of solemnity, to being oneself, a wedge-shaped core of darkness, something invisible to others . . . Beneath it all is dark, it is all spreading, it is unfathomably deep; but now and again we rise to the surface and that is what you see us by . . . This core of darkness could go anywhere, for no one saw it. They could not stop it, she thought, exulting. There was freedom, there was peace, there was, most welcome of all, a summoning together, a resting on the platform of stability. (62-3)

Here the feminine power that is regenerative and creative offers limitless wholeness and a sense of absolute harmony and stable well being; our collective core can be brought out from within us anywhere at any time. And it is often these moments that excite intense flashes of rhapsody: Mrs. Ramsay speaks of these "waves of pure lemon which curved and swelled and broke upon the beach and the ecstasy burst in her eyes and waves of pure delight raced over the floor of her mind and she felt, It is enough! It is enough!" (65).

This swell of joy could be associated with Kristeva's concept of "infantile language," or a "telescoping of parent and child . . . discourse of a child (boy or girl) . . . where his 'own' language is never totally rationalized or normated . . . but where it always remains an 'infantile language'" (*Desire in Language* 278). In either the unmitigated communication between parent and child, of adult self and child self, this sense of pleasure is born and a poetic voice emerges. For Maria DiBattista, "the non-sense spoken by the mad [is] no language at all, merely words languishing and dissolving into their constituent sounds—'ee um fah um so / foo swee too eem oo' (*MD* 80)—the sounds of the eternal, unreasonable world" (52). Here DiBattista evokes "the voice of no age or sex, the voice of an ancient spring spouting from the earth" (*MD* 80), embodied by the vagrant woman in the Regent's Park Tube station whom Peter Walsh overhears on his solitary-traveling journey. This woman sings of the transcendence of love "which has lasted a million years," and her infantile, "bubbling burbling song" becomes a nurturing, reviving force that "soak[s] through the knotted roots of infinite ages . . . fertilising, leaving a damp stain" (81). Once again, Woolf images the fecund, womb-like space in its eternal, vibrant wetness, and here actualizes the chora through the voice of a kind of mother-earth figure who appears to enjoy that "telescoping" power of connection with her child self. The voice is that of an earth song, one that Woolf also accomplishes in *The Years* as the "sound of the eternal waltz" like the "deep murmur [that] sang in [Kitty's] ears—the land itself, singing to itself, a chorus, alone." This choran song awaits those who seek it, and offers the potential for total happiness: "[Kitty] lay there listening. She was happy, completely. Time had ceased" (*TY* 129; 278). The choran moment here is tied with a maternal earth that is timelessly infused with pleasure.

    The renewing power of the maternal space is often reflected in music and art in Woolf's fiction, frequently evoking erotic intensity. Woolf actually wrote *The Waves* while being inspired by music, as she notes in a June 1927 diary entry: "I do a little work on it in the evening when the gramophone is playing late Beethoven sonatas. (The windows fidget at their fastenings as if we were at sea)" (*D3* 139); and in a letter to Bessie Trevelyan, "I always think of my books as music before I write them" (*L4* 426). The epigraph at the opening of my essay illustrates Woolf's chasing down of the choran space, particularly in the depiction of "some little language such as lovers use, broken words, inarticulate words . . . " (*TW* 342). Indeed Virginia's sister Vanessa Bell responded to the power of *The Waves* as follows, linking her reading experience with her feeling of giving birth: "For it is quite as real an experience as having a baby or anything else, being moved as you have succeeded in moving me . . . I know its only because of your art that I am so moved . . . if you wouldn't think me foolish I should say that you have found the 'lullaby capable of singing him to rest'" (Banks 296n). Vanessa even labored on a painting, eventually entitled *The Nursery*, which she hoped "would have some sort of analogous meaning to what you've done." As Mrs. Ramsay murmurs a song to herself while she reads a book in *To the Lighthouse*, "She felt that she was climbing backwards, upwards . . . so that she only knew this is white, or this is red. She did not know at all first what the words meant at all" (119). Here music is a gateway to her journey back to her infantile self, the self that does not understand the meanings of words. Woolf noted in a letter to Ethel Smyth in August of 1930 that she strives to "get my sense of unity and coherency and all that makes me wish to write the Lighthouse etc. unless I am perpetually stimulated" (*L4* 200). It seems that for Woolf, music is a constant source of inspiration that inspires and drives her quest for creating wholeness in her writing.

    In Woolf's other fiction, as in *The Years*, music creates a medium of erotic connection. Kitty basks in the glory of the opera, musing that "the music made her think of herself and her own life as she seldom did. It exalted her; it cast a flattering light over herself, her past . . . *He*, she thought, looking at the handsome boy, knows exactly what music means. He is already possessed by music. She liked the look of complete absorption that had swum up on top of his immaculate respectability" (183). In *The Voyage Out*, music becomes a culminating force of community. As Rachel plays the piano at the early morning dance, "their feet fell in with the rhythm [and] they showed a complete lack of self-consciousness ... Then they began to see themselves and their lives, and the whole of human life advancing very nobly under the direction of the music" (166-7). Through her talent for music, akin to Clarissa Dalloway's artistic ability of bringing people together with her parties, Rachel creates a nurturing space of non self-conscious repose.

In *To the Lighthouse*, Lily Briscoe offers a more prominent rendering of the choran space in the process of coming to her art. Although Lily questions why she continues to paint at all, she must battle the doubts that have permeated her self-concept as an artist just as she struggles with the "formidable" (158) space of the canvas. "Still the risk must be run; the mark made" (157). Rado argues that in Lily's moment of artistic inspiration, she represses "her body, her femaleness, her sexual identity" and "represents her mind as phallic" (155). I argue conversely that Lily reaches inside, into the core of her prelanguage and pregendered choran self for her artistic inspiration. Woolf's use of recurrent sexual imagery that ties the process of painting to a sense of erotic excitement is suddenly evident when her brush "for a moment ... stayed trembling in a painful but exciting ecstasy in the air." Finally, Lily's overwhelming initial hesitancy breaks and "as if some juice necessary for the lubrication of her faculties were spontaneously squirted" (159), she is able "precariously" to begin painting once again. The rhythm of her artistic illumination, once again tied to waves and water and thus the fluidity of life in the womb, becomes "strong enough to bear her along with it on its current" and becomes a kind of seductive dance between creator and vision: "She attained a dancing, rhythmical movement, as if the pauses were one part of the rhythm and the strokes another ... She was half unwilling, half reluctant" (158). Lily is finally able to surrender to the dance; she "lose[s] consciousness of outer things" so that her mind becomes androgynous and "throws up from its depths ... scenes, and names, ... and memories and ideas, like a fountain spurting over that glaring, hideously difficult white space, which she modeled with greens and blues" (159). Even Lily's painting is shaded with hues of the blue and green tones of water, reflecting the awesome power of the mind conjoined with the creative impulse; she might overflow with creative energy like the rapid water of the stream that floods over in a violent rainstorm.

Painting parallels existence for Lily, representing that reconnection with the choran space, that inner world of unfathomable memory that unifies art and life and originates poetry. Lily in fact incorporates the "wedge-shaped core of darkness" (62) and the "odd-shaped triangular shadow" (201) of Mrs. Ramsay, which is here metaphorical of the uterine space in its shape and tone, into her painting and thus her life. Life may not be the ideal she imagines for the canvas, but there are instead "little daily miracles, illuminations, matches struck unexpectedly in the dark" (161), inventing moments of perfect tranquillity in the possibility of permanence and connectedness. Lily exalts in the knowledge that "In the midst of chaos there is shape; this eternal passing and flowing . . . was struck into stability. Life stand still here, Mrs. Ramsay said." In Woolf's fiction, it is often the female artist who creates these instances of transcendent unity when "there is a coherence in things, a stability; something . . . is immune from change, and shines out . . . Of such moments . . . the thing is made that endures" (105). DiBattista notes that although her ultimate goal for the artist is androgyny, "traces of her feminine bias remain in Woolf's proposition that [Anon's] song 'fill[s] in the pauses' between acts of labor and continu[es] the emotion produced and experienced by the common voice [a]s a lullaby" (230). It seems that a "feminine bias" does exist in Woolf's depiction of a female artist whose ability to create and reconnect to the illuminating moment is so apparent. Yet according to Marilyn Brownstein, if we look at Woolf's writing as postmodern, it exists at the seam between pre- and postverbal because the prelanguage position is impossible to repossess once you've entered the symbolic: "For Woolf, the failure of language in this miracle of compression is the perpetuation of 'dumb yearning,' 'the primeval voice sounding in the ear of the present' as, perhaps, all there is to know" (86). Perhaps, then, it is really the maternally-bonded "song," the lull of the heartbeat we all experienced in utero, that smoothes over this gap and "fill[s] in the pauses" ("Anon" 230).

Woolf creates choran moments of jouissance[10] between married couples in her fiction as well. Determined herself "not to look upon marriage as a profession" and earnestly hoping for "a marriage that is a tremendous and living thing, always alive, always hot, not dead and easy in parts as most marriages are" (*L1* 496), Woolf explores in her fiction the paradoxes marriage offers. Although the imprint of marriage as a constrictive institution is perhaps her central thesis in *The Voyage Out*, at least by creating a heroine who falls ill and dies in the face of it, Woolf does offer a healthy alternative in the partnership between Ridley and Helen:

> "Tell me if there is a white hair, then?" she replied. She laid her hair in his hand.
> "There's not a white hair on your head," he exclaimed.
> "Ah, Ridley, I begin to doubt," she sighed; and bowed her head under his eyes so that he might judge, but the inspection produced

---

[10]I use this term as Cixous defines it ("sexual pleasure") in "Sorties" (Elaine Marks and Isabelle de Courtivron, eds., *New French Feminisms* [1975] 366-71).

only a kiss where the line of parting ran, and the husband and wife then proceeded to move about the room, casually murmuring.

"What was that you were saying?" Helen remarked, after an interval of conversation no third person could have understood. (196)

Their marital space encompasses a peaceful, unspoken connection that clearly binds their spirits.

A similar although more splendidly performed unspoken moment of connection happens between the Ramsays in *To the Lighthouse*. As Mrs. Ramsay finishes her knitting while Mr. Ramsay thinks "of Scott's novels and Balzac's novels," the frustrated atmosphere begins to transform; he "wanted her to tell him that she loved him. And that, no, she could not do" (123). As she gazes out the window " . . . he was watching her. She knew that he was thinking, You are more beautiful than ever. And she felt herself very beautiful. Will you not tell me just for once that you love me? He was thinking that, for he was roused" (123-4). Here is a heightened sensitivity that approaches eroticism expressed between husband and wife. We have been told earlier that "She had complete trust in him" (118), but here they participate in an unspoken dance of flirtation; he is expectant of her vocal declaration of love while she enjoys the fact that he watches her in anticipation, although "she could not say it" (124). The transient moment of anticipation is interrupted by her glance in his direction, becoming a flash of tacit "intercourse": "And as she looked at him she began to smile, for though she had not said a word, he knew, of course he knew, that she loved him. He could not deny it. And smiling she looked out the window . . . (thinking to herself, Nothing on earth can equal this happiness) . . . For she had triumphed again. She had not said it: yet he knew" (124). Although there is not any explicit sexual connection between Mr. and Mrs. Ramsay, their rapturous, unsaid communication illustrates another choran instance in Woolf's fiction. Woolf herself, upon her 25th wedding anniversary, wrote in her diary of "happiness . . . after 25 years cant bear to be separate . . . It is an enormous pleasure, being wanted: a wife . . . in a marriage so complete" (*D5* 120). Even in a marriage of no sexual love, Woolf offers proof here that a true partnership can do very well without.

Hermione Lee argues that "Woolf's sexual squeamishness, which plays a part in indirections and self-censorship of the novels, is combined with a powerful, intense sensuality, an erotic susceptibility to people and landscape, language and atmosphere, and a highly charged physical life. 'Frigid' seems a ridiculously simplistic description of this complicated, polymorphous self" (327). The same argument for polymorphous selves can be extended to Woolf's fiction, particularly in the character of Mrs. Dalloway. Clarissa Dalloway's absence of sexual desire is represented in the image of her bed: "The sheets were clean, tight stretched in a broad white band from side to side. Narrower and narrower would her bed be" (*MD* 31). The bed appears to close in on Clarissa until it becomes coffin-like in its stillness and cramped constriction. The metaphor of the coffin is further developed when Clarissa contemplates "what she lacked." She acknowledges that she has beauty and an intelligent mind, but does not possess that "something which broke up surfaces and rippled the cold contact of man and woman." Clarissa is unavailable sexually, at least for her husband, and could therefore be termed "frigid." And so Clarissa turns her thoughts to women. Clarissa's thoughts of the warmth that "broke up surfaces and rippled . . . " ironically break up her train of thought, and she begins to think "of women together." Although she feels somewhat guilty about her desires ("she resented it"), Clarissa here confesses that she "sometimes yield[ed] to the charm of a woman" (32), thereby expressing her homoerotic desire. She is seduced by their "power of sounds at certain moments," suggesting the link between ephemeral language of sound and the sensual experience.

It is at this moment of realization that she allows herself to feel like the stereotypical man finally overcome by the power of a woman's allure. Here, Clarissa experiences a brief erotic fantasy, what could be a moment of pure jouissance; yet Clarissa places herself entirely outside of it, perhaps to protect herself from the pain she inevitably ties with sexual pleasure. She feels a "tinge like a blush" and cannot help but "yield to its expansion" where she "quivered and felt the world come closer, swollen with some astonishing significance" (32). Woolf's poetic, sensual language here cannot be mistaken. And although Clarissa is thinking about and expressing her sexual desire, the narrative voice remains omniscient—there is no first person expressed to experience the immediacy of the moment. Yet the narrative technique here preserves a sense of anonymous distance as well, perhaps to invite the reader to participate in the splendor of an otherwise unclaimed moment. The "pressure of rapture . . . split its thick skin and gushed and poured . . . over the cracks and sores!" reminding Clarissa of the soothing power of fantasy to balm the anxiousness associated with her perplexing sexual orientation. For this fleeting instant she feels she has "almost expressed" significance in her vision of "a match burning in a crocus." This flash of heated illumination is symbolized in the fiery destruction of a flower, a traditional symbol of women's delicate genitalia. Flowers are important to Clarissa's happiness, as we see her warming over when she buys the flowers from Miss Pym at the beginning of the novel. The fact that here Clarissa associates the scorching crocus, preceded by the splitting and breaking of the flower's skin to produce the gush of rapture, with her moment of eroticism, simultaneously denotes the deep inner pain of desire's metaphorical birthing process and the image of rebirth connected with the vibrant early Spring flower.

Clarissa's confused fantasy soon incites the next wave of thought, which surrounds her memories of Sally Seton, her free-spirited confidante from her adolescent summer at Bourton. The conflicted passion she feels is associated with her revelatory memory of her kiss with Sally:

> Then came the most exquisite moment of her whole life passing a stone urn with flowers in it . . . And she felt she had been given a present, wrapped up, and told just to keep it, not to look at it—a diamond, something infinitely precious, which, as they walked (up and down, up and down), she uncovered, or the radiance burnt through, the revelation, the religious feeling!" (35-6)

This intimate, warm, lusciously choran moment is of course interrupted by Peter's "Star-gazing?"—the imaginary realm of feminine connection has been obliterated by the symbolic order of societal expectation, represented by the properly marriageable Peter. Although Clarissa loved both the freedom and reserve of Richard Dalloway and the overwhelming passion of Peter Walsh, the unabashed excitement of her love for Sally impressed upon her most. For she stood "in her bedroom at the top of the house holding the hot-water can in her hands and saying aloud, 'She is beneath this roof . . . She is beneath this roof!' . . . all because she was coming down to dinner in a white frock to meet Sally Seton! . . . She seemed . . . all light, glowing, like some bird or air ball that has flown in" (33-4). She allows herself to luxuriate in that semiotic moment revived in her memory, but will not ultimately permit herself to indulge in such a socially taboo relationship.

Woolf connected her friendships with women in her life with her writing, as a diary entry in November of 1924 indicates: "If one could be friendly with women, what a pleasure—the relationship so secret & private compared with relations with men. Why not write about it? Truthfully? As I think, this diary writing has greatly helped my style; loosened the ligature" (*D2* 320). Even Quentin Bell, that rather reticent biographer, acknowledges the significance of Virginia's girlhood relationship with Madge Symonds Vaughan, the oldest daughter of John Addington Symonds:

> Virginia was in fact in love with her. She was the first woman—and in those early years Virginia fled altogether from anything male—the first to capture her heart, to make it beat faster, indeed to almost make it stand still as, her hand gripping the handle of the water-jug in the top room at Hyde Park Gate, she exclaimed to herself: "Madge is here; at this moment she is actually under this roof." Virginia once declared that she had never felt more poignant emotion for anyone than she did at that moment for Madge. (60-61)

There are myriad similar moments depicted in Woolf's fiction; spiritualized, life-giving spaces appear, such as in *The Years* when "The Park was full of couples walking together. Everything seemed fresh and full of sweetness. The air puffed soft in their faces. It was laden with murmurs; with the stir of branches . . . and now and again the intermittent song of a thrush" (239). These are moments of supreme, uplifted romance that intermingle with sweet song and natural tranquillity. Woolf reflects her joy in writing *Mrs. Dalloway* in a December 1924 diary entry: "It seems to leave me plunged deep in the richest strata of my mind. I can write & write & write now: the happiest feeling in the world" (*D2* 323). She later writes about *The Years* that "the main feeling about this book is vitality, fruitfulness, energy. Never did I enjoy writing a book more, I think: only the whole mind in action: not so intensely as The Waves" (*D4* 361). Apparently, Woolf's feelings of that lively intellectual energy are projected onto the love relationships in her fiction.

It is in *Mrs. Dalloway* that Woolf first hints at celebration of a lesbian relationship, something she expands upon in her depiction of lovers in *Orlando*. I don't intend to state that lesbian desire is essentially androgynous—the particularization of same sex desire would undermine my entire thesis that choran ecstasy is available within the guise of *all* human connectedness, regardless of gender or sexual orientation.[11] Woolf does "conflate Clarissa's lesbian desires with androgyny" (Kaivola 248), but I asserted earlier in this essay that these transcendent moments take place between heterosexual relationships as well. Karen Kaivola aptly states that "Woolf develops strategies that enable her to negotiate the space between a dissembled Romantic androgyny and the hermaphroditic intermix that historically superseded it" (249). Additionally, for Lily, whose desire might also incidentally be described as lesbian, androgynous (choran) transcendent vision is enacted once she reconciles both sides of herself.

Virginia Woolf met poet, novelist, biographer, gardener and travel writer Vita Sackville-West in December of 1922, and they began a flirtatious friendship that would later turn into a passionate affair, in 1925. Woolf memorializes Vita in *Orlando*. Here she illustrates the same kinds of choran moments as in the novels previously discussed, but within the guise of androgynous desire. The sheer pleasure of desire for the self is realized when Orlando realizes that his body has transformed from a man's to woman's, as the trumpets outside "pealed Truth! Truth! Truth!" (137). An erotic moment occurs as Orlando stands "stark naked" in that the narrator, perhaps delving into the consciousness of the subject here, notes that "No human being, since the world began, has ever looked so ravish-

---

[11]For further discussion of the androgyny debate and its relation to *Mrs. Dalloway*, see Nancy Taylor, "Erasure of Definition: Androgyny in *Mrs. Dalloway*." *Women's Studies* 18.4 (1991) 367-377.

ing. His form combined in one the strength of a man and a woman's grace" (138). Orlando, once the "garment like a towel" thrown in the chamber has rather triumphantly fallen short of its target, "looked himself up and down in a long looking-glass, without showing any signs of discomposure." Woolf's wry observation of Orlando's metamorphoses here ends with a frank assertion of androgyny: "Orlando had become a woman—there is no denying it. But in every other aspect, Orlando remained precisely as he had been. The change of sex . . . did nothing whatever to alter their identity" (138). Woolf argues this point throughout the novel, claiming that "openness indeed was the soul of her nature," that "Different though the sexes were, they intermix. In every human being a vacillation from one sex to the other takes place" (189). Woolf light-heartedly continues the argument through Orlando's interactions with the social strata of the eighteenth, nineteenth and twentieth centuries, and does not concede the defeat of her push for androgyny.

Soon after Orlando becomes a woman and near the end of the novel as she contemplates her lover, Bonthrop, she thinks to herself,

> "I am a woman . . . a real woman, at last." She thanked Bonthrop from the bottom of her heart for having given her this rare and unexpected gift . . . for they knew each other so well that they could say anything they liked, which is tantamount to saying nothing . . . For it has come about . . . that our modern spirit can almost dispense with language . . . the most poetic [conversation] is precisely that which cannot be written down. (253).

Woolf writes in her diary about *Orlando* that "I never got down to my depths and made shapes square up, as I did in the *Lighthouse* . . . I want fun. I want fantasy" (*D3* 203). Yet once we look beyond the obvious comic camp in this passage, not only is the "rare and unexpected gift" (not unlike Clarissa's kiss) representative of that superior, communicative relationship akin to the Ramsays, but also their complete indifference to each other's sex. The comedy of Orlando's declaration of womanhood transforms that line into gender indifference. This unconsciousness in turn allows Orlando and Bonthrop a kind of "anonymous" relationship that transcends gender with its "poetic" communion. As DiBattista argues, "Orlando's sex-change represents an imaginative movement from repression to freedom" (122-3) and thus allows for the liberating concept of the "true self . . . compact of all selves we have it in us to be" (*O* 310). If Woolf precedes Judith Butler[12] and claims that the essence of self has no gender in *Orlando*, that gender is merely a performative shell that encapsulates our truly multiplicitous selves which emerge at certain moments of time and in response to particular situations, then the moments between lovers here point to a more radical vision of our collective connection to the chora.

Orlando emancipates her "true" self at this moment as a "real woman, at last," in her reconnection with this regenerative space that we can presumably all recreate through our vivid connection to memory. As Orlando muses, much like Clarissa Dalloway in their respective "middle age[s]": "It cannot be denied that the most successful practitioners of the art of life, often unknown people by the way, somehow contrive to synchronise the sixty or seventy different times which beat simultaneously in every normal human system so that when eleven strikes, all the rest chime in unison, and the present is neither a violent disruption nor completely forgotten in the past" (305). It is in the vibrant present moment of being in "Ecstasy!" (327) that we can merge again with our past.

It is in the "untamed forest" of Anon's artistic, poetic origins, the "moist and mossy floor [that is] hidden" ("Anon" 382) like Lily and Mrs. Ramsay's uterine, wedge-shaped core of existence that we can reclaim the chora as a space of unmitigated, supreme expression of pleasure. Like Nat Trotman, we can, as readers, "lean through, and . . . occupy [our] own space, yet . . . simultaneously exist" (9) in Woolf's work. We merge with the anonymous, androgynous force simultaneously as we reckon with the force of Woolf's words: "I am an image/androgyne, neither of the image, nor wholly separate from it" (Trotman 9). Here the text and thus the reader's internally spoken word echoes in the mind and becomes musical, and we are "lulled into complacency, rocked quietly off into a womb of language where all [we] feel and hear is the heartbeat language surrounding, caressing [us] . . . " (Trotman 11). I am struck by the "music" of reading Woolf's language "aloud" in my head; certainly the underlying music of Woolf's connection to the "uncouth jargon of [our] native tongue . . . Icham for woring al forwake / Wery no water in wore" ("Anon" 383) can be heard throughout her work, and awaits our convergence as intent readers. As Jean Wyatt argues in her discussion of *Mrs. Dalloway*, "the novel hits us not at the level of our social selves, but at the level of our primitive oral impulses: in Clarissa's blissful merging we experience our own desire to escape encasement in a circumscribed ego; to reinstitute our original boundless sense of a self merged"

[12]Gender theorist Judith Butler complicated the sex-gender debate in *Gender Trouble: Feminism and the Subversion of Identity* (1990) by arguing that all sexual difference (aside from purely anatomical difference) is culturally produced rather than natural. Sex and gender are cultural products as gender, and, for Butler, we are all caught in the hegemony of gender performance. *Orlando* begins to suggest the same, but I hope to extend the discussion by suggesting that Woolf offers her readers the chance to overcome the constrictions of gender, at least in the ethereal place where the reader and the text intersect, through the androgynous choran moments of her fiction.

(121).¹³ We are fortunate enough that Woolf has conceived these exquisite choran moments in her writing, and we can strive to reckon with them. While Woolf contemplates writing "Anon," she notes, "I am a little triumphant about the book. I think it's an interesting attempt in a new method. I think it's more quintessential than the others . . . I've enjoyed writing almost every page" (*D5* 340). This is the same "new method" of creating the complete experience she has evolved throughout her writings, right up to her final work.

Roland Barthes writes that "In a text of pleasure, the opposing forces are no longer repressed but in a state of becoming: nothing is really antagonistic, everything is plural." Woolf herself finds the drive to create texts of pleasure in a November 1928 diary entry: "And this shall be written for my own pleasure. But that phrase inhibits me; for if one writes only for one's own pleasure, I don't know what it is that happens" (*D3* 201). She answers her own inquiry soon after in her ruminations on *The Waves*: "What I want to do now is to saturate every atom. I mean to eliminate waste, deadness, superfluity: to give the moment whole; whatever it includes. Say that the moment is a combination of thought; sensation; the voice of the sea" (209).¹⁴ In giving us moments of wholeness in her work, Woolf is able to "hold up the creative, subconscious faculty" in her fiction (*D4* 281), and offers, then, a kind of opening up, a plurality of pleasure. She accomplishes what she fears she might lose—"But if I read as a contemporary I shall lose my child's vision and so must stop . . . What is the right antidote? . . . Writing to be a daily pleasure" (*D5* 347).

Virginia Woolf has given voice to the child-like "sonorous, rhythm obvious" of the "private world" ("Anon" 389) and "the primeval voice sounding loud in the ear of the present moment" (*BTA* 140) that creates a powerful instance of unified wholeness. She has reconnected her readers with the choran place of "no tension; no direction; but always movement, as the metre flings its curve of sound, to break, like a wave on the same place, and like a wave to withdraw, to fill again" ("Anon" 389). Like young James curled up in his mother's lap in *To the Lighthouse*, we too are "folded in this incantation [and] we drowse and sleep; yet [we] always see through the waters, something irradiate" (391). Virginia Woolf's writing indeed irradiates the whole choran experience; as Lily Briscoe reflects,

---

[13] Jean Wyatt argues that fusion with our childhood selves is desirable and natural in women's fiction, as opposed to Freud or Norman Holland's anxiety that one must defend the sense of autonomy that is lost in the state of symbiosis with the maternal body.

[14] Wyatt also contends that what Freud calls the "oceanic feeling" (which he deems a dangerous drowning sensation) is reclaimed by Kristeva's perception of the semiotic self. Her intriguing article identifies these kind of "oceanic" moments in *Mrs Dalloway*.

> One need not speak at all. One glided . . . Empty it was not, but full to the brim. She seemed to be standing up to the lips in some substance, to move and float and sink in it, yes, for these waters were unfathomably deep. Into them had spilled so many lives . . . some common feeling held the whole. (*TTL* 192)

Most remarkable here is the fact that both James and Lily respond to these instances of wholeness with the same revelry. Lily best exemplifies this union of seeming opposites once she concludes her painting: "With a sudden intensity, as if she saw it clear for a second, she drew a line there, in the centre. It was done; it was finished. Yes, she thought . . . I have had my vision" (209). Lily's painted line, as many critics have pointed out,[15] represents not a division of sides but instead a coupling of our masculine and feminine selves that finally renders them meaningless, and thus embodies an ultimate embracing of androgyny. In our "common" response to these "intense" flashes, binaries of gender are transcended and we, too, can have our vision and moreover "s[ee] it clear." Woolf's reading audience need only look deeply into these choran moments in her fiction and other writings to relive virtually, with our own androgynous understanding, our own unified past.

Thanks to both Jean Kennard and Robin Hackett for their patient willingness to read early drafts and for their insightful suggestions for revision. I'd also like to express my great appreciation for Charles Freeman's evocative perspective, without which I am sure that my essay would not have come as far.

---

[15]For an extremely useful reference guide on critical approaches to Woolf, as well as historical and biographical information on all that is Virginia Woolf, see Mark Hussey, *Virginia Woolf A-Z: The Essential Reference to Her Life and Writings* (NY: Oxford U P, 1995).

Works Cited

"'Anon' and 'The Reader': Virginia Woolf's Last Essays". Ed. Brenda Silver. *Twentieth-Century Literature* 25, 3-4 (Fall/Winter 1979): 356-437.

Banks, Joanne Trautmann, ed. *Congenial Spirits: The Selected Letters of Virginia Woolf.* NY: Harcourt Brace Jovanovich, 1989.

Barthes, Roland. *The Pleasure of the Text.* trans. Richard Miller, note Richard Howard. NY: Hill and Wang, 1975.

Bell, Anne Olivier, ed. and asst. Andrew McNeillie. *The Diary of Virginia Woolf.* 5 vols. New York and London: Harcourt Brace Jovanovich, 1978.

Bell, Quentin. *Virginia Woolf: A Biography.* 2 vols. NY: Harcourt, 1972.

Bhaba, Homi K. "The Commitment to Theory" *New Formations* 5 (1988).

Boone, Joseph Allen. "The Meaning of Elvedon in The Waves: A Key to Bernard's Experience and Woolf's Vision." *Modern Fiction Studies* 27.4 (Winter 1981-2): 629-651.

Brownstein, Marilyn L. "Postmodern Language and the Perpetuation of Desire." *Twentieth-Century Literature* 31 (1985): 73-88.

Caughie, Pamela. *Virginia Woolf and Postmodernism.* Chicago: University of Illinois Press, 1991.

Derrida, Jacques. *On the Name.* ed. Thomas Dutoit, trans. David Wood, John P. Leavy, Jr., and Ian McLeod. Stanford, CA: Stanford University Press, 1993.

DiBattista, Maria. *Virginia Woolf's Major Novels: The Fables of Anon.* New Haven and London: Yale University Press, 1980.

Freud, Sigmund. "The Psychology of Women." *New Introductory Lectures on Psychoanalysis.* trans. W. J. H. Sprott. New York: W.W. Norton, 1933. 153-85.

Garber, Marjorie. *Vested Interests: Cross-Dressing and Cultural Anxiety.* New York: Harper Collins, 1993.

Haberstroh, Patricia Boyle. *Women Creating Women: Contemporary Irish Women Poets.* Syracuse, NY: Syracuse U P, 1996.

Kaivola, Karen. "Revisiting Woolf's Representations of Androgyny: Gender, Race, Sexuality, and Nation." *Tulsa Studies in Women's Literature* 18:2 (Fall 1999): 235-61.

Kristeva, Julia. "A Question of Subjectivity—An Interview." *Women's Review* 12 (1986): 19-21. Rpt. *Modern Literary Theory: A Reader.* ed. Philip Rice and Patricia Waugh, New York: Arnold, 1996. 131-7.

——. *Desire in Language: A Semiotic Approach to Literature and Art.* ed. Leon S. Roudiez, transl. Thomas Gora, Alice Jardine, and Leon S. Roudiez. NY: Columbia U P, 1980.

——. *The Portable Kristeva.* ed. Kelly Oliver. New York: Columbia U P, 1997.

——. *Revolution in Poetic Language.* transl. Margaret Waller and intro. Leon S. Roudiez. New York: Columbia U P, 1984.

Lee, Hermione. *Virginia Woolf.* New York: Vintage Books, 1996.

Moi, Toril. *Sexual/Textual Politics*. New York: Routledge, 1985.
Morgan, Jas and Diana Trimble. "The Cocteau Twins: Obscured by Words" *Mondo Magazine* <www.cocteautwins.com> 1999.
Nicolson, Nigel and Joanne Trautmann, eds. *The Letters of Virginia Woolf*. 6 vols. New York and London: Harcourt Brace Jovanovich, 1978.
Rado, Lisa. *The Modern Androgyne Imagination: A Failed Sublime*. Charlottesville: UP of Virginia, 2000.
Schwartz, Beth C. "Thinking Back Through Our Mothers: Virginia Woolf Reads Shakespeare." *ELH* 38 (1991): 721-746.
Scott, Bonnie Kime. "The Word Split its Husk: Woolf's Double Vision of Modernist Language." *Modern Fiction Studies* 34.3 (Autumn 1988): 371-385.
Squier, Susan. "The Politics of City Space in *The Years*: Street Love, Pillar Boxes and Bridges." In *New Feminist Essays on Virginia Woolf*. 216-237. ed. Jane Marcus. Lincoln: University of Nebraska, 1981.
Suciu, Peter. "The Cocteau Twins Interviewed." *AM Archive* Issue 4-2 (October 1993).
Trotman, Nat. "The Burning Between: Androgyny/Photography/Desire." *Women's Studies* 28.4 (1999): 379-403.
Weil, Kari. *Androgyny and the Denial of Difference*. Charlottesville: UP of Virginia, 1992.
Woolf, Virginia. *A Room of One's Own*. 1929. foreword Mary Gordon. NY: Harcourt Brace [Harvest], 1989.
——. *Between the Acts*. 1941. NY: Harcourt Brace [Harvest], 1969.
——. *Jacob's Room* and *The Waves*. 1922 and 1931. NY: Harcourt Brace [Harvest], 1959.
——. *Mrs. Dalloway*. 1928. foreword Maureen Howard. NY: Harcourt Brace [Harvest], 1981.
——. *Moments of Being: Unpublished Autobiographical Writings*. ed. and intro. Jeanne Schulkind. Sussex: The University Press, 1976.
——. *Orlando*. 1927. NY: Harcourt Brace [Harvest], 2000.
——. "Professions for Women." 1931. In *The Pargiters*. ed. Mitchell A. Leaska, 1978.
——. *The Voyage Out*. 1920. NY: Harcourt Brace [Harvest], 1978.
——. *To the Lighthouse*. 1927. Foreword by Eudora Welty. NY: Harcourt Brace [Harvest], 1981.
——. "Women and Fiction." 1929. *The Forum* rpt. *Granite and Rainbow*.
Wyatt, Jean. "Avoiding self-definition: In defense of women's right to merge (Julia Kristeva and *Mrs Dalloway*)." *Women's Studies* 13 (1986):115-126.

Guide to Library Special Collections
This guide updates the information in volume 7.

Name of Collection: The Beinecke Rare Book and Manuscript Library

Contact: Vincent Giroud, Curator of Modern Books and Manuscripts
Patricia Willis, Curator of American Literature

Address: Yale University Library
P.O. Box 208240
New Haven, CT 06520-8240

Hours: Mon.-Fri. 8:30AM-5PM

Access Requirements: Register at the circulation desk on each visit.

Holdings Relevant To Woolf: General Collection includes autograph manuscript of "Notes on Oliver Goldsmith." Comments on Edward Gibbon, William Beckford Collection. Letters from Virginia Woolf in the Bryher Papers, the Louise Morgan and Otto Theis Papers, and the Rebecca West Papers. Related material: 41 letters from Vita Sackville-West to Violet Trefusis; files relating to Robert Manson Myers's *From Beowulf to Virginia Woolf* in the Edmond Pauker Papers.

Yale Collection of American Literature includes typewritten manuscripts of "The Art of Walter Sickert," "Augustine Birrell," "Aurora Leigh," "How Should One Read a Book?" "Letter to a Young Poet," "The Novels of Turgenev," "Street Haunting." Dial/Scofield Thayer Papers: manuscripts of "The Lives of the Obscure," "Miss Ormerod," and "Mrs. Dalloway in Bond Street." Letters from Virginia Woolf in the William Rose Benet Papers, the Benet Family Correspondence, the Henry Seidel Canby Papers, the Seward Collins Papers, the Dial/Scofield Thayer Papers, and the *Yale Review* archive. Material relating to translations of Woolf in the Thornton Wilder papers. Related material: Clive Bell, "Virginia Woolf" (Dial/Scofield Thayer Papers); 43 letters from Leonard Woolf to Helen McAfee (*Yale Review*); 11 letters from Leonard Woolf to Gertrude Stein.

Name of Collection: The Henry W. and Albert A. Berg Collection of English and American Literature

Contact: Isaac Gewirtz, Curator

Address: New York Public Library, Room 320
Fifth Avenue & 42nd Street
New York, NY 10018

Telephone: 212-930-0802
Fax: 212-930-0079
E-mail: igewirtz@nypl.org

Hours: Tues./Wed. 11AM -5:45PM
Thurs.-Sat. 10AM-5:45PM
Closed Sun., Mon. and legal holidays

Access Requirements: Apply for card of admission at Office of Special Collections, Room 316. Traceable identification required. Undergraduates working on honors theses need letter from faculty advisor.

Restrictions: Virginia Woolf's MSS are now made available on microfilm. N.B. *All the Berg's Woolf MSS are on microfilm published by Research Publications and available at many research libraries.*

Holdings Relevant To Woolf: Manuscripts of *Between the Acts, Flush, Jacob's Room, Mrs. Dalloway* (notes and fragments), *Night and Day, To the Lighthouse, The Voyage Out, The Waves, The Years*; 12 notebooks of articles, essays, fiction and reviews, 1924-1940; 36 volumes of diaries; 26 volumes of reading notes; correspon-

GUIDE TO SPECIAL COLLECTIONS 201

dence with Vanessa Bell, Ethel Smyth, Vita Sackville-West and others. Su Hua Ling Chen's Bloomsbury correspondence.

Name of Collection:	The British Library Manuscript Collections
Contact:	Manuscripts Enquiries
Address:	96 Euston Road London NW1 2DB England
Telephone:	0207-412-7513
Fax:	0207-412-7745
E-mail:	mss@bl.uk
Hours:	Present Hours: Mon 10:00-5:00PM Tue-Sat: 9:30-5:00PM
Access Requirements:	British Library Reader Pass (signed I.D. required and usually proof of post-graduate academic status, or other demonstrable need to use the collections—see www.bl.uk). In addition, access to most literary autograph material only available with letter of recommendation.
Restrictions:	Paper Copies, Microfilms, and Photography of selected items available upon receipt of written authorization for photo duplication from the copyright holder.
Holdings Relevant To Woolf:	Diaries 1930-1931 (microfilm); Mrs. Dalloway and other writings (1923-1925) three volumes; letter from Leonard Woolf to H. G. Wells (1941); two letters from Virginia Woolf and three letters from Leonard Woolf to John Lehmann (1941); letter written on behalf of Leonard Woolf to S. S. Koteliansky (1946); notebook in Italian kept by Virginia Woolf;

GUIDE TO SPECIAL COLLECTIONS 202

notebook of Virginia Stephen (1906-1909); A sketch of the past revised ts (1940); letters from Virginia Woolf in the correspondence files of Lytton and James Strachey; letter from Virginia Woolf to Mildred Massingberd; letter from Virginia Woolf to Harriet Shaw Weaver (1918); letters from Virginia Woolf to S. S. Koteliansky (1923-27); letter from Virginia Woolf to Frances Cornford (1929); letter from Virginia Woolf to Ernest Rhys (1930); correspondence of Virginia Woolf in the Society of Authors archive (1934-37); letter and postcard from Virginia Woolf to Bernard Shaw (1940); three letters (suicide notes) from Virginia Woolf (1941); two letters from Virginia Woolf and three from Leonard Woolf to John Lehmann (1941).

Collection of RPs ("reserved photo copies"–copies of manuscrips exported, some subject to restrictions).

Recent Acquisitions: "Hyde Park Gate News" 1891-92, 1895 (add. MSS 70725, 70726). Letters of Virginia and Leonard Woolf to Lady Aberconway, 1927-1941. Letter from Virginia Woolf to Frances Cornford.

Name of Collection: Harry Ransom Humanities Research Center

Contact: Research Librarian

Address: The University of Texas at Austin
P.O. Box 7219
Austin, TX 78713-7219

Telephone: 512-471-9119
Fax: 512-471-2899
E-mail: reference@hrc.utexas.edu

Hours: Mon.-Fri. 9AM-5PM
Sat. 9AM-NOON

GUIDE TO SPECIAL COLLECTIONS 203

Closed holidays; intersession Saturdays; one week each in late May and late August.

Access Requirements: Completed manuscript reader's application; current photo identification.

Restrictions: Photocopies of selected items available upon receipt of written authorization for photoduplication from the copyright holder.

Holdings Relevant To Woolf: The manuscript collection includes the typed manuscript with autograph revisions of *Kew Gardens,* and the typed manuscript and autograph revisions of "Thoughts on Peace in an Air Raid." The Center holds 571 of Woolf's letters, including correspondence to Elizabeth Bowen, Lady Ottoline Morrell, Mary Hutchinson, William Plomer, Hugh Walpole and others. Further mss. relating to Virginia Woolf include letters to her from T. S. Eliot and reviews of her work. A substantial collection of the first British and American editions of Woolf's published works, as well as 130 volumes from Leonard and Virginia Woolf's library and a collection of books published by the Hogarth Press, is also housed. An art collection holds a landscape painting of Virginia's garden and a series of Cockney cartoons in a sketch book, signed "V.W." The center also has extensive holdings of materials related to Leonard Woolf, Ottoline Morrell, Mary Hutchinson, Lytton Strachey, Dora Carrington, E. M. Forster, Clive Bell, Roger Fry, Vanessa Bell, Bertrand Russell, Elizabeth Bowen, William Plomer, Stephen Spender and Hugh Walpole.

Name of Collection: King's College Archive Centre

Contact: Rosalind Moad, Archivist

Address:	King's College Cambridge CB2 1ST
Telephone: Fax: E-mail:	01223-331444 01223-331891 archivist@kings.cam.ac.uk
Hours:	Mon.-Fri. 9:30AM-12:30PM and 1:30PM-5:15PM. *Closed during public holidays and the College's annual periods of closure.*
Access Requirements:	Proof of ID, letter of introduction, appointment in advance.
Holdings Relevant To Woolf:	Woolf MSS and letters: Minute book, written up by Clive Bell, of the meetings of a play-reading society, with cast lists and comments on performances by CB. Dec. 1907-Jan. 1909, Oct. 1914-Feb. 1915. Players included variously Clive & Vanessa Bell, Roger & Margery Fry, Duncan Grant, Walter Lamb, Molly MacCarthy, Adrian & Virginia Stephen, Saxon Sydney-Turner. *Freshwater, A Comedy*–photocopy of editorial typescript prepared from the MSS at Sussex University and Monk's House; photcopy of covering letter from the publisher to "Robert Silvers," 1.29.1976. Papers relating to the Virginia Woolf Centenary Conference held at Fitzwilliam College, Cambridge, 9.20-22.1982. TS with corrections of "Nurse Lugton's Curtain." Typed transcript of R. Fry's memoir of his schooldays. Correspondence with Clive Bell, Julian Bell, Vanessa Bell, Richard Braithwaite, Rupert Brooke, Mrs. Brooke, Katharine Cox, Julian Fry, Roger Fry, John Davy Hayward, J. M. Keynes, Lydia Keynes, Rosamond Lehmann, Charles Mauron, Raymond Mortimer, G. H. W. Rylands, J. T. Sheppard, W. J. H. Sprott, Thoby Stephen, Madge Vaughan. Woolf-related archival collections held: Charleston Papers; Rupert Brooke Papers; E. M. Forster Papers; Roger Fry

GUIDE TO SPECIAL COLLECTIONS 205

	Papers; J. M. Keynes Papers; J. T. Sheppard Papers; W. J. H. Sprott Papers. Various works of art by Vanessa Bell, Duncan Grant, and Roger Fry, held in various locations around King's College. Access via Domus Bursar's secretary.
Recent Acquisitions:	Roger Fry Papers: sketchbooks, 1880s-1920s. The papers of George Humphrey Wolferstan ('Dadie') Rylands (1902-99).
Name of Collection:	The Lilly Library
Contact:	Breon Mitchell, Director
Address:	The Lilly Library, Indiana University 1200 East Seventh Street Bloomington, IN 47405-5500
Telephone:	812-855-3143
Fax:	812-855-3143
E-mail:	liblilly@indiana.edu, mitchell@indiana.edu
Hours:	M-F 9-6; Sat. 9-1; Closed Sundays and Major Holidays
Access Requirements:	Valid photo-identification; brief registration procedure.
Restrictions:	Closed stacks; material use confined to reading room; wheelchair accessible reading room and exhibitions (but no wheelchair-accessible restroom)
Holdings Relevant to Woolf:	Corrected page proofs for the British edition of *Mrs Dalloway*; letters to Woolf from Desmond and Mary (Molly) MacCarthy; 77 letters (published in *Letters*) from Woolf to correspondents including Donald Clifford Brace, Robert Gathorne-Hardy, Barbara (Strachey) Halpern, Richard Arthur Warren Hughes, Desmond MacCarthy and Molly MacCarthy; "Preliminary Scheme for the formation of a

Partnership between Mr Leonard Sidney Woolf and Mr John Lehmann to take over The Hogarth Press" (includes contract signed by Lehmann, LW, and VW, and receipt for Lehmann's payment to VW to purchase VW's share in the Hogarth Press); photographs of VW, LW, Lytton Strachey, Strachey family, Roger Fry, and Vanessa Bell (Hannah Whitall Smith mss.); (Richard) Kennedy mss. (four hand-colored lithographs of VW: artist's proofs for RK's portfolio, VIRGINIA WOOLF: "AS I KNEW HER"; Sackville-West, V. mss. (10,529 items: includes the correspondence of Vita Sackville-West, and Harold Nicolson); MacCarthy mss. (ca. 10,000 items: papers of Desmond and Molly MacCarthy); correspondence between LW and Mary Gaither regarding publication of *A Checklist of the Hogarth Press* (1976, repr. 1986); Todd Avery, *Close and Affectionate Friends: Desmond and Molly MacCarthy and the Bloomsbury Group* (The Lilly Library / Indiana University Libraries, 1999).

Name of Collection: Archives and Manuscripts, University of Maryland, College Park, Libraries

Contact: Beth Alvarez, Curator of Literary Manuscripts

Address: University of Maryland Libraries
College Park, MD 20742

Telephone: 310-405-9298
E-mail: ra60@umail.umd.edu
Hours: Mon.-Fri. 10AM-5PM, Sat. Noon-5PM.

Access Requirements: Photo ID.

Holdings Relevant to Woolf: Papers of Hope Mirrlees contain five autograph letters and postcards (1919-28) from Virginia Woolf to Mirrlees. Also in the collection are 113 letters from

GUIDE TO SPECIAL COLLECTIONS 207

T. S. Eliot to Mirrlees, and three letters from Lady Ottoline Morrell to Mirrlees.

Name of Collection: Monks House Papers/Leonard Woolf Papers/Charleston Papers/Nicolson Papers

Contact: Dorothy Sheridan, Head of Special Collections

Address: University of Sussex Library
Brighton
Sussex BN1 9QL
England

Telephone: 01273-678157
Fax: 01273-678441
E-mail: Library.Specialcoll@sussex.ac.uk

Hours: By appointment

Access Requirements: Letter, to be received *before* visiting. Photocopying strictly controlled.

Holdings Relevant to Woolf: The University of Sussex holds two large archives relating to Leonard and Virginia Woolf: The Monks House Papers, primarily correspondence and MSS of Virginia Woolf, including the three scrapbooks relating to *Three Guineas*; and The Leonard Woolf Papers, primarily correspondence and other papers of Leonard Woolf. (Monks House Papers are available on microfilm in many research libraries.) The Charleston Papers consist in the main of letters written to or by Clive and Vanessa Bell and Duncan Grant which had accumulated in their home; the library houses Quentin Bell's photocopied set. Also included are c. 900 letters from Maria Jackson to Julia and Leslie Stephen (Charleston Papers Ad. 1); letters from Roger Fry, Maynard Keynes, Lytton Stachey, Virginia Woolf, Vita Sackville-West, E. M. Forster, T. S. Eliot, Frances Partridge and others.

The Nicolson Papers complement these three Sussex archives relating to the Bloomsbury Group, and consist of Nigel Nicolson's correspondence relating to his editorial work as principal editor of the six-volume *Letters of Virginia Woolf*, published between 1975 and 1980.

The Bell Papers. A. O. Bell's correspondence relating to her editorial work on Virginia Woolf's Diaries. A parallel collection to Nicolson Papers.

Name of Collection: Archives & Manuscripts

Contact: Michael Bott, The Archivist

Address: The University of Reading, The Library,
Whiteknights
P.O. Box 223
Reading RG6 6AE
England

Telephone: 0118-931-8776
Fax: 0118-931-6636
E-mail: g.m.c.bott@reading.ac.uk

Access Requirements: Appointment needed to consult material. Permission required to consult or copy material in the Hogarth Press and Chatto & Windus collections from Random House, 20 Vauxhall Bridge Road, London SW1V 2SA, UK.

Holdings Relevant to Woolf: Hogarth Press (MS2750): editorial and production correspondence relating to publications of the Press including Woolf's own titles. Production ledgers 1920s-1950s. Correspondence between Leonard Woolf and Stanley Unwin about progress with his collected edition of the works of Freud.

Chatto & Windus (MS2444): small number of letters 1915-25; 1929-31.
George Bell & Sons (MS1640): 5 letters from Leonard Woolf 1930-66.
Routledge (MS1489): Reader's report by Leonard Woolf on George Padmore's "Britannia rules the blacks" (1935); "How Britain rules Africa."
Megroz (MS1979/68): 2 letters from LW, 1926.
Allen & Unwin (MS3282): Correspondence with LW 1923-24; 1939-40; 1943; 1946; 1950-51, including letters concerning a reprint of *Empire and Commerce in Africa*, and concerning ill-founded rumors about the Hogarth press.

Name of Collection: Frances Hooper Collection of Virginia Woolf Books and Manuscripts/Elizabeth Power Richardson Bloomsbury Iconography Collection.

Contact: Karen V. Kukil, Associate Curator of Rare Books

Address: Mortimer Rare Book Room
William Allan Neilson Library
Smith College
Northampton, MA 01063

Telephone: 413-585-2906
Fax: 413-585-4486
E-mail: kkukil@smith.edu

Hours: Mon.-Fri. 9AM-5PM

Access Requirements: Appointment to be made with the Curator.

Holdings Relevant to Woolf: The Hooper Collection emphasizes Woolf as an essayist but also includes many Hogarth Press first editions, limited editions of Woolf's works, and translations. The collection includes page proofs of *Orlando*, *To the Lighthouse*, and *The Common*

Reader, corrected by Woolf for the first American editions, a proof copy of *The Waves* that Woolf inscribed to Hugh Walpole, and the proof copies of *The Years* and of *Flush*. The Collection also has one of the deluxe editions of *Orlando* that was printed on green paper. Other items include twenty-two pages of reading notes from 1926, three pages of notes on D. H. Lawrence's *Sons and Lovers*, thirty-three pages of notes for *Roger Fry*, a six-page ms. "As to criticism," a five-page ms. of "The Searchlight," and a fourteen-page ms. of "The Patron and The Crocus." The Hooper Collection also owns 140 letters between Woolf and Lytton Strachey as well as other correspondence, including a 13 February [1921] letter to Katherine Mansfield and ten letters to Mela and Robert Spira.

The Richardson Collection is a working collection of books and materials used by Richardson in preparing her *Bloomsbury Iconography*. It includes Leslie Stephen's photograph album, ninety-eight original exhibition catalogs dating back to 1929, clippings and photcopies of such items as reviews of early Woolf works, and Bloomsbury material from British *Vogue* of the 1920s. The Collection also has three preliminary pencil drawings by Vanessa Bell for *Flush*.

The Mortimer Rare Book Room also owns Woolf's 1916 Italian ms. notebook and her corrected typescripts of "Reviewing" and "The Searchlight." In addition, there is a 1923 photograph of Woolf at Garsington. Original cover designs for Hogarth Press publications include *The Common Reader*, *On Being Ill*, and *Duncan Grant*. The Mortimer Rare Book Room also has a Sylvia Plath Collection that includes eight of Woolf's books from Plath's library, several of which are underlined and annotated, as well as Plath's notes from her undergraduate

English 211 class at Smith (1951-2) in which she studied *To the Lighthouse*.

Name of Collection:	Woolf/Hogarth Press/Bloomsbury
Contact:	Robert C. Brandeis
Address:	Victoria University Library 71 Queens Park Crescent E. Toronto M5S 1K7 Ontario Canada
Hours:	Mon.-Fri. 9AM-5PM
Access Requirements:	Prior notification; identification.
Restrictions:	Limited photocopying.
Holdings Relevant to Woolf:	This collection, the most comprehensive of its kind in Canada, contains all the work of Virginia and Leonard Woolf in various editions, issues, variants and translations; all the books hand printed by Leonard and Virginia Woolf at the Hogarth Press, including many variant issues and bindings, association copies and page proofs; a nearly comprehensive collection of Hogarth Press machine printed books to 1946 (the year Leonard Woolf and the Press joined Chatto & Windus) including presentation copies, signed limited editions, page proofs, variants as well as substantial amounts of ephemera. The collection is also very strong in Bloomsbury art, especially the decorative arts, and contains important examples of Omega Workshops publications and exhibition catalogues. Vanessa Bell correspondence/MSS; Leonard Woolf correspondence; Ritchie family materials and correspondence re: Anne Thackeray Ritchie/Stephen family. Vanessa

Bell dustwrapper designs for Woolf novels; Quentin Bell correspondence; S. P. Rosenbaum mss. 97 additional items: Ephemera Collection.

Recent Acquisitions: Bronze bust of Lytton Strachey by Stephen Tomlin (1901-37). A companion piece to Tomlin's bronze of Virginia Woolf already in the collection. More than 100 additional items including translations of Virginia Woolf's work.

Name of Collection: Library of Leonard and Virginia Woolf (Washington S U)

Contact: Laila Miletic-Vejzovic, Head
Manuscripts, Archives and Special Collections

Address: Washington State University Libraries
Pullman, WA 99164-5610

E-mail: www.wsulibs.wsu.edu/holland/masc/masc.htm

Hours: Mon.-Fri. 8:30AM-5PM

Access Requirements: Letter stating nature of research preferred; student or other identification.

Restrictions: Materials must be used in the MASC area under supervision. Photocopying or photographing is permitted only when it will not harm the materials and is permitted by copyright.

Holdings Relevant to Woolf: WSU has the Woolfs' basic working library including many works which belonged to Virginia's father, Sir Leslie Stephen, and other family members. Over 800 titles came from their Sussex home, Monks House, including some works bought at auction soon after Leonard Woolf died in 1969. Later additions include: 1,875 titles from his house in Victoria Square, London; 400 titles from his nephew Cecil Woolf; and over 60 titles from Quentin and Anne

Olivier Bell. WSU has been actively collecting: all works in all editions by Virginia; all titles by Leonard; works published by the Woolfs at the Hogarth Press through 1946; books by their friends and associates, especcially those by Bloomsbury authors and about Bloomsbury artists; relevant correspondence and original works of art. Original artwork by Vanessa Bell; scattered letters by Vanessa Bell, E. M. Forster, Roger Fry, Leslie Stephen, Lytton Strachey, and Leonard Woolf. Original artwork by Richard Kennedy for illustrations in his book *A Boy at the Hogarth Press*; scattered letters by Roger Fry, Leslie Stephen, Ethel Smyth, and Leonard Woolf.

Virginia Woolf's initialed copy of *Cornishiana*; Leonard Woolf's annotated copy of *An Anatomy of Poetry* by A. William-Ellis; Leslie Stephen's copy of *Lapsus Calami and Other Verses*, inscribed by James Kenneth Stephen. Several letters from Virginia Woolf, including two written in 1939 to Ronald Heffer, and a letter to Edward McKnight Kauffer. New in the Hogarth Press Collection are a copy of E. M. Forster's *Anonymity, an Enquiry*, bound in cream paper boards, and what Woolmer calls the third label state of Forster's *The Story of the Siren*.

Name of Collection: Yale Center for British Art

Contact: Elisabeth Fairman, Associate Curator for Rare Books

Address: 1080 Chapel Street
P.O. Box 208280
New Haven, CT 06520-8280

Telephone: 203-432-2814
Fax: 203-432-9695

E-mail:	elisabeth.fairman@yale.edu
Hours:	Tues.-Fri. 10AM-4:30PM
Access Requirements:	Permission needed in order to reproduce.
Holdings Relevant to Woolf:	Rare Books Department: 94 letters from Vanessa Bell and Duncan Grant to Sir Kenneth Clark. Prints & Drawings Department: 2 designs by Vanessa Bell and 2 studies by Duncan Grant. Paintings Department: 1 painting by Vanessa Bell, 2 by Duncan Grant (including a portrait of Vanessa Bell).

Reviews

Outside Modernism: In Pursuit of the English Novel, 1900-30.
Lynne Hapgood and Nancy L. Paxton, Eds.
(London: Macmillan Press, 2000) xii + 223 pp.
Katherine Mansfield & Virginia Woolf: A Public of Two
Angela Smith (Oxford: Clarendon Press, 1999) ix + 230 pp.

Both *Outside Modernism: In Pursuit of the English Novel, 1900-30* and *Katherine Mansfield & Virginia Woolf: A Public of Two* focus on issues of inclusion and exclusion, on being inside or outside certain recognized, and likely all too inflexible, boundaries. Hapgood and Paxton's collection of eleven essays considers, as their title suggests, a number of "non-modernist" English novelists and their texts, analyzing their relationships to literary modernism and, ultimately, to modernity itself. The essayists either contest the positioning of these authors and works as "outsiders" when it comes to the modernist project or, in rarer instances, celebrate such a placement. Smith's work, on the other hand, assumes her central subjects, Virginia Woolf and Katherine Mansfield, to be in the thick of the modernist movement, securely on the inside, even as they themselves existed as "liminars" (11), each a resident of an "in-between zone" (13). In their existence as "threshold people" (Turner 95) and in their creation of worlds and characters that embodied such an existence, Smith postulates that Woolf and Mansfield were uncannily linked (a "queer sense of being 'like'" [*D2* 45] was Woolf's own phrase) in life experiences and in creative approach.

The "outsiders" of *Outside Modernism: In Pursuit of the English Novel, 1900-1930* are generally writers termed "realists," or, in the vocabulary of Virginia Woolf in "Mr. Bennett and Mrs. Brown," "Edwardians" (95), ones whose "business is not our business," whose "conventions are ruin," whose "tools are death" (*CDB* 110). Throughout *Outside Modernism*, Virginia Woolf garners considerable attention not only as an originator of modernist thought but also as one whose dismissal of realism in art altered the vision of how to express modernity. Hapgood, Paxton and their fellow essayists follow many feminists, postmodernists and others who have variously sought to examine the concept of "high modernism," its canon, its vocabulary, its critical stances and political implications, its movers and "shapers." However, they claim as their own particular goal the "rais[ing] [of] provocative questions about the effects of overly zealous periodization" (4) and about what they see as an unnecessary resort to hegemony in defining the modernist period. Nancy L. Paxton, in the chapter entitled "Eclipsed by Modernism," calls also for a recognition of the nationalism "that continues to shape the research practices and critical assumptions of many students and scholars of modernism, especially at a time when we rely more upon electronic data bases that are nationally, and often quite exclusively, organized" (7).

All the essayists represented in this collection set out to reconsider a number of "non-modernist" English novels of the representative period "which have been assigned to a space outside modernism, and to interrogate the cultural work performed by prevailing definitions and critical methodologies inherited from modernism" (vii). Wide-ranging studies, from wide-ranging critical perspectives and arranged in sections labeled History/Time, Gender/Sexuality, and Geography/Space, examine over twenty literary texts, from those of Frederic Manning and Radclyffe Hall to those of John Galsworthy and Maud Diver. Each critic strives to de-stabilize the modernist/realist hierarchy and to recognize those who, while utilizing the realist form, also "struggled to set a new literary agenda and, in doing so, found themselves working at the interface of literary modes" (ix).

Ultimately, the Hapgood/Paxton text serves to spotlight both the enormous diversity of the so-called "modernist" period, a diversity often belied by its apparent roots in Victorian formalism, and the highly revolutionary nature of early twentieth-century realism. In "Transforming the Victorian" Lynne Hapgood, for example, seeks to disrupt the reading of Victorian/Edwardian/Georgian or traditional/modern as unquestioningly linear or progressive. Such a reading, Hapgood insists, delimits the work *and* the politics of the period; marginalizes novels outside the Jamesian mode, such as socialist novels like William Morris's *News from Nowhere*; devalues or ignores the many transformations and the rich literary diversifications always underway. She insists that modernism and the modern need not and should not be unequivocally "synonymous" and argues that "the way is open to consider the Victorian realist tradition as a site of diversity and continual change" (27).

John Lucas's closing essay, "From Realism to Radicalism: Sylvia Townsend Warner, Patrick Hamilton and Henry Green in the 1920's," focuses on realism as a revolutionary technique. In this analysis, Lucas closely scrutinizes Green's *Blindness*, Townsend Warner's *Lolly Willowes* and Hamilton's *Craven House*, all published in 1926, to display not so much their conventional form as their "radical inventiveness" (204). All these seemingly realistic novels, Lucas contends, ultimately exploit and subvert the techniques of realism to offer a variety of strongly formulated social and political challenges. All move through disrupted and surprisingly uncontained narrative to offer "radical readings of post-war society" (221).

Aside from its overriding premises, a major strength of *Outside Modernism* as a whole lies in its useful and enriching readings of many lesser known texts. John Rignall's "Continuity and Rupture in English Novels of the First World War: Frederic Manning and R.H. Mottram," for example, argues that these authors' writings explode the modernists' view of World War I as an entirely pivotal and disruptive moment in history. And further, through his examination of these writings, Rignall seeks to explode the modernist myth that the war experience was "ultimately incommunicable" (47). He asks the reader to question "how far this myth corresponded to historical reality" (44). He goes on to state that the "war created fears, or hopes, of revolution but brought about few radical changes, and the insistence on rupture masks continuities of class and custom, of economic and social conditions, and of artistic and literary conventions which need to be recognized" (44). Examining Manning's and Mottram's respective war novels, *The Spanish Farm Trilogy* (1924-6, 1927) and *The Middle Parts of Fortune* (1929), Rignall posits them as examples of both continuity and rupture in narrative practice *and* life as a result of the Great War. "The unspeakable rupture," according to this critic, "is contained within the bounds of formal convention" (47). However, despite such conventions, he maintains that the novels do not end conventionally, therefore that within their realism lies a flexibility that flirts with and anticipates modernist practices.

In another interesting example, "G.K. Chesterton and the Terrorist God outside Modernism," Robert L. Caserio takes Chesterton's *The Man Who Was Thursday* (1908) and reads the work both as an example of what he terms "double-writing" (66) and of "terrorism." In doing so, he deconstructs what might be considered a traditional or realistic approach to a narrative by an apparently conservative author and claims for the work the ambiguity characteristic of modernism. In *The Man Who Was Thursday*, Caserio argues, Chesterton "uses uncertainty to gain certainty" (76) and places his law-abiding protagonist Gabriel Syme clearly within, not outside of, the "terrorist-centred tradition" (77) as embodied in the character of anarchist and modernist, Lucian Gregory.

William Greenslade, in "'Pan' and the Open Road: Critical Paganism in R. L. Stevenson, K. Grahame, E. Thomas and E. M. Forster," likewise relates how seemingly realistic literary texts respond to ongoing cultural debates and questions by harboring revolutionary attitudes. Greenslade argues that Stevenson, Grahame, Thomas and Forster each used contemporary "paganist" philosophy in their works as acts of rebellion against "the modernizing of Britain" (145). They did so, he asserts, amidst a "particular symbolic geography which was far from nostalgic" (145) and quite "out of centre" (153).

Chapters that follow, "Engendering Modernism: The Vernacular Modernism of Radclyffe Hall," by Richard Dellamora, and "Writing Around Modernism:

May Sinclair and Rebecca West," by Lyn Pickett, likewise re-evaluate the apparent conservatisms of their respective writer subjects, here females, only to reveal them as highly resistant to any easy appropriation. In comparing "Miss Ogilvy Finds Herself" to *The Well of Loneliness*, Dellamora uncovers the radicalism embedded in Hall's "realism." He postulates that Hall's apparent acceptance of Havelock Ellis's "third sex" theory in *The Well of Loneliness* actually "predicts the end of the theory of sexual inversion upon which it is modelled" (100). The work, he claims, registers "the approaching end of the oppressive institutions of domestic and social dominance whose traces characterize third-sex theory" (100) by looking both backward and forward to times when alternate life styles were/are possible. Pykett, similarly, argues that both Sinclair and West produced narratives linked with the New Woman novels that were so rife not only with "female self-sacrifice" (115) but also with mysticism and the richness of visionary or intuitive experience. Hence, they lay far afield from the entirely "realistic" mode to which they were generally relegated. In order to arrive at such a conclusion and to fully consider the modernist period writing of West and Sinclair, however, Pykett declares that it is necessary both to expand existing definitions of modernism and "to disrupt conventional literary periodization" (109).

Other substantial chapters complete this collection. In "Reconsidering Colonial Romance: Maud Diver and the 'Ethnographic Real,'" Nancy L. Paxton compares Maud Diver's *Lilamani: A Study of Possibilities* (1910) and the three subsequent novels of this series with E. M. Forster's *A Passage to India*. She suggests that Diver's utilization of the "ethnographic real" and her depiction of a cross-cultural romance counters the uneasiness of the modernists in approaching or dealing with the colonized, especially in India. Paxton sees Diver's work as revolutionary and "modernizing," despite its upholding of certain existing class and gender hierarchies. Diver, unlike Forster and others, presents the Rajput widow Lilamani not as an English New Woman but rather as her "superior alternative" (188) *and* as the appropriate partner for her English husband, a sensitive artist. "*Lilamani* insists that class identity has the power to override the racial differences that otherwise would separate the colonizing British from elite, cultured, educated, upper class Indians, and especially from the reputedly more 'martial races' of Northern India" (189-90).

Two essays in this collection run a slightly different course. Ann Ardis's essay, "Delimiting Modernism and the Literary Field: D. H. Lawrence and *The Lost Girl*," differs from previous articles by singling out a text from amongst an admittedly high modernist's other works and by revealing how this anomalous "realistic" novel directly engages in a debate about modernism and modern aesthetics. She suggests that Lawrence's often neglected *The Lost Girl* represents his own tension over the rift between high and low modernism, between high and low culture. Lawrence does this, she writes, by presenting in *The Lost Girl* the "competition" between "different forms of expressive culture at the turn of the century" (128), namely, between music hall theater, the cinema and, ultimately, literature itself.

Perhaps the most provocative argument of the collection comes with Lynne Hapgood's "The Unwritten Suburb: Defining Spaces in John Galsworthy's *The Man of Property*." In this critique, Hapgood juxtaposes Galsworthy's "realism, in its Victorian guise" (168), and his revisionary "construction of the suburbs" (170). But her argument differs in this way: all other articles ultimately valorize "conventional" views of modernism by seeking to prove that "outsider" works really belong *inside* standard definitions of modernism, that they are ambiguous, disruptive, formally subversive, and intentionally revolutionary. Hapgood, on the other hand, in locating Galsworthy's text in a metaphoric and literal "literary suburb," seems to find the "outside" location a position of potential, power and *evolution*. Galsworthy, out in the suburbs, enhances the geography of modernism without necessarily falling into its abyss. "*The Man of Property* is a strongly political statement about the failure of political imagination to realize a new kind of social organization relocated beyond the city in the new world of the suburbs" (177).

One final caveat, however, must be presented in relation to this rich text. Virginia Woolf, as previously mentioned, gets much of the credit for helping to define modernist thought, especially through her "Mr. Bennett and Mrs. Brown" and a few other texts. But, too often in *Outside Modernism*, terms such as "modernist, "non-modernist", even "realist" are used indiscriminately. While a few authors offer the specific definitions against or with which they work, too many assume their terms to be universally understood. That there are such assumptions, in fact, seems to be an integral and well-taken aspect of the Paxton/Hapgood argument, but in order to work to expand or eliminate questionable concepts, one must at least know what they are. In any case, the undefined terminology weakens and/or risks confusing an otherwise strong argument.

All of this brings us to Angela Smith's *Katherine Mansfield & Virginia Woolf: A Public of Two*, where the accent as to the modernist project falls somewhat differently. Angela Smith does not seek to expand the definitions of modernism nor does she argue, in the main, for her authors' positions in it. Her assumption is that she does not need to do so. Instead, she examines Woolf's and Mansfield's particular "inflection" (vii) of modernism. She insists on her subjects' comparable liminal states, their common experiences of a limbo-world (or worlds) where they remain neither inside nor outside but "betwixt and between" (11). Drawing on, among others, Freud's theories of the uncanny in *Das*

Unheimliche; Kristeva's theories of the semiotic, of the abject and "the foreignness . . . within" (181); and Victor and Edith Turner's cultural studies of ritual, she traces her subjects' affinities in life and in fiction.

In drawing parallels between the two gifted writers, Smith certainly does not enter uncharted waters. Many have gone before her—Smith herself notes the excellent work of Patricia Moran in *Word of Mouth* (1996) and of Nóra Séllei in *Katherine Mansfield and Virginia Woolf: A Personal and Professional Bond* (1996), for example—but she does develop a strong argument for the sources and extent of Woolf and Mansfield's extraordinary state of "*communitas*" (13). She traces especially thoroughly the remarkable similarities in the various personal displacements the two women artists suffered. They are almost breathtaking. Both were the daughters of successful and overbearing fathers, of stressed and often distant mothers. Both, in the middle of large families by birth order, felt like foreigners at home. Both were bisexual and experienced difficult sexual encounters. Both struggled as adults with debilitating illnesses that constantly threatened their artistic productivity. Both married strong male writers who survived them, ultimately editing their works and shaping their literary reputations for generations to come. Both women remained childless, often regretting the fact, but bore remarkably similar attitudes concerning creativity and the writing process. And, above all, both admitted the enormity of the influence that one had upon the other. The jealousy not infrequently expressed by each one for the other can be read, in fact, as an obvious sign of their mutual respect.

Smith does her best work, however, when moving beyond the theoretical and the biographical, where weak transitions in her arguments sometimes lead to redundancies and ponderously long paragraphs (often she goes on for pages without a break), to the analytical. In her fourth chapter she begins at last to relate Mansfield's and Woolf's mutual experiences of the fractured self to specific and complementary texts. In successive chapters, she traces the "sense of echo" (90) between Mansfield's *Prelude* and Woolf's *To the Lighthouse*; examines the early writings of each author and discusses them as rites of passage; looks at the "single day" as presented in *At the Bay* and *Mrs. Dalloway*; reviews the cinematic imagery in "The Daughters of the Late Colonel" and *Jacob's Room* and considers the short stories, Woolf's "An Unwritten Novel" and Mansfield's "The Stranger," as examples of stories in which "a journey becomes the medium for inner exploration" (225), a passage through liminal territory.

While discussing a wide range of Mansfield texts, Smith limits her discussions to Woolf's earlier works, considering them to be the ones most directly influenced by Mansfield, who died of a pulmonary hemorrhage in 1923. (Woolf would continue writing until her death in 1941.) While this assumption seems somewhat regrettable (the "Daughters of the Late Colonel" seems to beg to be read with *The Years*, for instance), Smith's critical readings of the texts she selects are insightful, even if occasionally less cohesive than they might be. Particularly effective and persuasive is Chapter 6, "A Single Day: 'At the Bay' and *Mrs. Dalloway*." Here, Smith brings to bear on the Mansfield and Woolf texts the precepts of Post-Impressionist painting. According to Smith, they—Cézanne, Van Gogh and Gauguin—offered questions, not answers, through their respective canvases, and they did so "partly by eschewing both realism and the emphasis on narrative" (155) that was a characteristic of Victorian art/writing. Mansfield and Woolf, in works such as *At the Bay* and *Mrs. Dalloway*, Smith argues, "framed" their works in a similar way. Like Post-Impressionist painters, their projects involved "not realism but a heightening of people or objects to give an experience equivalent to the impact made by people or objects in life" (149). According to Smith, who continuously argues her case for Mansfield and Woolf as a "public of two," "[p]aint is applied differently [in their works] from the way in which other modernist novelists use it: it is no accident that on the day that Woolf records in her diary that she has finished *Mrs. Dalloway* she also comments: 'The thought of Katherine Mansfield comes to me . . . '" (192). Smith also duly notes that both Leonard Woolf and John Middleton Murry were involved with the Post-Impressionist Exhibition of 1910, assuring that their wives, even had they *not* had other connections as well, would have been more than conversant with the exhibition, its painters and its ideologies. Nonetheless, that Mansfield's and Woolf's respective works comprise numbers of colorful, bold and "framed" portraits and encompass a physical and psychic landscape more "real" than real cannot be denied.

Overall, in reading *Katherine Mansfield & Virginia Woolf: A Public of Two* and *Outside Modernism: In Pursuit of the English Novel, 1900-30*, a reader cannot help but be awed by the complexity of the "modernist" period and the works and artists that operated both "within" and "without" its apparent parameters. Both critical works convince one that our understandings and delineations of any period can and must be expanded. Linking the Hapgood/Paxton work to Smith's brings to mind Bonnie Kime Scott's provocative diagram of the "Tangled Mesh of Modernists" (10). The artistic framework of the great modernist period is indeed far more elaborate and expansive than we may initially have perceived it to be. Look in dark corners; look beyond boundaries. Such is the mutual message of these timely and useful scholarly studies.

—Susan H. Fox, *California State University, Hayward*

Works Cited

Kristeva, Julia. *Strangers to Ourselves*. Trans. Leon S. Roudiez. London: Harvester Wheatsheaf, 1991.

Scott, Bonnie Kime, Ed. *The Gender of Modernism*. Bloomington: Indiana UP, 1990.

Turner, Victor. *The Ritual Process*. New York: Aldine. De Gruyter, 1995 (1969).

Woolf, Virginia. "Mr. Bennett and Mrs. Brown." *The Captain's Death Bed and Other Essays*. New York: Harcourt Brace Jovanovich, 1978 (1950).

——. *The Diary of Virginia Woolf. Vol. II*. Ed. Anne Olivier Bell, assisted by Andrew McNeillie. London: Harcourt Brace Jovanovich, 1978.

Approaches to Teaching Woolf's To The Lighthouse.
Eds. Beth Rigel Daugherty and Mary Beth Pringle.
(New York: MLA, 2001) 211 pp.

In her now-classic essay, "Lupine Pedagogy: Teaching Woolf to Terrified Students," Annis Pratt[1] described her students' inability to read Virginia Woolf's novels:

> On the first day of a semester-long course I taught on Virginia Woolf for twenty years, I could always sense terror pervading the room, radiating off students' bodies in a wave, and from the back of my mind I could hear strains of "Who's Afraid of Virginia Woolf" to the squealing tune of those nervous little pigs from my childhood. Where did the students' fear come from? (Pratt 91)

Annis Pratt's undergraduates are not unusual. As *Approaches to Teaching Woolf's* To the Lighthouse makes clear, students in many classrooms the country over fear and resent reading the works of Virginia Woolf, repeatedly complaining to their teachers that Woolf is "boring," that "nothing happens," that Woolf's sentences are too long and complicated, and that she doesn't include them in her works. Further, not only do students resist reading Virginia Woolf, many teachers may feel reluctance to teach Woolf's works. For example, Laura Davis probably speaks for others when she says, "Until I approached *To the Lighthouse* with indexing,[2] I was wary of both sharing this novel with a less than enthusiastic audience and of imposing my own views on student readers" (83). If, like those represented in this volume, you are a teacher who seeks useful strategies to meet students' reluctance to read Virginia Woolf's work, you will most likely find in *Approaches to Teaching Woolf's* To the Lighthouse a practical and thought-provoking resource.[3]

In deciding to focus on *To the Lighthouse*, the editors discovered that it was taught in an array of classrooms through divergent methodologies (xii). One of the most helpful features of this book is that the editors have gathered lesson

---

[1] An excellent essay by Annis Pratt is included in this volume.
[2] Indexing is a methodology to empower the reader and to facilitate writing in response to the text.
[3] Before I proceed further, however, I want to acknowledge that in this text my work on *To the Lighthouse*, along with that of others, is viewed as foundational. I do not think this fact has prejudiced me in the book's favor, for it is one of the many strengths of this anthology that it incorporates much more than one point of view.

plans geared to a variety of students in varied classroom settings. Women returning to the classroom after raising families, full-time workers who take no more than two courses per term, students in rural colleges, students on urban campuses, students in seminars in their colleges' Honors Programs, students in large introductory courses in fiction and British fiction are all represented in *Approaches to Teaching Woolf's* To the Lighthouse. Students' concerns, questions, resistance, are addressed by a plethora of pedagogical responses. Clearly the editors are veteran teachers whose primary question is "How can we be useful to students?"

Approaches to Teaching Woolf's To the Lighthouse presents practical methods for using Woolf's novels, essays, memoirs, letters, diaries, and feminist polemics to teach freshmen English, creative writing, Women's Studies, Cultural Studies, New (and old) Historicism, Lesbian Studies, Family Systems theory, autobiography and memoir, Narrative theory, the history of the novel, the History of the British novel, Peace Studies, New Criticism, among others. As one would expect, many of the approaches overlap. For example, many strategies underpinning various methodologies incorporate writing into the reading process. Indexing (Davis), Reading Journals (Neverow), open-ended response sheets (Levenback), undergraduate reports (Bazin), life-writing preparation (Folsom) can be used in numerous methodological approaches. Helping students overcome resistance to what they may perceive as bewildering and impenetrable stylistic devices, some teachers focus on close textual analysis to reveal patterns and help students create meaning (Barrett, Davis). As a way to encourage students' pleasure in hearing Woolf's style, other teachers have students read Woolf's works aloud to one another (Lawrence), and dramatize the texts (Pratt). In other settings, students may lead class discussions (Bazin, Neverow) and share interpretive tasks in small groups (Pinkerton, Pratt) in order to make the text their own. Numerous teachers contextualize Woolf's works in historical and aesthetic settings (Oxindine, Bazin, Braendlin, Levenback, Hussey, Currier), often through multimedia approaches (Yunis, Bishop). Enhancing Woolf's relevance to personal and community history, some teachers weave Woolf's writings into students' personal histories (Bazin, McVicker), incorporate *To the Lighthouse* into theories explaining family systems (Cobb), and connect *To the Lighthouse* to multicultural examples of memoir (Folsom). These classroom practices can be adapted to diverse settings and methodological approaches, but what they share is an inspiring focus on student centered learning.

The Virginia Woolf who insisted that the common reader must "trespass at once" was more than a great Modernist/Postmodernist stylist. The majority of the essays in this book demonstrate practical ways in which to use Woolf's works to strengthen students' critical awareness and inquiry. How and in what ways is

Woolf to be defined as a feminist theorist and activist, and how might this question structure classroom interaction is a question investigated by, among others, Eileen Barrett, Toni McNaron, Nancy Topping Bazin, Vara Neverow, Marcia M. Folsom, and Mark Hussey. Can Woolf be claimed as a lesbian, and how might students grapple with this question in Woolf's texts, in a college classroom setting, and in their personal lives is a question that informs some of the teaching strategies of Toni McNaron, Eileen Barrett, and Vara Neverow. Students may resist Woolf because they resent what they see as her class and racial privilege. Louise DeSalvo and Patricia Laurence's essays challenge Woolf's texts, acknowledging students' questions about privilege and power and thus modeling methods of interrogating text and cultural context. As Karen Levenback's essay demonstrates, the questions that Woolf's texts raise about war should prove useful to those students whose philosophical backgrounds or economic circumstances may encourage enlisting in the military. Through hands-on experience in the campus print shop, Edward Bishop's students take on the roles of printer and publisher, exploring how the material practice of writing and the money it produced directly affected Woolf's relation to her art.

The editors to the volume specifically requested that contributors focus on practical means of making Woolf accessible to resisting, first time readers of Woolf. Hence, "[r]eaders looking for cutting-edge criticism or radical pedagogies will not find them here" (31). This is at once the volume's great strength and a possible limitation. Ironically, although the preponderance of those included in this volume have published numerous and frequently-cited ground-breaking theoretical essays in Woolf studies, only a few essays (for example, those by Jeanette McVicker, Pamela Caughie, and Mary Pinkerton) demonstrate incorporating advanced theoretical discourse into the classroom. Some of the teachers represented here, in fact, eschew the introduction of theoretical critical analysis, instead using Woolf's diaries, letters, and essays to expand students' interpretive repertoire. The focus on the practical rather than on contemporary literary theory is deliberate. The editors' chosen audience consists of "instructors new to teaching, new to translating critical theory into classroom strategy, or new to teaching this novel, as well as to instructors confronting a wide range of undergraduates reading Woolf for the first time" (xii). For this reason, the text has an extensive bibliography for diverse methodological approaches (6-19), distinguishes between and appraises the various available teaching editions of *To the Lighthouse* (3-6), makes note of teaching tools other than print materials (19-22), and includes helpful introductory essays to each of the pedagogical approaches.

As I read this book, I found myself wishing that all state legislators who hold the purse strings of public universities and trustees at embattled private colleges would be required to read this book (and then have to pass a standardized test on it). In it they would see real concern for students, for here is a book that presents practical lesson plans that facilitate teaching students to think for themselves, as Woolf herself would have wanted.

Adult engagement with the work of challenging students in sustaining and nurturing settings is what this text both demonstrates and encourages. *Approaches to Teaching Woolf's* To the Lighthouse shows teachers helping students build up their skill and knowledge base, increasing students' ability and willingness to ask questions, to work with others in respectful if sometimes heated debate, and to synthesize and generate meaning. Doing so, this text presents more than a range of highly effective classroom management techniques. It inspires teachers and reminds us why we became teachers in the first place—for the joy of the unexpected and the delight in helping others develop a love for learning, inquiry, books, and writers that we so cherish ourselves.

Jane Lilienfeld, *Lincoln University*

Work Cited

Pratt, Annis, "Lupine Pedagogy: Teaching Woolf to Terrified Students."
Virginia Woolf: Themes and Variations. Selected Papers from the Second Annual Conference on Virginia Woolf. Eds. Mark Hussey and Vara Neverow-Turk. New York: Pace UP, 1993. 90-97.

Virginia Woolf: Reading the Renaissance.
Ed., Sally Greene. (Athens: Ohio UP, 1999) 295 pp.

The dust jacket, designed by Inari, of this extraordinarily handsome book, harmonizing with the burgundy hard cover, reproduces Duncan Grant's *Venus and Adonis* (1919) as emblematic of Woolf's "'free translations' of her Renaissance sources" (x). Grant had remarked that his painting was "not in any way an illustration of the subject, but a rhythm which came out of the subject," which was "the so-called Simonetta Vespucci (sometimes called *Cleopatra*) by the early Renaissance artist Piero di Cosimo" (x). The text itself is enhanced by a small illustration serving as a visual epigraph: "Elephant and Castle" (iv), reminding us of the burial site of Shakespeare's sister. Larger relevancies such as the Cornelius Ketel/Federigo Zuccaro "Queen Elizabeth" and "Sabrina Disenchanting the Lady" from *Comus: A Mask with Eight Illustrations by William Blake* as well as parallel images of a Gisèle Freund portrait of Woolf and a seventeenth century portrait of Montaigne reinforce the multifaceted approach the readerly writers take.

Sally Greene rightfully acknowledges that "[i]mportant groundwork" for all the contributors to "the collection was established by Alice Fox in *Virginia Woolf and the Literature of the Renaissance* (Oxford, 1990)" (ix-x). As for the ten essays themselves, as well as Greene's introduction, they are unashamedly documented and generous with acknowledgments, e.g., David McWhirter's thanks to "the anonymous Renaissance scholar-reader for Ohio UP" (261). These essays demonstrate the humility of seasoned scholars who are wise enough to recognize that they stand on the shoulders of giants. Despite Diana E. Henderson's statement that "[t]he scholarship on Woolf has become too compendious for anyone to acknowledge all that is of value or influence" and her assertion that she has cited essays primarily to clarify where her "reading diverges from or complements related essays," she nonetheless provides readers with six pages of notes to a nineteen page essay (155).

Sally Greene's essay, "Michelet, Woolf, and the Idea of the Renaissance," explores the changes in our conception of as well as nomenclature for the "Renaissance," now more appropriately termed "the early modern period." Cogently, Greene explores the multifaceted way Woolf has plundered Michelet, despite his vertigo-inducing style, for ideas as well as images of historic development. Greene's citing of the images of a twentieth-century Renaissance in *Night and Day* through which Katherine Hilbery and Ralph Denham dream by themselves and seek "an ideal of 'communication'" with each other provides a satisfying angle of perception on this novel not only as "a romantic comedy," but as a novel wherein perceptive characters mine the aesthetic past to gain a purchase on their baffling present. Greene's description of Michelet's tombstone—his words "*'L'histoire est une résurrection'* are inscribed . . . above a figure of a female body rising from the mortal male body" (n. 64, 39)—relates to Woolf's metaphorically expressed ideas in A Room of One's Own such as Judith, Shakespeare's sister. As Greene observes, "Like Michelet, Woolf celebrates—with all the accuracy of poetry—the possibility of individual achievement, while holding that genius is the result of "many years of thinking in common, of thinking by the body of the people" (29).

The collection was serendipitously useful to me during the months I prepared this review as when I chose among Nicola Luckhurst's quotes from Montaigne and included his picture as a handout for World Literature I. I also used passages from Anne E. Fernald's essay on the memory palace in an introductory lecture for the early modern period. In another instance, I incorporated Diana E. Henderson's treatment of *Mrs. Dalloway* in a lecture for a colleague's novel course.

Nicola Luckhurst's essay, "To quote my quotation from Montaigne," like Greene's, again treats Montaigne's identification with his work in ways that draw parallels with Woolf's attitudes toward herself as writer. In Luckhurst's words, "a strong corporeal equation of body and book" characterizes the "readerly writing of both Woolf and Montaigne" (46-47). Luckhurst argues convincingly that Virginia Woolf's reading (in contrast with Leonard's "making of him, by conflating text and author, a symbol with which to mark part of a large schematic argument") is "peculiarly modern in its appreciation of Montaigne's dialogic and digressive aesthetic" (42). Luckhurst's delineation of conversational elements in both Montaigne's and Woolf's thought on the essay is masterful in its historical reconstruction (49-52). But Luckhurst goes farther and lays the groundwork for that elusive genre which Woolf claims not to have been written, "that new genre—which itself might look remarkably like an *essai*—women's autobiography" (59).

Anne E. Fernald's essay is particularly useful not only in its acknowledgment of the work of Frances Yates (1966) and Mary Carruthers (1990), but also in its delineation of parallels with Woolf's description of the dome of the Reading Room of the British Library. Fernald argues that Woolf subverts/compares doodles to "the reading room, with its radial symmetry" which "resembles Renaissance memory diagrams and represents a fantasy of an organized and complete mind" (107). Her essay explores memory palaces and national libraries—most aptly the British Museum. Fernald's essay is, in fact, a memorial to the old Library of the British Museum which has been succeeded by the new British Library at St. Pancras.

In "Rough with Rubies: Virginia Woolf and the Virgin Queen," Reginald Abbott presents an engaging exploration of Woolf's use of jewels, particularly rubies, and her various engagements with Queen Elizabeth which are ultimately realized in *Between the Acts* when "these two halves of an icon of female power [woman as ruler and woman as artist] are presented in a complex, but not competitive, proximity to each other as two distinct characters: Mrs. Manresa and Miss LaTrobe" (65). Once again, *Night and Day* figures prominently in the pattern of the essay, in this instance as providing "the first important ruby ring in Woolf's fiction" (70).

In her elegantly argued essay, "Circe Resartus," Kelly Anspaugh explores William Browne of Tavistock's *Circe and Ulysses: The Inner Temple Masque* (1614) in concert with *To the Lighthouse* (1927), citing Beverly Ann Schlack's argument concerning how Woolf had "employed Milton's *Comus* as a hypotext for her first novel, *The Voyage Out*" (161). Anspaugh builds a convincing case for Browne's masque informing "her text on the level of character, imagery, theme—even genre" (163). Indeed, some scholars have argued that Milton's *Comus* "owes a good deal to *Circe and Ulysses*" despite the probability that it was never performed (164). *Circe and Ulysses*, then, was written for "private, fraternal delectation" (165). Browne's Circe is a white magician as his sirens are "creatures . . . transformed into the docile and devoted (literally henlike) handmaidens of Circe, and their song brings . . . everlasting joy" (169). With a bow to Alice Fox, Anspaugh cites Woolf's quoting a modified version of the sirens' song ("Steer, hither steer your winged pines, all beaten Mariners") as Mrs. Ramsay reads haphazardly in an anthology and makes a metaphoric climb through branches of red and white flowers. Moreover, Anspaugh convincingly suggests that the character of Mrs. Ramsay owes a little something to Browne's Circe even as Woolf *"revises"* Browne's "truculent Triton into a sort of guardian angel" in Mr. Carmichael (175). As Circe had been maligned, dating from Homer, so Mrs. Ramsay has been disliked by Mr. Carmichael until he bows to her in tribute while he recites "Luriana, Lurilee." Moreover, Anspaugh credits Woolf for recognizing Browne's "humane (protofeminist?) rehabilitation of the figure of Circe" (188). Within this frame, Browne "would have understood both Mrs. Ramsay and Lily, would have appreciated both the red of the rose and the white of the lily. He would have known it was only a matter of connecting the two, of bringing them into harmony." Anspaugh's brief concluding sentence related to the genre of the masque is as notably well phrased as the other concluding sentences in the collection with its abundance of felicitous endings for its essays: "Then all dance" (188).

Rebecca Laroche discusses the Elizabethan sonnet along with *A Room of One's Own* in "Laura at the Crossroads." Sir Sidney Lee figures prominently in her delineation of the masculinist history of sonnet scholarship until the recent contributions of Rachel Bowlby, Heather Dubrow, Ilona Bell, and Barbara Estrin. Laroche perceives in "*A Room of One's Own*, which reads literary history for silenced female voices . . . a composite figure made up of the female beloved, the woman writer, and the female scholar" (195). Her rewarding essay configures "the freedom of my mind," the commanding phrase of the "immancl'd" Lady of *Comus* which Woolf quotes in her rage at being locked out of the library enclosing Milton's manuscript of "Lycidas."

Lisa Low draws on Milton in "'Listen and save': Woolf's Allusion to *Comus* in Her Revolutionary First Novel" and defends him against his ill-deserved reputation as "the father of modern female doom" by following the clue provided by the poetry of Milton's masque. Arguing that Richard Dalloway's kiss is a pivotal point in the novel reviving and reifying Rachel's [and Woolf's] memories of childhood "sexual molestation" (121), Low credits "a supposedly misogynist Milton" with "less a justification for than a critique of the patriarchy" through the Lady's "unmovably fierce self-reliance and imperturbable calm more typical of Milton's Christ than of his Eve" in her ordeal with Comus, "an evil orgiast" (123, 119). Low overcomes reductive anti-Miltonic readings of "mainline feminist criticism" to suggest that in the "mournful tale of Sabrina she [Woolf] saw a sighting on Milton's part, of a matriarchy to come" (133).

Diane Gillespie's magisterial "Through Woolf's 'I's': Donne and *The Waves*" unites Woolf's notion of the multiplicity of character, including her own, with Donne's poetry and prose to make a convincing delineation of one of her five epigraphs: "I did mean that in some vague way we are the same person, and not separate people. The six characters [in *The Waves*] were supposed to be one" (Woolf to G. L. Dickinson, October 27, 1931). One can connect ideas of multiplicity as well as simultaneity as Gillespie cites Woolf's intention of making the six characters as one in *The Waves* with Anspaugh's quote from Woolf about the merit of reading many books—Woolf writes "six"—at once.

Michael McWhirter's concluding essay, "Woolf, Eliot, and the Elizabethans: The Politics of Modern Nostalgia," differentiates between "Eliot's backward-looking nostalgia for dehistoricized origins" and Woolf's "historicity, [which] by 'thinking differently,' reaches toward an always unconcluded future" (261). Eliot, one soon realizes thanks to McWhirter's examples, has oversimplified the British past though his desire for hierarchy and orthodoxy. The ideas several generations of graduate students absorbed—"dissociation of sensibility," for example—can be read as supporting Eliot's preferences and personal taste. Woolf's respect for varieties of literature, including unpublished writers who may in fact be women, suggests a Renaissance Faire thriving on the Bakhtinian carnivalesque as her posthumously published novel, *Between the Acts*, suggests. McWhirter juxtaposes Eliot's *The Rock*, "a pageant commissioned by the Church of England in 1933 to support a number of church restoration projects" (256), with Woolf's village pageant for *Between the Acts* with its more modest goal of installing electric light in the parish church. He finds that Woolf's depiction of the Rev. G. W. Streatfield echoes "her affectionate dismissals of 'poor old Tom'" (258).

Greene's anthology is a treasury of contemporary scholarship and insight about "the period Woolf loved the best" (208 n. 12). One might go so far as to say that it is a revenant of Judith Shakespeare who has now been given a scholarly dimension if not voice.

—Evelyn Haller, *Doane College*

Virginia Woolf's London. A Guide to Bloomsbury and Beyond.
Jean Moorcroft Wilson
(London and New York: Tauris Parke, 2000) 256 pp.
Virginia Woolf.
Nigel Nicolson (New York: Viking Penguin, 2000) 193 pp.

Jean Moorcroft Wilson brings a Londoner's eye to Virginia Woolf's own London. The reader of Woolf's work already comes to this book with a sense of the importance of place and finds that sense enhanced by Wilson's careful and respectful approach. She underlines Woolf's exuberance about London with a careful nuancing of the meaning and context of specific areas of the city in the light of Woolf's personal and intellectual history.

The first chapter re-introduces the reader to the specifics of places in Virginia's life. The events are familiar; the point of view adds a visual sensation to the events. The Leonard McDermid illustrations of Woolf's homes are perhaps better than photographs would have been since they add time to location. It is lovely to see them without the automobiles and clutter that twenty-first century visitors find. It is also such a pleasure to find images of the less visited or impossible-to-visit sites, among them Little Talland House, Asham House, and the Round House at Lewes.

Wilson puts the Bloomsbury spots in relation to one another, offering a sense of the ease of visiting and maintaining an ongoing conversation. She offers a fair and kind assessment of the Bloomsbury group and friends and colleagues as well as fun-loving sparring partners. She adds insight into the day-to-day neighborhoods, if one may call them that, that Virginia walked and enjoyed so thoroughly. She also, and intentionally, acknowledges a clear sense of class in neighborhoods and areas of London, much of which would be lost on the contemporary visitor; time and gentrification have made the changes from Woolf's time to our own.

Wilson next tackles the London in Woolf's writing and the symbolism it may embrace. She posits that Virginia "divided London mentally into three—the centre, the suburbs, and the slums," with the Richmond suburb quite at the bottom of Woolf's preferred list. Wilson takes specific areas of the city and offers an analysis of what Woolf may have thought of each. Although less than complete, the addition of what areas were like in Woolf's day does add to the reader's insight when returning to the novels. Although that same reader might legitimately disagree with some of Wilson's interpretation, there is mental food aplenty for the tasting. A specific and thought provoking section, for example, involves the explication of place as the basis of unity in the simultaneity of events in *Jacob's Room*.

The heart of this book is the central section which contains seven guided Virginia Woolf walks with easy-on-the-eye maps by Tamson Hickson. They make a straightforward way for the London visitor to walk the streets of London with the work of figuring them out already done. The streets of the Bloomsbury walk will be familiar to Woolf scholars, but the very specific relationships between homes become clearer. The walks based on the novels—a *Mrs. Dalloway* walk, Martin and Sally Pargiter's walk in *The Years*, Ralph Denham's walk in *Night and Day*, Mr. and Mrs. Ambrose's walk in *The Voyage Out*—are quite fun to undertake. Woolf's city walk gives a pleasant organization to the London walker.

The walk which may provide the most unexpected delight, particularly to the repeating visitor, is the Hampstead walk. I would heartily encourage people with a bit more time to try this one. The walk itself is lovely, with the possibility of visiting Hampstead Heath. The climbing, narrow, rambling streets are quite different from inner London and a sense of quiet and calm still pervades the area. The heath itself will give one a whole new sense of what London is.

Apart from the simple joy of the walk, the Woolf reader can become acquainted with a part of London frequented by Virginia but rarely acknowledged in biographies. The home of Margaret Llewelyn Davis and Lillian Harris is here. Janet Case lived nearby. Keats' house is on this walk and the sightseer could augment the trip by reading Virginia's essay about it. "All traffic of life is silenced. The voice of the house is the voice of leaves brushing in the wind; of branches stirring in the garden." And, oh yes, the lavender, for those who love it, thrives at Keats' house. It is well worth taking the book on a trip to London to enjoy the walks or parts of them.

This is a knowledgeable and respectful work, shedding light and delight on Virginia Woolf's London. The few inaccuracies are a product of this American edition being published without an update from the earlier British. But these are not substantive and do not impede either the learning or the enjoyment. The style is eminently readable, with a light touch aimed more for conversation than discourse. That is to its credit and to its salutary accessibility to multiple readerships.

Woolf readers and scholars owe an inestimable debt to Nigel Nicolson for his work with Joanne Trautmann Banks in editing the six volumes of Virginia Woolf's letters. In this book he takes a more personal approach in writing a biography colored by recollection and introspection. This pastiche produces a maddening combination of little known details about Woolf's life and questionable analysis.

It is intriguing, for instance, to consider that Harold Nicolson's *Some People* may be the seed of the genre Woolf used in *Orlando*. Nigel Nicolson suggests that we reread Woolf's review of *Some People* (available as "The New Biography" in the fourth volume of Woolf's *Essays* edited by Andrew McNeillie). And there are convincing passages. "For here he has devised a method of writing about people and about himself as though they were at once real and imaginary," writes Woolf. "*Some People* is not fiction because it has the substance, the reality of truth. It is not biography because it has the freedom, the artistry of truth." The argument is reasonable and it is well worth following the suggestion to reread Woolf's essay.

Nicolson does add some intriguing detail in his biography—imagining Woolf paddling down the Ouse in an inflatable canoe; or considering Orlando as "Vita in Wonderland." On the other hand, Nicolson identifies his own most troublesome point of view. "I am writing the life of a woman for whom I had great affection and whom I much admire. I am obliged to argue against her profoundest convictions on a subject central to her life." And so he spends several pages in a rebuttal of *A Room of One's Own*, and more in one of *Three Guineas*. What is outwardly a biography of Woolf, then, becomes part biography of Virginia and part biography and testament of Nigel. This weakness persists throughout the book.

The way these two volumes handle Virginia's relationship with Ethel Smyth, for instance, illustrates the gulf between their points of view. Nicolson contends that "although Ethel Smyth undoubtedly loved Virginia with a sick passion, Virginia tolerated her . . . as a diversion, and then a burden which she could not easily shake off." Wilson's approach is far differently rooted. Virginia, she says, "found it easier to confide in her than in any other correspondent during this period [the 1930's] and her letters are full of revelations about past experiences."

Though both these books are comparatively short and an easy read, Wilson's adds the most information, particularly to those readers interested by the context of Virginia's life.

—Krystyna Colburn, *University of Massachusetts, Boston*

The Eye's Mind: Literary Modernism and Visual Culture
Karen Jacobs (Ithaca: Cornell UP, 2001) v + 311 pp.

The Eye's Mind will appeal to readers engaged with Woolf and modernism from a wide variety of interests, even though the direct discussion of Woolf is limited to one chapter. Jacobs approaches her analysis of literary modernism *vis a vis* a focus on the shifts taking place in visual relations "as they are represented in American, British and French modernist texts from 1900 to 1955" (2). The multi-discursive context brings psychoanalysis, anthropology, photography and cinema into strategic dialogue with literary production in the period, yielding a multi-layered discussion that reconstellates Woolf not only with Walter Benjamin, but also Henry James, Vladamir Nabokov, Sigmund Freud, Maurice Blanchot, Zora Neale Hurston, Ralph Ellison, and Nathanael West, to name only those writers dealt with extensively in individual chapters. What links them in Jacobs's analysis is "the diminished faith these disparate writers share regarding the capacity of vision to deliver reliable knowledge, as they critique the forms of violence that vision inevitably seems to entail" (3). Jacobs's theoretical framework, indebted to the work of Foucault, draws on a wide range of post-structuralist, feminist, and postcolonial theorists, foregrounding the construction of the gendered, racialized body; it also notes the work of a vast number of literary, visual and cultural scholars, yet its critical sophistication never gets in the way of the reader. This is a lucid, well-researched and documented book that successfully contributes to the critical reimagining of the field of Modernism that has been taking place for the past 20+ years. Having said that, I nevertheless find a key weakness in the book due to the general absence of an *ontological* framing of the politics and metaphorics of vision, which I will articulate at the end of this review.

Taking as its point of departure the role of the first half of the 20th century in deepening and multiplying "lines of fracture in [the] fantasy of the transparent subject"—a fantasy constructed through Descartes's formulation of a disembodied observer as both seer and knower—Jacobs notes the simultaneous "escalating dominance of the image and a growing uneasiness about its penetration and mediation of every sphere of social life." The modernist period "may be understood as registering the emergence of that body as an afterimage, exposed in repeated betrayals of its situated partiality, its culturally determined distortions, its will to dominance and even violence, that cumulatively have become the basis for anti-Enlightenment critique" (2). The analysis engages with what Jacobs determines to be "three related cultural developments contemporary with the rise of modernism": a growing philosophical skepticism expressed most overtly by psychoanalysis, phenomenology and existentialism; the "impact of visual technologies" and their intersection with consumerism, especially as this alters perception; and the emergence of the human sciences, especially sociology and anthropology, "which together consolidate new visual techniques and ways of knowing, most notably, through the participant-observer method" (2-3).

Through this multi-situated analysis, Jacobs divides the writers noted above into three sections, though each section speaks to and enriches the others, resisting a strictly linear development of a thesis. Instead, Jacobs's discussion of the gendered and racialized body, the crisis of representation, and the metaphorics of multiple kinds of external and internal gazes takes the form of critical juxtaposition, reading one text/discourse against another, in order to "differently highlight three conceptual problems of special significance for modernist visuality: the changing status of the authorial gaze . . . , the construction of objects of the gaze and their links with the problem of embodiment, and the representation of viewing subjects or spectators and their intervention into questions of agency" (37).

Jacobs foregrounds the modernist novel in her analysis in order to think about its "unrivaled supremacy as a popular form since the turn of the century," even as she notes that most of the novels she discusses were not in fact "popular." "I understand the significance of the novel's popularity more narrowly as an index of its ideological typicality," she writes, suggesting that the novel is "a kind of vast discursive container, filled with semiautonomous, contradictory languages derived from diverse social strata" (6). Such an understanding allows Jacobs to situate the novel within discourses of power, though she foregoes any attempt to say that the novel is either complicitous with or subversive of politics. "The goal of comprehending the novel's hybrid languages through the crude lenses of complicity or critique may be less valuable . . . than the attempt to track the myriad, irreducible ways cultural and technological changes are processed into its symbolic form" (7). By positioning literary and critical works within each of the sections, Jacobs thus locates the modernist novel within the knot of discourses both challenging and competing for cultural, social, political and scientific authority as the upheavals of the century take place.

Chapter 6, "Spectacles of Violence, Stages of Art: Walter Benjamin and Virginia Woolf's Dialectic" juxtaposes *Between the Acts* with Benjamin's *Arcades Project*, though other texts by both writers are utilized in the 40-page chapter. Jacobs begins with a discussion of Benjamin's effort to achieve a politicization of art in the 1936 essay, "The Work of Art in the Age of Mechanical Reproduction," noting that for Benjamin, "to politicize art is to recreate spectacle, at least potentially, as an active mechanism for change" (204). Jacobs considers *Between the Acts* as a narrative exploration of this idea: "the novel investigates the crowd as theatrical audience; its distracted consideration of its annual village pageant—part airy entertainment, part history play—raises fundamental questions about whether aesthetic spectacle can further political aims by exposing ideological biases and galvanizing the audience into significant political activity" (204). Invoking Benjamin's theories of constellation and the dialectical image (as elaborated in "The Origin of German Tragic Drama," "Theses on the Philosophy of History" and *The Arcades Project* primarily) as the framework for reading Woolf's text, Jacobs "aims to delineate the contradictory mechanisms by which aesthetic events can serve a didactic purpose—both for the audience depicted within *Between the Acts* and for its larger audience of readers—without surrendering fully their artistic integrity" (204-205). Noting the work of many Woolf scholars who have fruitfully constelled Woolf with Benjamin (she especially cites the work of Patricia Joplin and Michael Tratner), Jacobs situates her own discussion as paying heightened critical attention to the role of vision in Benjamin's aesthetic theories, which she then uses as the ground for a critical juxtaposition with Woolf's final novel. Her discussion of Benjamin's *Arcades Project* is illuminating and rich, especially as she attempts to read the place of vision within his study of the Paris Arcades, the 19th-century forerunner of department store, against the discourse of fascism (the study, left unfinished at the time of his suicide, took up the greater part of the period between 1937-1940).

The discussion of Woolf's late work is also rich and illuminating, drawing on "Anon," "A Sketch of the Past," and "Thoughts on Peace in an Air Raid" to offer a reading of Woolf's dialectical understanding of the relationship between art and history, the individual and the collective, the "fragment as constellatory unit" and a narrative of progress in *Between the Acts*. Woolf uses the fragment skeptically to comment on, to interrogate, and perhaps to demystify, both our experience of historical differences as a narrative of progress and our experience of historical sameness as a narrative of universality and transcendence. By reconstellating the dialectical oppositions of difference versus sameness against the backdrop in which village theater meets the theater of war, Woolf aims to deconstruct, to "blast . . . out of the continuum of history's course" (as Benjamin puts it) the false polarities which, with luck, may yield a flash of historical insight (220).

Jacobs finds a "thinking in common" between Woolf and Benjamin both in terms of their aesthetic/narrative theories and their political positions: "Against the fascist politics they hoped to undermine, Benjamin and Woolf aim to transform the observer's relation to the image from the passive complacency of aesthetic contemplation or commodified desire to a more active, transformative relation" (217).

I found each of the sections interesting, particularly the reading of Blanchot's pivotal 1955 essay "The Gaze of Orpheus" and the discussion of Hurston's conflicted anthropological and literary use of the Boasian participant-observer method. The book yields multiple ways for rethinking the discourses of modernism and modernity and engages productively with recent work from feminist, postcolonial, and post-structuralist critics and theorists.

However, the near absence in the book of a critique of the ontological foundation of vision is not only extremely troubling, it weakens the analysis rather seriously, in my view (her reliance on Martin Jay's discussion of "ocularcentrism" is, perhaps, telling). While utilizing the philosophies of Sartre and Merleau-Ponty, she relegates to a footnote the work stretching from Nietzsche through Bergson and Heidegger, on which they relied: "There is, however, a complex philosophical history of the development of embodied, culturally mediated accounts of vision which precedes [Sartre and Merleau-Ponty], which I can do no more than gesture toward here" (17n32). Because of her focus on "image," Jacobs completely misses the significance of (to take only one example) Heidegger's "The Age of the World Picture" (1938) which she invokes fleetingly only to forget: "not only is the modernist era of epistemological doubt commensurable with an allegiance to images, it would seem in fact to be dependent on them as a means of knowing a world 'conceived and grasped,' as Heidegger put it in 1938, 'as a picture'" (18-19).[1] By neglecting a substantive discussion of the metaphysical dimensions of the visual, Jacobs virtually erases one of the most significant—and violent—ways in which the gendering and racializing of bodies (are forced to) find their "proper places" in the fractious discourses of modernism (and western culture generally). The absence is overtly revealed in lines such as this one: "What is striking is the degree to which these aesthetic aims, expressed not only in photographic discourse but also in literary modernism, resemble the clinical ambitions of nineteenth-century taxonomic projects" (27). If she had fully articulated the ontological grounding of Foucault's critique of the human sciences (and his debt to Heidegger and

---

[1] As a kind of corrective, I refer readers to two important texts by Heideggerian critic William V. Spanos which clearly foreground the ontological force of the "eye" and the violence it enables: in terms of modernist narrative structure, "The Detective and The Boundary: Some Notes on the Postmodern Literary Imagination" (*Repetitions: The Postmodern Occasion in Literature and Culture* [Baton Rouge: Louisiana State UP, 1987] p. 13-39); and as it has manifested itself in the imperial impulse from the Romans to the present, *America's Shadow: An Anatomy of Empire* (Minneapolis: University of Minnesota Press, 2000).

REVIEWS

Nietzsche) in *The Order of Things* (a text, I might add, that inexplicably does not show up in her bibliography), she could *hardly* be surprised at such a resemblance, nor could her discussion of anthropology and sociology proceed in the same way. The virtual absence of the ontological as part of her theoretical framework thus seriously weakens what could have been an extremely important book. Still, as I hope I've suggested, there is a great deal to recommend this book, which offers a valuable meditation on the complexities of modernism.

—Jeanette McVicker, *State University of New York College at Fredonia*

A Route to Modernism: Hardy, Lawrence, Woolf
Rosemary Sumner (New York: St. Martin's Press, 2000) 228 pp.

Rosemary Sumner posits, at the beginning of her study, that there are essentially two kinds of modernism: that which struggles to understand or grasp the unknowable, the inconsistent, and that which is analytical and patterns human experience. Sumner argues that Joyce, Stein, and Pound fit into the latter description, whereas the titular trio of Hardy, Lawrence and Woolf represent those who struggle to name the unnamable. There is no doubt as to which form of Modernism Sumner prefers. She agrees with Lawrence that Joyce's work is "'utterly without spontaneity or real life'" (2). Instead, she prefers "the inconsistent, the irrational, the unresolved, the unknown" (2). Unfortunately, modernism, even the Anglo-American kind, comes in many shapes and sizes. Sumner's neat categorizations tend to provide a rather limited context. The reader often has the uncomfortable feeling while cozily considering several points which Hardy, Lawrence, and Woolf share in common that there are multiple packs of modernism at the door clamoring to burst in and disrupt the rather neat argument. Sumner herself suspects these potential intruders. She refers to the "distinction between Hardy, Lawrence, Woolf, and some of their contemporary modernists" (5). It is not revealed who these individuals may be; although Conrad's name is brought forward, this keen observer of the uncertain and irrational is quickly dismissed.

Such exclusivity extends itself into the very argument of the text, so that, despite the work's title, Woolf's works are never discussed with quite the same fervor granted Hardy and Lawrence. Indeed, only one of Woolf's novels, *Between the Acts*, meets Sumner's requirements that the novel must address the oscillation between binaries such as the known/unknown, abstract/concrete, conscious/unconscious. She finds *Mrs. Dalloway* and *The Waves* too "tight" and "time-based," novels that do not allow for the necessary clash between harmony and discord (154). However, Sumner is unfair to both Woolf and herself, for her discussion of the interludes in *The Waves* and their changing point of view is astute and brings into focus the whole problem of seeing, of visual selection and focus in the novel.

Woolf's role in this study is to serve us a kind of handmaiden to the colossi of Hardy and Lawrence. These male writers take chances; they are bold. Their writings were censored, even burned, and their struggle with the contradictions inherent in existence and human relationships is seen as propelling the British literary world into the troublesome realm of modernism. Sumner goes so far as to call Hardy a surrealist, a startling label until she shows us some of his drawings for *Wessex Poems*, drawings that emphasize what the artist/writer sees rather than what he "knows" is real. Hardy's way of seeing challenges our sense of reality and order. He presents us with a world whose structure is constantly threatened by unpredictable and bizarre events, such as a pig's pizzle flying through the air or a fossilized trilobite staring significantly into the eyes of a man hanging in mid-air. Sumner suggests that Hardy fashioned his strong plots in order to find a publisher. Yet he constantly pushed the envelope of respectable meaning in an attempt to explore the juxtaposition between form and chaos.

In some regards, Lawrence had an easier time of it, since it was Hardy who had introduced the unexpected into systematic form. As Sumner notes Lawrence owes much of his love of contraries and abstractions to Hardy. The "Study of Thomas Hardy" is replete with oscillating images battling to achieve harmony only to dissolve into discord. An experienced reader of Lawrence will find only a few new insights here. Like H. M. Daleski in *The Forked Flame*, Sumner argues that Lawrence, like his character Rupert Birkin, sought "an alarming kind of contradictory wholeness" (134). So much emphasis is placed upon the teetering binaries that comprise both the content and the form of *Women in Love*, that one begins to wish that the argument would itself totter into some sense of resolution.

In fact, Sumner begins to yearn for some kind of resolution between the differences that comprise her argument. It is difficult, when speaking of abstract concepts and contradictions, not to lapse into defining them with their own terms. Although her argument stresses the dissonances of life, humans like and seek harmony and wholeness, and her own argument is no exception. There are particular difficulties in discussing the "abstract" (140). One interesting method Sumner sees her authors as using to counter this difficulty is their use of the negative, which helps to keep the indefinable from being defined. Whatever the method used, the problem of discussing that which is immutable is never resolved by the critic or her subjects. The difficulties in naming and knowing that Sumner sees as comprising the works of the authors in her study is curiously untheorized. Here is another reason why readers might feel as if Sumner has removed them from the bustle of Lawrence's "day world." Denied a contemporary or cultural context, these authors are, for the most part, removed from the intense theoretical conversation that has surrounded them in recent years. Despite her emphasis on the unknown, Sumner's argument is, in many ways, too familiar. It is enclosed and orderly and no uncategorized modernist or disruptive theorist is allowed to introduce chaos into the book's tight structure.

A Route to Modernism: Hardy, Lawrence, Woolf is a work that presents the three authors in intriguing juxtaposition. Although Woolf enthusiasts may be disappointed at the lack of balance in the structure (she certainly doesn't get anything like the suggested third of the critical pie), nevertheless, there are many interesting points raised, especially concerning Hardy's modernism. Given Woolf's acquaintance with and appreciation of Hardy, Sumner's work is an inspiring introduction to a full-length study of Hardy and Woolf, a study that has yet to be written but one that will profit from her valuable insights.

—Helen Wussow, *Brooklyn College, CUNY*

On the Winds and Waves of the Imagination: Transnational Feminism and Literature
Constance S. Richards (New York: Garland, 2000) xv + 177 pp.

In current feminist critical practice formulaic theories of a universal female subject caught within a predictable patriarchy are happily giving way to explorations of a broad range of female subjectivities in different culturally specific contexts. Negotiating difference in academic feminism's new dispensation frequently calls for evaluations that deploy counterpoint to advance the multi-dimensional quality of female experience. Women inhabit multiple spaces and as subjects of study, they bring with them different cultures, geographies, and political realities to stand in an uneasy relation to one another. The turn to disparate texts to explicate the testaments of womanhood is, therefore, a welcome move, but it is still a tense time for feminist critics. Compared to the consensus-driven struggle against patriarchy, the question of same-sex difference in feminist discourse provokes deep anxieties about positionality or the pervasiveness of racial and class privilege within patriarchal systems.

Constance S. Richards' book *On the Winds and Waves of Imagination: Transnational Feminism and Literature* offers an inspiring example of how to navigate the impasse. With the winds of postcolonial theory at her back, Richards enters this contested realm determined to forge a closeness not only in the worlds her project opens up but also between herself, as a representative Western feminist critic, and the ever-expanding vistas of post-second-wave feminism. Her subject is "a transnational feminist praxis," posited as a useful paradigm for what readers can learn from "artistic production from multiple peripheries" and about literature as "a political act." A series of searching questions sets the framework and tone of her analysis, their cascading energy weaving together a variety of voices and histories: "[H]ow do Virginia Woolf's critical essays, in which she claims that, as a woman, she has no country, influence how we read her satiric portrayal of British colonial mind-set in her fiction? How does knowing that Zoe Wicomb identifies herself as a black South African, rather than deploy the 'Coloured' title assigned under apartheid, inform how we read her exploration of the privilege her 'Coloured' protagonist exploits by expatriating to England? And what does knowing that Alice Walker re-creates a psychic connection to the African continent as an intervention into the disruption of the slave trade say about her construction of African people in her novels?"

In a reassuring show of confidence, Richards identifies the converging interests of a select sample of canonical and counter-culturalist texts that endorse postcolonial principles in their articulation of feminist struggle. The book's developmental trajectory begins with a summary of certain "approaches to postcolonial studies," which are offered as analogues for the acts of cultural resistance that for Richards mark a desirable threshold in feminist writing and reading practices. In this introductory chapter titled "Towards a Transnational Feminist Writing and Reading Practice" she presents an array of theoretical issues that underscore the ideological triumph of the postcolonial intellectual order and explicitly enhance the value of her call for a political marriage of feminist and postcolonial scholarship. Examples abound of alternative practices of reading and new interpretive possibilities for assessing the power dynamics of textual production. Familiar arguments in postcolonial critical theory, ranging from the vexing questions of language and identity to the deconstruction of empire and nationhood, are rehearsed with sufficient enthusiasm to clarify the extent to which the field is a boon for feminist criticism. It is a winning strategy, one that takes Richards to the frontiers of the discourse. But there is a declining sense of Richards' grasp of the strong body of transnationally-conscious feminist criticism that helped to reshape the priorities of Western feminist praxis and broaden the canvas for feminist scholarship. Wide-ranging critiques by Chandra Mohanty, Carole Boyce Davies, Gay Wilentz, Françoise Lionnet and Rajeswari Sunder Rajan, for example, must resonate with any attempt at mapping out new critical terrain in feminism. The lack of proportional representation of ideas by internationally-minded feminist critics in Richards' survey of the field creates the impression that she is venturing into an uncharted terrain.

The subsequent chapters on Woolf, Wicomb, and Walker examine the legitimate challenges these writers' conceptual and cultural journeys hold for feminist criticism. Together the authors and the texts selected for discussion represent a series of escalating steps toward merging feminist and postcolonial perspectives. The second chapter, titled "Virginia Woolf: A Critique from the Center of Empire," tackles an issue of abiding interest to Woolf scholars: how the writer juggled her insider/outsider position within empire. About Woolf's construction of the "Orientalized Other" in *The Voyage Out*, Richards asks: ". . . does she use the racialized and colonized 'other' to construct the identity of the dominant, colonial 'self'?" The question does not draw a direct or full response, only sympathetic speculation about Woolf's celebrated ambiguity. Richards realizes how complexly difficult it is to impute motive to Woolf because she does not draw clear lines. But even between the lines of Woolf's novel, she finds nothing but silence: "The purposeful use of silence in *Voyage* points not an ability to speak but a refusal to speak for colonized populations." This tightly scripted reading of the novel is partly relieved by amplifying references to *Between the Acts* and *Mrs. Dalloway*, but on the whole Richards seems to be circumspect in her analysis of Woolf's engagement with race.

Chapters three and four carry the weight of the book's authority. Richards gives more scrutiny to the ways Wicomb and Walker stake a claim to transnational feminist praxis. In these chapters the thorny problem of speaking for others takes center stage. The Wicomb chapter, "Transnational Feminist Reading: The Case of Cape Town," begins with a personal narrative about Richards' coming into the maturing awareness that positionality constitutes an important subtext in the reading of women's stories, real and imagined. "The first time I read South African feminist and author Zoe Wicomb's *You Can't Get Lost in Capetown* (1987), it became clear that the novel required of me, a white, U.S. academic, feminist reader, a politically engaged reading practice," she writes. Influenced by the book's multivalent representation of the struggle against oppression in South Africa, Richards expands her own angle of vision to give full expression to the writer's fierce act of self-definition within South Africa's fragile social fabric. Wicomb's construction of South African women's "multiple subjectivities," her decentering of colonial and national master narratives, and her unaffiliated quest for new truths receive high praise from Richards. *You Can't Get Lost in Cape Town* brings up and explodes the vestiges of a bygone era, exposing the nation's disturbing divides to new kinds of determinations that do not fit into neat binary oppositions. For this reason, Richards believes, it is a "a novel for the new South Africa." Wicomb's new novel, *David's Story*, published by the Feminist Press in 2001, will no doubt draw the attention of readers like Richards.

The fourth chapter, "Exoticism to Transnational Feminism: Alice Walker," presents the writer as personifying the transnational feminist ethic given the fact that her fiction revitalizes the relationship between culturally different worlds and at the same time recognizes the strains in the relationship. By expanding the ground on which ideological issues are fought, Walker allows her ideas to travel as far as she does to combat historical and cultural complacency. It is no surprise that she is Richards' choice for embodying Maria Lugones' metaphor of "world traveling" without the cultural baggage of "arrogant perception." Expanding her venture in Africa, however, has been difficult because while she feels a deep connection to her ancestral homeland, she has refused to give it uncritical praise. Encoding Africa's cultural difference in her fiction, particularly in the novel *Possessing the Secret of Joy*, has opened her up to charges of insensitivity but Richards sees a more lasting impact in her sense of justice and emancipatory politics.

Richards generates a tremendous amount of enthusiasm in her book. By catching the currents of postcolonial thought and cross-linking them with feminist literary criticism, she gives another boost to the scholarship in the field.

—Tuzyline Jita Allan, *Baruch College, CUNY*

Virginia Woolf in the Age of Mechanical Reproduction
Pamela Caughie, Ed. (New York: Garland, 2000) xxxvi + 310 pp.

The Virginia Woolf and the Walter Benjamin industries are each roughly thirty years old.[1] The word "industry" would, of course, suggest that both Woolf and Benjamin studies either have been coopted by capitalism or have become capitalist enterprises in their own right. Much as critics may aim to argue on behalf of Woolf's and Benjamin's challenges to the marketplace, the very written expressions of their arguments add to the burgeoning "'intelligentsia economics,' or the 'intellect industry' (a concept akin to the overworked 'culture industry')" (5). I suspect that none of the contributors to *Virginia Woolf in the Age of Mechanical Reproduction* would deny her or his own involvement in primarily the Woolf industry. They certainly do not deny Woolf's involvement in the intellectual marketplace. However, just as the contributors regard Woolf's engagement as alert and critically-informed, their own outlook is conscious and constructive.

This outlook is enhanced by reading Woolf in light of Benjamin,[2] a reading that would seem inevitable. Starting as a Marxist filter in the 1970s, Benjamin's works have become a point of reference in modernist and postmodernist literary studies. But the similarity between the two writers is also noteworthy. Woolf is a cultural and modernist icon herself now, and like Benjamin, was a practicing cultural critic and a politically engaged intellectual. She was from approximately the same generation, born ten years earlier and dying one year later, and from a similar background, born into privilege and at the same time inhabiting outsider status.

The ten essays included in *Virginia Woolf in the Age of Mechanical Reproduction* explore the intersections between Woolf and Benjamin, with a focus on the thesis of Benjamin's most famous essay, "The Work of Art in the Age of Mechanical Reproduction," published in 1936. The 1920s and 1930s witnessed the rise of new media technologies; they were also Woolf's most productive decades. The aim of *Virginia Woolf in the Age of Mechanical Reproduction* is to demonstrate the way Woolf's work in those years, like Benjamin's essay, exemplifies the relationships between the new media technologies and the arts.

---

[1]The number of articles, books and dissertations on Woolf began to flourish at the same time that translations of Benjamin reached the English-speaking world in the 1970s.
[2]When will a book on *Benjamin* In a Room of His Own appear?

In a collection centering on one of Benjamin's major concerns, the replacement of the aura unique to art by mass-produced representation, one might expect, if not fear, significant repetition. However, that danger is successfully avoided here. In their exploration of the way "modernist techniques and new technologies mutually shap[ed] one another" (xxv), the contributors also examine the interplay between other parallel, opposing, or adjacent categories, including class and gender, intelligentsia and marketplace, in front of and behind the camera, inside and outside, artistic aura and mechanical reproduction, and past and present. This multiplicity of approaches complements rather than echoes one another.

This complementary enhancing begins in the first part of the collection, "Intellectuals in the Marketplace," consisting of Hankins's "Virginia Woolf and Walter Benjamin Selling Out(Siders)" and Sonita Sarker's "*Three Guineas*, the In-corporated Intellectual, and Nostalgia for the Human." Both Hankins and Sarker center on the Woolf and Benjamin intersection. Hankins splendidly contrasts the ways Woolf's focus on gender and Benjamin's on class form their differing attitudes toward notions of inside and outside, public and private, *flâneur* and *flâneuse*. Sarker, whose essay is also informed by feminism, examines Woolf's and Benjamin's analyses of mass media technology. While Benjamin located the human in the past, before the era of mechanical reproduction, Woolf uses mechanical reproduction as a tool to maintain the integrity of the human. For example, as Sarker deftly argues, Woolf used the corporation of the Hogarth Press to resist anonymity, or incorporation into larger bodies.

Apart from a few exegeses on the appearance of the Benjaminian concepts of aura and shock in Woolf's writing, the five essays in Part II move away from a sustained discussion of the interconnections between the two writers. Following Melba Cuddy-Keane's lead essay on the changing phenomenon of sound reception, the next four in Part II treat Woolf's aesthetic and critical responses to and engagement with specific modes of mechanical reproduction and new technology: the gramophone, film, the telescope, and the car. Readers interested in the historical and contextual background of the 1920s and 1930s will find this section especially appealing. Some of the highlights include Cuddy-Keane's argument to attend to sound *as* sound, as Woolf did in many of her own works. Cuddy-Keane proposes the term "auscultation" to describe the act of listening. A new critical vocabulary, such as the coining of words like "auscultation," is necessary for us to be able to distinguish, for example, "between listening to the gramophone as an intermediary for music and listening to the sounds of the gramophone as the music itself" (75). Concluding with a discussion of the subversive use of the gramophone in *Between the Acts*, Bonnie

Kime Scott's essay more narrowly focuses on the history of the gramophone and its role in the Woolf household.

Like Scott, Michael Tratner addresses the radical potential of technology in *Between the Acts*, but to a far greater extent. Tratner deepens his argument with an analysis of the uses to which fascists put film and technology in the service of hero-worship, masculinity, and war. Woolf, in *Between the Acts*, uses filmic techniques to hypnotize the audience, but not into the worship of stage figures; rather, into experiencing the aura of the everyday, of the close. The pageant in *Between the Acts* resists fascist art, which, "glorifying a 'boyish' cult of heroism and an idealized, nontechnological nature, ironically unleashes the most dehumanizing effect of technology" (122). Fittingly, Holly Henry's "From Edwin Hubble's Telescope to Virginia Woolf's 'Searchlight'" follows Tratner's "Why Isn't *Between the Acts* a Movie?" Like Tratner, Henry both examines the way emerging technologies—like the telescope and the searchlight—infuse Woolf's aesthetics, and notes the way Woolf critiques the fascist application of these technologies "to comment on the inanity of human aggression" (149).

A subtext of Part II is the way Woolf, though not among the first wave, embraced the new technologies. If she were writing now, no doubt she would be adept at the computer. She and Leonard acquired a gramophone, watched films, and had a strong fascination with the telescope. In 1928 they bought a car, and it changed Woolf's life, and aesthetics, forever, as Makiko Minow-Pinkney, using a strongly informed psychoanalytic approach, argues in "Virginia Woolf and the Age of Motor Cars." Minow-Pinkney goes on to explain how the flood of impressions one experiences in a car can be overwhelming. As a writer, though, Woolf felt obligated to be receptive to stimuli, and not to erect defenses against them, because stimuli can prompt shocks that can lead to spiritual, mystical visions. Thus it is that we all can experience the auratic through technology.

The first essay in Part III's focus on "Virginia Woolf on Both Sides of the Camera" is the most compelling in the collection. In "Virginia Woolf, Intellectual Harlotry, and 1920s British *Vogue*," Jane Garrity examines the way popular culture then (*Vogue*) and now (Bass Ale ads) transformed and continue to reify Woolf's status as an icon of high culture for commercial purposes. Along with publishing her essays, *Vogue,* as a magazine appealing to the upper-class lady, included photographs that portrayed Woolf as a "modernist Madonna" (193), that is, "in terms of a historically regressive model of femininity" (204). However, Woolf's appearance in these pages did not represent a total sell-out; the essays she wrote for *Vogue* did not add to the chorus of the magazine's other articles. Garrity's reading of both the photos and the essays is thorough. That is not quite true of Maggie Humm's treatment of Woolf's photograph album-making in "Virginia Woolf's Photography and the Monk's House Albums." Though

Humm's thesis is noteworthy—"Woolf's album making mirrors her aesthetics" (220)—she does not develop her analysis of either the few photographs that are reproduced in her essay or the tantalizing citations from Woolf on photography, such as her praise of the Zeiss camera for its being "'unrivalled in the portrayal of the human—if mine can be said to be human—face'" (227).

Mark Hussey's "How Should One Read a Screen?" takes us right up to our present age of electronic reproduction. How do Woolf's texts fit into the age of hypertexts? Woolf, Hussey reminds us, was intimately involved with the publishing of her own work. Its physical layout, with its spaces and blank spots, is unreadable by the machine. The body of the text is erased; the text then becomes, at best, "a kind of container for identity, so [that] language is treated as merely a vehicle for information" (258). Furthermore, as Hussey writes, "what is not on the page is not missed" (264), and so we lose the experience of "reading" what is not written.

Hussey acknowledges that he shares Benjamin's ambivalence toward the brave new world of technology, an ambivalence shared, it would seem, by most of the other contributors to the volume. That apprehension—and toward the market system as well—may account for why critics are drawn to Benjamin, and for the same reasons, to Woolf. Leslie Hankins has suggested that just as Woolf and Benjamin were able to hold "in dialectical tension the conflicted roles of cultural inheritor and outsider" (9), perhaps we academics can strive to emulate their practice of inventing "ways to survive without being absorbed into the system of rewards and the market" (29).

—Jeanne Dubino, *Plymouth State College*

British Women Writers of World War II: Battlegrounds of Their Own
Phyllis Lassner (Macmillan, 1997) 293 pp.

As her title suggests, Phyllis Lassner, in *British Women Writers of World War II: Battlegrounds of Their Own,* circumscribes a space for the recuperation of women writing about the Second World War, part of the continuing efforts of women scholars to answer Virginia Woolf's question in *A Room of One's Own*: where are the books by women? As Lassner cogently argues, the growing recognition of women's responses to war is necessarily reshaping the critical debates about war literature and helping to restock at least one section of Woolf's imagined bookshelves with works by ignored women authors. Lassner initiates the direction of her argument in contradiction to Salman Rushdie's claim that: "'If you think of World War II—America, Germany and Italy all produced extraordinary novels about it; England didn't'"(1). For Lassner, Rushdie's point, typical of masculinist assumptions about writing during the period of the war, completely ignores a wealth of women's writing which has not only *not* been taken seriously but which has also fallen largely out of print. To counter such assumptions, Lassner summarizes and critiques works by Vera Brittain, Stevie Smith, Dorothy Sayers, Ethel Mannin, Storm Jameson, Naomi Mitchison, Vita Sackville-West, and Katharine Burdekin, among others. In Lassner's view, British women's World War II writing has value as "a distinguished and multi-form literary tradition and as individual novels of political and social analysis" (2).

Lassner insists that women writers before and during the war period consistently broke through conventional ideological assumptions about their roles and right (or lack thereof) to inhabit public space. The writers she examines refused to be denied their struggle for self-determination as revealed in their "histories and self-representations" (7). In other words, Lassner points out, "British women writers interpret their World War II experiences in ways that unsettle our conceptions of political differences, social change and gender" (8). In studying English women's home front novels, Lassner is able to demonstrate the ways in which the writers redefined patriotism as emotional and political and committed themselves to a nation they could try to change. The women Lassner chooses, for example, wrestled with the politics of identification, demonstrating a feminine capacity to identify "with" aliens and others with whom they were lumped anyway within a nation "at war with itself" (18). Indeed the women writers themselves wrestled with feelings of ambivalence in regard to the nation and to the "Other," a problematization of the historical moment, which as Alison Light describes, exists on a large scale: "'... novels not only speak from their own cultural moment but take issue with it, imagining new versions of its problems, exposing ... its confusions, conflicts and ... desires, the study of fiction is an especially inviting and demanding way into the past'" (22).

Taking Woolf's *Three Guineas* as the "ur-text of feminist anti-war writing" (29), Lassner argues that the validation of Woolf's voice appears to have situated her as the only credible feminist writing about war when, in fact, there are a complicated set of responses to World War II, a chorus of female voices of which Woolf's was but one. Lassner is right, I think, to sketch the intense ambivalence of Woolf's political and personal responses to the growing threat of war, to see Woolf as a bit more complacent about her cultural identification with British gentility in 1930, but increasingly tormented, as war grew closer, by what she viewed as the destabilization of culture and identity brought on by male militarism.

At least one area, in Lassner's view, where women make a substantial literary contribution during this period is in female dystopias. Masculinist culture claimed Huxley's *Brave New World* and Orwell's *Animal Farm* as models of the dystopian genre, thereby causing the obscurity and neglect of Orwell's and Huxley's female contemporaries. Storm Jameson's *In the Second Year,* Naomi Mitchison's *We Have Been Warned,* and Katharine Burdekin's *Swastika Night* are among Lassner's examples of female dystopias which are unabashedly political, which examine the very form itself, and which question the despair of Huxley and Wells, preferring to analyze the ideologies and conditions which have produced the dystopian moment. Burdekin's *Swastika Night* (1930), for example, a work brought back into print through the efforts of scholars like Daphne Patai, sums up, Lassner claims, many female dystopias of the time. Indeed reminiscent of the much more recent *The Handmaid's Tale* by Margaret Atwood, *Swastika Night* suggests the inevitable fate of the human race if masculinist aggression, in the form given it by Hitler's Germany, can carry out its program of eugenics, turning women into increasingly deformed "breeders" decreasingly giving birth to girls.

When she turns to explore women's writing depicting the home front, Lassner examines, among others, Woolf's *Between the Acts.* The novel is an enactment of Woolf's theories on war and masculine aggression articulated so powerfully in *Three Guineas.* Lassner perceptively acknowledges the power of Woolf's interweaving of nature's violence with cycles of building and destruction not only within the family unit but also on the grander scale of civilizations. Lassner is especially effective in her reading of this novel when she imagines the motion of the novel as a downward spiral into a vortex, in other words, a re-descent into barbarism brought on by masculine desire for death and destruction. Lassner's reminder that Pointz Hall was built in a hollow and inhabited by "parvenu" Olivers who faintly resemble cavemen blends with her analysis of Lucy Swithin's continuous action of reading an "Outline of History" for its depiction of the prehistoric era and Woolf's suggestion that, rather than progress, human history is a backward march to the tarpits of its origins. Linked to this notion of backwardness, Woolf has also definitively inscribed the destructive heritage of patriarchy in the line of Bart Oliver as traced through his son, Giles, by evoking SS stormtroopers' boots through Giles's action of stomping on the grotesque ring created by a snake choking on a toad. This very powerful image, along with that near the end of the novel where the players hold up mirrors to the audience, reinforces Woolf's message that the greatest threat to peace may lie in the homeland itself.

Lassner continues to guide her reader through discussion of fictions which recreate a perpetuation of "civil war" as women writers seek to reinscribe their social space in the aftermath of war and as they embrace a common experience with the countries in Europe overrun by Hitler's forces. In her closing chapter, Lassner takes up the treatment, especially in the work of two women writers, of Britain's Others, the Jews. Lassner writes eloquently of women like Phyllis Bottome and Olivia Manning, who recognized that Britain and Europe could not be restored to psychological health without fighting against the victimization of "those alien to the British [and certainly European] political imagination" (217). Bottome's 1937 blockbuster, *The Mortal Storm,* for example, which champions Jews at a moment in history when six million were on the verge of being exterminated has been largely forgotten by contemporary readers, and to recuperate it for this audience, Lassner provides a trenchant analysis embedded in her discussion of Bottome's antifascist political activities.

Lassner's far-ranging recovery of a female tradition writing against war which has been lost to view in our (yes, even today!) patriarchal culture sustains and continues a major effort of feminist scholarship while remaining grounded by examining works which are inseparable from their historical moment. Her argument for such "a distinct tradition" (252), is compelling as is her commemoration of these women for whom the war served as a defining moment, creating the opportunity for heroism and the "moral and political victory enacted by the individual and collective voice of so many" (252).

—Merry Pawlowski, *California State University, Bakersfield*

Virginia Woolf and Fascism: Resisting the Dictators' Seduction
Merry Pawlowski, Ed. (London: Palgrave, 2001) xiv + 241 pp.

This engaging essay collection continues the revaluation of Woolf's place in the public sphere, positioning her politics felicitously with the Fabian and co-operative movement activities of her husband, sensibly to the left of Labour insiders Oswald Mosley and Harold Nicolson and somewhere between, and perhaps beyond, the liberal and radical feminism of the day. As the subtitle suggests, militancy is purposeful when individuals of both sexes stand together against such "forms of terrorism" (to quote Jane Marcus's "Afterword") as are evident in the world today, successors to state fascism in Italy and Germany in the 1930s and during World War II. With one or two exceptions, the essayists interrogate their subjects handily and with more or less equal effectiveness.

Somewhat uncomfortably on point in Part I: "Fascism, History, and the Construction of Gender," Quentin Bell reiterates his well-known preference for *A Room of One's Own* over *Three Guineas*, and he holds his own on the contradictory evidence of the latter's total pacifism *vis-à-vis* the limited pacifism (like Leonard's) of Woolf's diaries of exactly the same time. As the only male in the chorus, Bell contends that "it would be entirely unjust to suggest that, amongst the British, either sex actually *wanted* war in 1938," and, as if relishing the last word in a private quarrel with his aunt, concludes that she was lucky to have been spared embarrassment by not seeing Margaret Thatcher "joyfully leading her country into a short but bloody war" in the Falkland Islands (20).

On the other hand, Marie-Luise Gättens argues persuasively that Woolf's *Three Guineas* gives a theoretical account of the relationship between men and women that goes far toward explaining fascist ideology in a non-democratic country such as Nazi Germany. Most interesting is Gättens' view of Woolf's underestimation of "the desire that many women feel for the splendor of the [male] procession" (34). The essay focuses on the complicity of some women in the suppression of women, such as Gertrud Scholtz-Klink, head of Hitler's Women's Bureau, and director Leni Riefenstahl, who staged the 1934 National Socialist Party congress for the propaganda film *Triumph of the Will* to exaggerate the significance of the rulers over the ruled and to mythologize German "male victory." (See the still frame on the dust jacket.) This distortion of gender roles in fascist ideology is treated nearer to England by Merry Pawlowski and Vara Neverow in essays, respectively, that either ridicule the abrasive criticism of the misguided Wyndham Lewis or try to understand psychoanalysis from Woolf's perspective of Freud, as Professor von X. in *A Room of One's Own*, the caricature of a pathology and argument from which she both deduced and assailed the fascist mentality in *Three Guineas*. Both Pawlowski and Neverow offer close readings of Woolf acutely informed by selected readings in juxtaposed subjects, in Lewis's *Hitler* and Freud's *Totem and Taboo*, for example.

Part II of *Virginia Woolf and Fascism*, "Preludes to War: Politics in the Novels, Aesthetics in the Nonfiction," also profits as an ensemble of chapters that cohere in themselves and also advance the cumulative argument of the book as a whole. For convenience, the reviewer addresses this part in pairs. The first one is recommended reading with David Bradshaw's essay on *Mrs. Dalloway* and Italy in this volume of *Woolf Studies Annual* . Read together, Leigh Coral Harris's essay on Woolf's response to Mussolini's invasion of Abyssinia and Lisa Low's treatment of the effect of the rise of fascism on female consciousness in *Mrs. Dalloway* contribute to our understanding of how much Italy, and particularly Rome, meant to Woolf as a "private, peaceful place of spiritual renewal" (Harris 75), a place threatened by disruption and depression since Mussolini's rise to power in 1922 and rapid transformation of the country into "an authoritarian State" (Low 93). The invasion of 1935 and antecedent crackdown on legal rights in the 1920s are assaults upon the body and mind by the "barbarian," as Leonard and Virginia Woolf disdainfully referred to the excessively masculine state fascism in their day. Objection to Il Duce's call for a fascist art is registered in Virginia's diaries, letters, travel jottings, and essays (again, especially *AROO* and *TG*) but also in *Mrs. Dalloway*. Resistance to seduction by a "sterile fascist regime" might also emerge from the fertility of Italy's native and traditional "moral courage" (Harris 91). But it is a pity Bradshaw's connection between Septimus Smith and British World War I combat veterans of the Italian campaign at Vittorio Veneto lies outside the historic background Low outlines (92-94). For the key to the thesis (or keys) evidently resides nearer to hand in Woolf's circle of male friends.

Equally enlightening is the second half of Part II, comprised of chapters by Jessica Berman, on Woolf in relation to the proto-fascism of Oswald Mosley's New Party, and Natania Rosenfeld, on the reaction of both Leonard and Virginia Woolf against images of dictatorship. Assumptions about the Woolfs as a writing couple are probably as basic to Berman's exposition as they are to Rosenfeld's understanding of Leonard and Virginia as "ardent individualists" who resist the amorphous "I" of anti-democratic group psychology (135). Berman's review of New Party rhetoric is most interesting in light of the role Harold Nicolson played as editor of the New Party journal *Action*, recruiting contributors for it from among the habitués of Bloomsbury, including his wife (Virginia's closest friend), Vita Sackville-West. Mosley's connection with the Labour Party's leadership before his expulsion and before Nicolson's fortunate return to his senses makes fascinating, if enigmatic, literary history. Generally, the wives (including Cynthia Mosley) remained disengaged by choice. Leonard and Virginia had nothing to do with the matter whatsoever and their writings show that they would have disapproved of it. Berman's analysis of *The Waves* (and the cult of Percival) complements Rosenfeld's interpretation of an incident in *Between the Acts*, in which a snake's disgusting effort to swallow a crushed toad betides a "monstrous inversion" of birth. The monstrosity of charismatic dictators recalls Leonard's satirical portrayal in *War for Peace* and *Quack, Quack!*, as Rosenfeld points out, in the manner of her recent book, *Outsiders Together* (2000), and reminiscent of an essay by Patricia Laurence (1998). (The general sympathy of such like-minded scholars is noted by Berman, by coincidence, in her review of Rosenfeld's book in the *Virginia Woolf Miscellany*.)

With less point but equal commitment, the third section of *Virginia Woolf and Fascism*, "Voices against Tyranny: Woolf among Other Writers," delivers the concluding arguments of the book. Although it is not clear how the comparatist method of the last four chapters differs from others, it is generally true here that Woolf functions as a stimulus for reading *other* women writers on the tyranny of fascism. For example, Maroula Joannou mainly interprets Margaret Atwood's *The Handmaid's Tale* after a synopsis of Woolf's opposition in *Three Guineas* and after establishing a parallel context for Atwood in the antifeminist reaction of the 1980s. Likewise, Lia Giachero, in occasionally fractured English and in Italian translated in the notes, writes almost entirely about an artist, Benedetta Cappa Marinetta, who, seduced by fascism, has nothing in common with Woolf, proving, evidently, that Italy in the 1930s made impossible not only a Judith Shakespeare but also a native Virginia Woolf. Molly Abel Travis's essay overcompensates for the swerve away from Woolf by repeating the by-now-too-familiar glosses of *Three Guineas* to vindicate her against the supposed "Ur-fascism" of critical opponents F. R. and Q. D. ("Queenie") Leavis as sex constables. The zeal of the argument tends to link semblances that are not the same: "machismo Freikorps ideology," the "classicism" of select Modernists (but not Eliot, for some reason), and the "meliorative rationalism" of the Bloomsbury Group itself except Woolf and Keynes (167-68). After all, one might prefer James or Conrad to Woolf and still not be a fascist. However, though overdemonstrated, an essay committed to a good cause is attractive politically. Speaking for Woolf and a dozen assembled scholars, Travis is "impelled by conviction that fascism could be resisted, a conviction shared by this writer and the other writers in this volume" (177).

A testament is clearly warranted just as convention calls for a peroration, the affirmation of a thesis or creed with a closing appeal to the citizens of the republic. Using Keynes as an epigraph, Loretta Stec picks up Travis's observation that Bloomsbury rationalism (as "Utopianism") lacked an adequate sense of evil to meet the challenge to civilization that the Fascisti and Nazi ideologues posed to ordinary people. The seductive promise of a golden age, with women in an allotted place at home for "the increase and preservation of the species and the race," as Hitler said in *Mein Kampf* (qtd. Stec 180), involves utopianism turned inside out, "depraved," "demonic," "apocalyptic." Thus, Katharine Burdekin's *Swastika Night*, Woolf's *Three Guineas* (once again), and Rebecca West's *Black Lamb and Grey Falcon* are cast as examples of dystopian Modernism that respond to the idea of world war by embracing utopian feminism without name. Recalling Woolf's "rather premature and optimistic" burning of the word *feminist* (Marcus, qtd. 187), Stec takes this suggestion to be a "prescient advancement in feminist thinking that sees the need to move beyond gender-based identities to create real change" (187). Thereafter, she strikes exactly the right note to end an earnest book on progress and hope, on the resistance to lies told by dictators. She concludes that "Modernity has bequeathed us a state of deep skepticism as well as a desperate need to believe, nonetheless, in a utopian future" (193). Inimitably, Marcus's epilogue sustains and extends the appeal to a universal audience: "If our students learn to read *Three Guineas* the way Merry Pawlowski and her colleagues in this volume do, they will find a usable critique of the world around them" (194). In short, this book is inspiring.

—Wayne Chapman, *Clemson University*

Works Cited

Bradshaw, David. "'Vanished, Like Leaves': The Military, Elegy and Italy in *Mrs Dalloway*." *Woolf Studies Annual* 8 (2002): 107-125.

Laurence, Patricia. "A Writing Couple: Shared Ideology in Virginia Woolf's *Three Guineas* and Leonard Woolf's *Quack, Quack!*" *Women in the Milieu of Leonard and Virginia Woolf: Peace, Politics, and Education*. Eds. Wayne K. Chapman and Janet M. Manson. New York: Pace UP, 1998. 125-43.

Rosenfeld, Natania. *Outsiders Together: Virginia and Leonard Woolf*. Princeton: Princeton UP, 2000. [Rev. by Jessica Berman in *Virginia Woolf Miscellany*, Fall 2001: 7-8.]

Daily Modernism: The Literary Diaries of Virginia Woolf, Antonia White, Elizabeth Smart, and Anaïs Nin
Elizabeth Podnieks (Montreal & Kingston: McGill-Queen's University Press, 2000) 407 pp.

"Someday I want to write about this, as a tribute to a much despised form of literature, as an answer to those who have shrugged their shoulders when they saw me bending over a mere diary," wrote twenty-year-old Anaïs Nin on the eve of her departure for Paris (*Early Diary* 3:32-33). In *Daily Modernism: The Literary Diaries of Virginia Woolf, Antonia White, Elizabeth Smart, and Anaïs Nin* Canadian scholar Elizabeth Podnieks fulfills the young diarist's wish. She pays tribute to the diary, that "much despised" and widely misunderstood form of life writing, and, in the process, contributes significantly to diary scholarship, genre scholarship, feminist scholarship, and the study of modernisms.

Podnieks' project is ambitious and her research extensive. Her four-fold aim is to 1) elevate the diary as a literary genre; 2) define it as a quintessential women's genre, particularly in the twentieth century; 3) move the diary to the center of twentieth century modernisms; and, in the process, 4) challenge conventional genre categories (such as autobiography, diary, and fiction). Podnieks devotes separate chapters to the vastly different "modernist" diaries of Woolf, White, Smart and Nin, but first she lays the theoretical foundation for her treatment in three preliminary chapters.

The book's opening two chapters—"Blurring Boundaries: Mapping the Diary as Autobiography and Fiction" and "That profoundly female, and feminist, genre"—are, to my mind, the richest in the volume. In her brief "Introduction" and "Blurring Boundaries" chapters, Podnieks provides a much-needed history of the diary written in English. Giving a brief nod to the Japanese "pillow" diaries of 794 to 1185 C.E., she informs us that in the English tradition, the term "journal" first appears in the *Oxford English Dictionary* in 1355-1356 in an ecclesiastical context: "A service-book containing the day-hours = DIURNAL" (14), while "diary" was first used by William Fleetwood in a 1581 letter: "Thus most humbly I send unto yor good Lo. this last weeks Diarye" (15). Podnieks' point in "Blurring the Boundaries" is that in the English tradition, the diary developed at the same time as most of the other literary prose genres (the novel, autobiography, biography, and modern essay), but we have failed adequately to recognize its similarities to these forms. While the other genres have been considered public and intentionally literary, diaries have been treated erroneously all these years as private, spontaneous, and (therefore) artless. Podnieks builds on Lawrence Rosenwald's seminal 1988 volume *Emerson and the Art of the Diary*, and from their debunking work it is apparent that the only diarists who sincerely wish their diaries to be private are those who burn their texts before death. Most diaries are "written for some form of posterity" (28); indeed, the fascination of diaries is that they manage to be both private and public spaces, and they often have complex and multiple "audiences."

Podnieks draws the title of her second chapter from Adrienne Rich's observation that the diary is "That profoundly female, and feminist, genre." Here she traces the much-neglected female diary tradition in English, starting with Lady Margaret Hoby (1571-1633) whom Harriet Blodgett calls the first English woman diarist and Podnieks "Pepys's Sister" in a pointed bow to Judith Shakespeare. One of the many joys of *Daily Modernism* is the wit Podnieks exhibits in many of her section headings ("Mr Bennett and Mrs Woolf," "Tradition and the Individual Diarist") that delight as they insert the diary (and women) into the literary scene. Diary scholarship is not extensive, and in this chapter Podnieks brilliantly challenges prior critical assertions. She notes, for example, that Hoby penned her diary long before John Evelyn or Samuel Pepys, who are usually cited as the founders of the English diary tradition, and that it was Hoby (not Pepys) who first used the famous diary phrase "And so to bed."

Even more distressing is Podnieks' assertion that, although Woolf claimed women *novelists* didn't disturb the household peace, women *diarists* apparently did—and this may account for their present under-representation among the so-called "great English diarists." The over-esteemed Pepys destroyed his wife's diary, and Jane Carlyle opened her diary (which both Woolf and Antonia White read) with the line: "I remember Charles Buller saying of the Duchess of Praslin's murder, 'What could a poor fellow do with a wife who kept a journal but murder her'" (49). Even Henry James objected to the publication of his sister Alice's journals, although they were written specifically for publication.

In 1923, the British diarist and diary scholar Arthur Ponsonby asserted, "If a census of diary keepers could be made, it would probably be found that [ministers] and soldiers headed the list" (21). Podnieks disputes this claim. She believes that by the twentieth century, English-speaking women were probably keeping more diaries than English-speaking men. Indeed, she points out that diaries in the West tend to be marketed to women rather than men. Podnieks' careful stance on gender and the diary is that the differences in men's and women's lives "have rendered the diary not a more female than male space, but a more necessary and meaningful site for women than for men" (6). Women's diaries, she believes, offer "'protective' modes . . . the supposedly private nature of the form allows writers to express themselves freely without the immediate fear of censorship" (6).

Woolf, White, Smart, and Nin all kept diaries during the 1920s and 1930s—Woolf, White, and Smart in London. The four had much in common besides their diarizing, but their paths crossed only obliquely—in ways Podnieks fascinatingly documents. In the chapters devoted to each diarist, Podnieks' effort is to demonstrate each diary's similarities to its author's fiction, each diary's modernist qualities, and each diary as a site of struggle where its author rewrote the "womanly woman's narrative" (144). Podnieks examined the manuscript versions of each diary, and a special strength of these chapters is her careful descriptions of the original physical diaries themselves which range from Nin's rich leather volumes to Woolf's carefully bound, covered, and ruled diaries to Smart's simple student notebooks. Each chapter is full of provocative ideas, and while readers may not agree with Podnieks' every assertion, her chapters are important starting places for the conversation.

Podnieks believes Woolf "used her journal to play out the multiple roles" identified in Hermione Lee's 1996 biography *Virginia Woolf*, and that it is in the diary that Woolf's many "colours" are most vibrant (98, 163). I find this thesis persuasive; however, in the interest of full disclosure, I should admit to a personal stake as I too am writing a book on Woolf's diaries. My own research leads me to challenge just three of Podnieks' assertions. I worry her chapter gives the impression that Woolf's diaries are more elaborately rewritten than they are. Podnieks wishes to show that Woolf wrote her diary "with aesthetic awareness," a fact few would dispute (108). My own impression of the Berg Collection manuscripts coincides with that of Anne Olivier Bell, who noted in her "Editor's Preface" to volume one of the *Diary* that "There is remarkably little crossed out or altered in these pages, considering the speed at which Virginia wrote; indeed the pace at which she wrote precluded these corrections and additions which are so striking a feature of her more pondered manuscripts" (x). Podnieks underplays the diary as an exercise in free writing, a characteristic that not only makes Woolf's diary "modernist," but that also sets it so remarkably apart from most of the other great diaries of the world.

Podnieks follows Olivier Bell in attributing the gaps in Woolf's diary to "psychological depression" (101). Compared to most great diaries, Woolf's diary *is* spare. The 2,179 entries across her lifetime average out to only 60 entries a year in the years she kept a diary, and during the 1920s (often considered the peak of her artistry) to only 40 entries a year. One wonders if Woolf's gaps were not also her savvy answer to the diary's constitutional hazard: repetition.

Finally, Podnieks' chapter perpetuates the view of Judy Simons and others that Woolf's diary is a reticent one. What are our standards for diary "openness"? Have they been shaped by Pepys's gleeful and guileless confessions of beating his wife and diddling servant girls? Are our standards those of our current age—that of twenty-first century tabloid journalism? Avowals of Woolf's diary reticence arise, I believe, from our wish to find in Woolf's diary explicit details of her sexual abuse and her love affair with Vita Sackville-West. Although it lacks these desired revelations, Woolf's diary is extraordinarily open and honest in many areas: in articulating her jealousy of Vanessa, in suggesting struggles with Leonard as well as her love and admiration for him, in charting her views of her many acquaintances, in revealing her insights and anguish as a writer, in speaking of menopause. Podnieks herself quotes the stunning passage from the 1926 diary in which Woolf captures hauntingly for all time the experience of oncoming depression (*D*3 110-111). In judging a diarist's reticence or openness, the diary's function for its writer must be consulted more than our own curiosity.

For the British novelist Antonia White, the diary functioned as a personal couch for psychoanalysis, according to Podnieks. Comparing White's diary to Freud's *Dora: An Analysis of a Case of Hysteria*, Podnieks suggests that White's diary allowed her to be both patient and analyst, to "exploit . . . psychoanalysis as a modernist literary aesthetic" (166), and to try to "wrest . . . her female subjectivity from a Freudian discourse" (195). Future studies of White's diary may choose to accentuate the difficulty and ultimate failure of this latter endeavor. Podnieks astutely notes that White's turn from her trained male analyst of the 1930s to the untrained female therapist Dorothy Kingsmill in the late 1940s enabled her to detach herself from her father, "trace her writing self through her maternal lineage" and enjoy a few years of productivity (217). Why the maternal could not be sustained is a compelling question.

In "'Keep out / Keep out / Your snooting snout': The Irresistible Diaries of Elizabeth Smart," Podnieks focuses on fellow Canadian Smart's creation of a diary steeped in humor and literary allusion. As with White, future studies might explore the way in which these devices imprisoned Smart's artistry as well as framed it. In "'I was born to hear applause': Self-Promotion and Performance in the Diaries of Anaïs Nin," Podnieks confronts a diary that is still emerging in unexpurgated form, has multiple versions, and whose historical unreliability has been thoroughly documented. Nin seems indeed to have created a new form, the "fictive diary" (to join Binjamin Wilkomirski's and Lauren Slater's "fictive memoirs") for Podnieks foregrounds a diary written not to record but obsessively to transform Nin's daily reality.

In surveying the vast spectrum of diaries, from the uncorrected to the extensively revised, we find the diaries most often esteemed have tended to be, not surprisingly, those diaries that have been rewritten—often extensively and years after the fact: Evelyn's, Pepys's, Fanny Burney's, Nin's, even Anne Frank's. In this light, Woolf's comparatively unrehearsed diary seems even more remarkable as a literary achievement. *Daily Modernism* is a worthy book unfortunately titled, for the word "Daily" perpetuates yet another myth about diaries—that they are kept daily—a myth that may inhibit many a would-be diarist. None of Podnieks' four diarists wrote every day—even the prolific White and Nin. Nevertheless, Podnieks' lucid and engaging book makes good on her assertion that the diaries of Woolf, White, Smart, and Nin "are valid and valuable modernist achievements" (12). More than this, she convinces us of what Woolf herself so clearly recognized in her review of John Evelyn's journal, that "as an artistic method this of going on with the day's story circumstantially ... has its fascination" ("Rambling Round Evelyn" 118-119).

—Barbara Lounsberry, *University of Northern Iowa*

Works Cited

Blodgett, Harriet, ed. *"Capacious Hold-All": An Anthology of Englishwomen's Diary Writings.* Charlottesville: University Press of Virginia, 1991.

Freud, Sigmund. *Dora: An Analysis of a Case of Hysteria.* Ed. Philip Rieff. New York: Macmillan, 1963.

Lee, Hermione. *Virginia Woolf.* London: Chatto & Windus, 1996.

Nin, Anaïs. *The Early Diary of Anaïs Nin.* Vol. 3: 1923-27. Ed. Rupert Pole. London: Peter Owen Publishers, 1983.

Ponsonby, Arthur. *English Diaries.* London: Methuen, 1923.

Rich, Adrienne. *On Lies, Secrets, and Silence: Selected Prose, 1966-1978.* New York: W. W. Norton, 1979.

Rosenthal, Lawrence. *Emerson and the Art of the Diary.* New York: Oxford U P, 1988.

Simons, Judy. *Diaries and Journals of Literary Women from Fanny Burney to Virginia Woolf.* Iowa City: U of Iowa P, 1990.

Woolf, Virginia. *The Diary of Virginia Woolf.* Vol. 1: 1915-1919. Ed. Anne Olivier Bell. Intro. Quentin Bell. Harmondsworth: Penguin, 1979.

———. *The Diary of Virginia Woolf.* Vol. 3: 1925-1930. Ed. Anne Olivier Bell. Asst. Andrew McNeillie. Harmondsworth: Penguin, 1982.

———. "Rambling Round Evelyn." *The Common Reader.* First Series. London: Hogarth Press, 1948: 110-20.

Notes On Contributors

David Bradshaw is Hawthornden Fellow and Tutor in English Literature at Worcester College, Oxford, and a Fellow of the English Association. Editor of the Oxford World's Classics editions of *Mrs Dalloway* (2000) and *The Mark on the Wall and Other Short Fiction* (2001), as well as editions of *The White Peacock* (1997) and *Women in Love* (1998) in the same series, he has also edited *Decline and Fall* (2001) and *The Good Soldier* (2002) for Penguin Classics, and *The Hidden Huxley* (1994), *Brave New World* (1994), and *The Concise Companion to Modernism* (2002). He is the author of many articles on Modernist literature, politics and ideas and is an editor of *The Review of English Studies*.

Stuart Christie teaches in the Department of English Language and Literature at the Hong Kong Baptist University. He is currently at work on a book-length manuscript analyzing E. M. Forster's BBC broadcasts.

Emily M. Hinnov is a second-year student in the University of New Hampshire's PhD Literature program. Her primary scholarly interest is in studying the theme of mothering in British and American women's fiction from the mid-nineteenth century through the 1940s. She is also interested in the female bildungsroman and in her MA thesis examined motherhood and sexuality in the novels of the Brontës and gendered body images in Victorian literature. Her dissertation will examine both the pleasure and the anguish in Julia Kristeva's conception of the chora, and how both aspects are revealed in women's writing about motherhood in the Victorian and Modern female novel.

Maggie Humm teaches in the School of Cultural and Innovation Studies, University of East London. Her writing on Woolf is in her books *Feminist Criticism* (1986), *Border Traffic* (1991), *Practising Feminist Criticism* (1995) and *Feminism and Film* (1997), and chapters in *Writing a Woman's Business*, eds. K. Fullbrook and J. Simons (1998), *Virginia Woolf in the Age of Mechanical Reproduction*, ed. P. Caughie (2000), *Transformations*, eds. S. Ahmed et al. (2000). She is researching the photography and visual aesthetics of Woolf, Bell and other modernists for her book *Modernist Women and Visual Cultures: Woolf, Bell and Borderline Modernisms (*Edinburgh UP).

Michael Lackey Having earned M.A. degrees in German, philosophy, and English and a PhD in English from the University of Kentucky, Michael Lackey has recently been awarded the Alexander von Humboldt fellowship to do research at the University of Siegen in Germany (2001-02). He has published articles in a number of journals, including *Virginia Woolf Miscellany*, *Journal of the History of Ideas*, *Philosophy and Literature*, *Studies in Short Fiction*, *Victorian Poetry*, and *Crossings: A Counter-Disciplinary Journal*, and is currently completing a book on Modernist atheism. He is an assistant professor at SUNY-Brockport.

Rishona Zimring is an Assisant Professor of English at Lewis and Clark College in Portland, Oregon. Her publications include essays on Conrad and espionage, Jean Rhys and cosmetic consciousness, and the Booker Prize.

Policy

Woolf Studies Annual invites articles on the work and life of Virginia Woolf and her milieu. The Annual intends to represent the breadth and eclecticism of critical approaches to Woolf, and particularly welcomes new perspectives and contexts of inquiry. Articles discussing relations between Woolf and other writers and artists are also welcome.

Articles are sent for review anonymously to a member of the Editorial Board and at least one other reader. Manuscripts should not be under consideration elsewhere or have been previously published. Final decisions are made by the Editorial Board.

Preparation of Copy

1. Articles are typically between 25 and 30 pages, and do not exceed 8000 words.

2. A separate page should include the article's title, author's name, address, telephone & fax numbers, and e-mail address. The author's name and identifying references should not appear on the manuscript.

3. A photocopy of any illustrations should accompany the manuscript. (Black-and-white photographs will be required for accepted work.)

4. Manuscripts should be prepared according to most recent MLA style.

5. Three copies of the manuscript and an abstract of up to 150 words should be sent to: Mark Hussey, English Dept., Pace University, One Pace Plaza, New York NY 10038-1598. Only materials accompanied by a self-addressed, stamped envelope (or international reply coupon) will be returned.

6. Authors of accepted manuscripts will be asked to submit two hard copies and an electronic version. Authors are responsible for all necessary permissions fees.

Please address inquiries to: Mark Hussey, English Department, Pace University, One Pace Plaza, New York NY 10038. mhussey@pace.edu
Fax: (212) 346-1754.

www.ingramcontent.com/pod-product-compliance
Lightning Source LLC
Chambersburg PA
CBHW021822300426
44114CB00009BA/281